Practical Digital Forensics

Get started with the art and science of digital forensics
with this practical, hands-on guide!

Richard Boddington

PUBLISHING

BIRMINGHAM - MUMBAI

Practical Digital Forensics

First published: May 2016

Production reference: 1200516

Published by Packt Publishing Ltd.
Livery Place
35 Livery Street
Birmingham B3 2PB, UK.

ISBN 978-1-78588-710-9

www.packtpub.com

Credits

Author
Richard Boddington

Reviewer
Colin J. Armstrong

Commissioning Editor
Veena Pagare

Acquisition Editor
Divya Poojari

Content Development Editor
Sanjeet Rao

Technical Editor
Vishal K. Mewada

Copy Editor
Madhusudan Uchil

Project Coordinator
Judie Jose

Proofreader
Safis Editing

Indexer
Hemangini Bari

Graphics
Jason Monteiro

Production Coordinator
Aparna Bhagat

Cover Work
Aparna Bhagat

About the Author

Richard Boddington commenced general policing with the London Metropolitan Police in 1968 and joined the Royal Hong Kong Police in 1971, later serving as a chief inspector in the Special Branch. In 1980, Richard moved to Australia and worked as a desk officer and case officer with the Australian Security Intelligence Organization. He later worked in several federal and state government agencies, including the Western Australia Department of Treasury and Finance, as a senior intelligence officer.

In 2008, he commenced developing and coordinating information security and digital forensics undergraduate and postgraduate courses at Murdoch University, where he was responsible for the creation of a digital forensic and information security degree offering. He provided a unique online virtual digital forensics unit for postgraduate students at the University of Western Australia in 2014.

Between 1991 and 2015, Richard was a security analyst and digital forensic practitioner, providing independent consultancy services for legal practitioners and organizations requiring independent digital forensic examinations and reports. This included analyzing case evidence in criminal and civil cases heard at Magistrate, District and Commonwealth Courts. His work included the compilation of digital forensic reports and testifying as an expert witness on complex technical matters to assist the jury in understanding digital evidence presented during trial.

Recent forensic examinations undertaken by him include analyzing digital evidence recovered from computers, mobile phones, and other digital devices and then preparing expert testimony relating to a broad range of criminal and civil cases, including:

- Child pornography and child exploitation
- Cyberstalking
- Aggravated burglary and false imprisonment
- Analysis of CCTV video digital evidence of assault and rape cases
- Alleged homicide, suicide, and other crimes of violence

- Bomb threats
- Family law disputes and Australian Vietnamese Relief Organization (AVRO) breaches
- Workers' compensation disputes
- Suspected forgery or manipulation of digital video and mobile phone evidence
- Industrial espionage and sabotage and intellectual property theft

Since 2015, Richard has continued his digital forensics examinations on behalf of TSW Analytical Pty Ltd in Western Australia, where he now heads the Digital Forensics and Data Recovery Team.

He is also the General Manager for Research and Training at eReveal Technologies Pty Ltd (TSW Global Company) and is responsible for designing and coordinating online digital forensics, multimedia forensics, and e-discovery training courses for a broad range of organizations.

Richard is presently developing online digital forensics and e-discovery academic postgraduate course for the evolving Institute for Applied Forensic Science, associated with TSW Analytical, as part of broader postgraduate forensic course offerings in Australasia and overseas.

In 2010, Richard authored two digital forensics chapters in *Digital Business Security Development: Management Technologies*. He has also written a number of journal articles on the validation of digital evidence, his ongoing research area.

In 2015, he authored an online video cast series, *Emerging Forensic Tools for Locating and Analyzing Digital Evidence*, on behalf of IGI Global Video Lecture E-Access Videos (`http://www.igi-global.com/video/emerging-forensic-tools-locating-analyzing/134946`).

Acknowledgment

I would like to acknowledge the constant love, support, and faith shown to me from my beautiful wife, Meiling, and our close family unit, which has helped me throughout my research and writing of the book, which I now dedicate to them.

The inspiration, technical brilliance, and forensic expertise of Jim Baker of Xtremeforensics and my colleague-at-arms, Dr. Richard Adams, have been the driving force behind my renewed dedication to digital forensics that has resulted in the writing of this book. James McCutcheon's leading work in testing forensic image containers was inspirational and I am pleased to share some of his grossly unrecognized research along with Dr. Adams' work on the ADAMS model. I hope some small but important mention of their work in this book goes some way to publicizing their research. I hope it will encourage other like-minded practitioners to get involved in some really helpful and needed research for the discipline.

Dr. Colin Armstrong's help in the technical review of the book has always been positive and encouraging and helped me reach my final goal, and I thank Colin for his time and constructive feedback to the publishers.

Finally, I am grateful for the support and encouragement from the academics and forensic practitioners and technicians at TSW, who had implicit faith in my forensic experience and provided me with a supportive environment in which to complete the book.

About the Reviewer

Colin J. Armstrong has extensive business experience in communications and information technology, information systems and services, security, and forensic science education, spanning the aviation, transport, hotel and catering, tertiary education, and charitable industries. His experience derives not only from industry roles, but studies acquiring bachelor, masters, and doctoral degrees, participation in the Australian Standards Expert Committee, memberships to various professional industry bodies, board memberships, and company directorships.

www.PacktPub.com

eBooks, discount offers, and more

Did you know that Packt offers eBook versions of every book published, with PDF and ePub files available? You can upgrade to the eBook version at www.PacktPub.com and as a print book customer, you are entitled to a discount on the eBook copy. Get in touch with us at customercare@packtpub.com for more details.

At www.PacktPub.com, you can also read a collection of free technical articles, sign up for a range of free newsletters and receive exclusive discounts and offers on Packt books and eBooks.

https://www2.packtpub.com/books/subscription/packtlib

Do you need instant solutions to your IT questions? PacktLib is Packt's online digital book library. Here, you can search, access, and read Packt's entire library of books.

Why subscribe?

- Fully searchable across every book published by Packt
- Copy and paste, print, and bookmark content
- On demand and accessible via a web browser

Table of Contents

Preface

This book will provide you with a clear understanding of digital forensics, from its relatively recent emergence as a sub-discipline of forensics to its rapidly growing importance alongside the more established forensic disciplines. It will enable you to gain a clear understanding of the role of digital forensics practitioners and their vital work in cybercrime and corporate environments, where they recover evidence of criminal offences and civil transgressions. Examples of real case studies of digital crime scenes will help you understand the complexity typical of many cases and the challenges digital evidence analysis poses to practitioners.

During the past 10 years or so, there has been a growing interest in digital forensics as part of tertiary courses and as a career path in law enforcement and corporate investigations. New technologies and forensic processes have developed to meet the growing number of cases relying on digital evidence. However, it has been apparent that the increasing complexity, size, and number of cases is creating problems for practitioners, who also face resource and costing restrictions and a shortage of well-trained and experienced personnel. The book will describe these challenges and offer some solutions, which hopefully will assist and empower current and prospective practitioners to manage problems more effectively in the future.

These are truly exciting and challenging times for practitioners seeking to enhance their skills and experience in recovering evidence and assisting the legal fraternity in making sense of their important findings. For those wishing to enter the discipline, they do so at a time when banality, complacency, and fatigue are disappointingly quite common. The enthusiasm of entering the profession can rapidly dissipate because of tedium and heavy caseloads, notwithstanding the inherently exciting and important nature of the work. Presented in this book are new and more effective ways to reduce tedium and time wastage, reinvigorate practitioners, and restore the excitement of the hunt for evidence heralded by fresh winds of change.

What this book covers

Chapter 1, The Role of Digital Forensics and Its Environment, describes the digital forensics environment—an emerging discipline within the broader field of forensic science. It outlines the main digital forensics environments of criminal and civil law cases and describes the role of digital forensics practitioners.

Chapter 2, Hardware and Software Environments, presents the basic working of computer hardware, operating systems, and application software and describes the nature of recovered digital evidence. A basic introduction to filesystems and files commonly recovered during forensics examination is given as well as an insight into file encryption and password protection.

Chapter 3, The Nature and Special Properties of Digital Evidence, describes the special characteristics of digital evidence, including the nature of files, file metadata, and timestamps, which form an essential part in the reconstruction of suspected offences. The complex nature of digital evidence is introduced, and the expectations of the courts as to its admissibility in legal hearings is explained.

Chapter 4, Recovering and Preserving Digital Evidence, explains the importance of preserving digital evidence in accordance with legal conventions. It describes forensic recovery processes and tools used to acquire digital evidence without undue contamination under different forensic conditions.

Chapter 5, The Need for Enhanced Forensic Tools, emphasizes the redundancy of conventional forensic imaging and the indexing of increasingly larger datasets and introduces new forensic processes and tools to assist in sounder evidence recovery and better use of resources. The chapter introduces the disruptive technology now challenging established digital forensic responses and the overreliance on forensic specialists, who are themselves becoming swamped with heavier caseloads and larger, more disparate datasets.

Chapter 6, Selecting and Analyzing Digital Evidence, introduces the structure of digital forensic examinations of digital information through the iterative and interactive stages of selecting and analyzing digital evidence that may be used in legal proceedings. The chapter introduces the stages of digital evidence selection and analysis in line with acceptable forensic standards.

Chapter 7, Windows and Other Operating Systems as Sources of Evidence, provides you with an understanding of the complexity and nature of information processed on computers that assist forensic examinations. The chapter looks at the structure of typical Windows, Apple, and other operating systems to facilitate the recreation of key events relating to the presence of recovered digital evidence. It touches on malware attacks and the problems encountered with anti-forensics tactics used by transgressors.

Chapter 8, Examining Browsers, E-mails, Messaging Systems, and Mobile Phones, looks at Internet browsers, e-mail and messaging systems, mobile phone and other handheld devices, and the processes of locating and recovering digital evidence relating to records of personal communications such as e-mails, browsing records, and mobile phones. The value of extracting and examining communications between persons of interest stored on computer and mobile phones is described.

Chapter 9, Validating the Evidence, emphasizes the importance of validating digital evidence to ensure that as thorough as possible an examination of the evidence is undertaken to test its authenticity, relevance, and reliability. Some common pitfalls that diminish the admissibility of digital evidence, as well as the evidentiary weight or value of evidence, are discussed, as is the need for open-minded and unbiased testing and checking of evidence to be a routine matter. The presentation of digital evidence and the role of the forensic expert is outlined in the chapter.

Chapter 10, Empowering Practitioners and Other Stakeholders, provides a summary of the book and reflects on the changes presently occurring within the discipline. It offers some new processes and tools that enhance the work of practitioners and reduce the time spent on each case as well as untangling the complexity of analyzing large datasets.

What you need for this book

No software is required for the book.

Who this book is for

This book is for anyone who wants to get into the field of digital forensics. Prior knowledge of programming languages may be helpful but is not required and is not a compulsory prerequisite. This is a helpful guide for readers contemplating becoming a digital forensic practitioner and others wishing to understand the nature of recovering and preserving digital information that may be required for legal or disciplinary proceedings. The book will appeal to a range of readers requiring a fundamental understanding of this rapidly evolving discipline, including:

- Police, law enforcement, and government investigative bodies
- Corporate investigators
- Banking, business, and forensic auditors
- Security managers and investigators
- IT security professionals
- Taxation compliance investigators

- Defense and intelligence personnel
- The legal fraternity and criminologists

Conventions

In this book, you will find a number of text styles that distinguish between different kinds of information. Here are some examples of these styles and an explanation of their meaning.

Code words in text, database table names, folder names, filenames, file extensions, pathnames, dummy URLs, user input, and Twitter handles are shown as follows: "MS Word document, a file denoted by the .docx extension."

New terms and **important words** are shown in bold. Words that you see on the screen, for example, in menus or dialog boxes, appear in the text like this: "The exact view of file is shown in the following screenshot, which displays the **Properties** sheet."

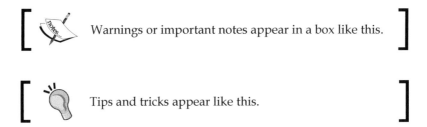

Warnings or important notes appear in a box like this.

Tips and tricks appear like this.

Reader feedback

Feedback from our readers is always welcome. Let us know what you think about this book—what you liked or disliked. Reader feedback is important for us as it helps us develop titles that you will really get the most out of.

To send us general feedback, simply e-mail feedback@packtpub.com, and mention the book's title in the subject of your message.

If there is a topic that you have expertise in and you are interested in either writing or contributing to a book, see our author guide at www.packtpub.com/authors.

Customer support

Now that you are the proud owner of a Packt book, we have a number of things to help you to get the most from your purchase.

Downloading the color images of this book

We also provide you with a PDF file that has color images of the screenshots/ diagrams used in this book. The color images will help you better understand the changes in the output. You can download this file from `https://www.packtpub. com/sites/default/files/downloads/PracticalDigitalForensics_ ColorImages.pdf`.

Errata

Although we have taken every care to ensure the accuracy of our content, mistakes do happen. If you find a mistake in one of our books—maybe a mistake in the text or the code—we would be grateful if you could report this to us. By doing so, you can save other readers from frustration and help us improve subsequent versions of this book. If you find any errata, please report them by visiting `http://www.packtpub. com/submit-errata`, selecting your book, clicking on the **Errata Submission Form** link, and entering the details of your errata. Once your errata are verified, your submission will be accepted and the errata will be uploaded to our website or added to any list of existing errata under the Errata section of that title.

To view the previously submitted errata, go to `https://www.packtpub.com/books/ content/support` and enter the name of the book in the search field. The required information will appear under the **Errata** section.

Piracy

Piracy of copyrighted material on the Internet is an ongoing problem across all media. At Packt, we take the protection of our copyright and licenses very seriously. If you come across any illegal copies of our works in any form on the Internet, please provide us with the location address or website name immediately so that we can pursue a remedy.

Please contact us at `copyright@packtpub.com` with a link to the suspected pirated material.

We appreciate your help in protecting our authors and our ability to bring you valuable content.

Questions

If you have a problem with any aspect of this book, you can contact us at `questions@packtpub.com`, and we will do our best to address the problem.

1
The Role of Digital Forensics and Its Environment

The purpose of this book is to provide you with a clear understanding of digital forensics from its relatively recent emergence as a subdiscipline of forensics to its rapidly growing importance alongside the more established forensic disciplines. This chapter will enable you to gain a clear understanding of the role of digital forensic practitioners and the cybercrime and corporate environments, where they are actively seeking evidence of crimes and civil offences. A small sample of case studies of digital crime scenes will enable you to understand the complexity typical of many cases and the challenges posed to the forensic practitioner.

During the past 10 years or so, there has been a growing interest in digital forensics as a part of tertiary courses and as a career path in law enforcement and corporate investigations. New technologies and forensic processes have developed to meet the growing number of cases relying on digital evidence. However, it has been apparent that the increasing complexity, size, and number of cases is creating problems for practitioners, who also face resource and costing restrictions as well as a shortage of well-trained, experienced personnel. The book will describe these challenges and offer some solutions that have helped me in my practice and research endeavors, and which will hopefully assist and empower current and prospective practitioners to manage problems more effectively in the future.

Inherent security problems associated with personal computers, tied to their popularity in the workplace, have spawned new problems for law enforcement. For example, organizations undertaking criminal investigations or completing internal audits typically encounter the tedious examination of computer records to recover digital evidence. Such examinations urgently require new forensic processes and tools to help practitioners complete their examinations more effectively.

These are exciting times for those practitioners seeking to enhance their important role in assisting the legal fraternity. For those wishing to join the discipline, they will be doing so at a time when practitioners are at a crossroads in terms of changes affecting evidence recovery and management. Banality, complacency, and fatigue are common within the discipline, and the enthusiasm of entering the profession can rapidly dissipate because of the tedium and heavy caseloads, notwithstanding the inherently exciting and important nature of the work. What will be shared with you are new and more effective ways of reducing tedium and time wastage, reinvigorating practitioners, and restoring the excitement of the hunt for evidence, heralded by the gentle winds of change sweeping across the discipline that will eventually turn into a whirlwind if some challenges are left unattended.

The following topics will be covered in the chapter:

- An outline of the history and purpose of forensics and, specifically, digital forensics
- Definitions of the discipline and its role vis-à-vis more established forensic disciplines
- Descriptions of criminal investigations and the rise and nature of cybercrime
- An outline of civil investigations and the nature of e-discovery, disputes, and personnel disciplinary investigations
- An insight into the role of digital forensic practitioners, the skills and experience required, and the challenges confronting them
- A presentation of case studies of noteworthy digital forensic crime scenes to highlight the topic

Understanding the history and purpose of forensics – specifically, digital forensics

Forensic evidence is used in courts of law or in legal adjudication, although some purists do not see forensics as a science. The term could be misleading but may be applied to the technologies related to specific sciences rather than the science itself. There are areas of specialization in forensics, such as questioned expert, forensic dentist, civil engineer, auto crash investigator, entomologist, fingerprint expert, and crime scene reconstruction expert.

The origin of forensics

In 1879, Paris police clerk Alphonse Bertillon introduced a process of documenting crime scenes by photographing corpses and other evidence left behind at the scene. Bertillon's novel photographic records of crime scenes and his precise cataloging and measurement of corpses provided the foundation for the forensic science relating to sudden deaths and homicides. It assisted in the identification of the deceased and provided important information during postmortems to assist in determining the circumstances of the events leading up to the death of the deceased.

Bertillon espoused a radical notion in criminal investigation at the time, positing that science and logic should be used to investigate and solve crime. His scientific work greatly influenced one of his followers, Edmond Locard.

Locard's exchange principle

Locard's exchange principle is a fundamental forensic tenet based on the common exchange of physical traces at a crime scene. For example, fingerprints or DNA traces may be left at the scene, or gunpowder residue from a gunshot may spread onto an attacker's clothes. Although circumstantial by nature, these traces help reconstruct what occurred at the crime scene and may identify those present. We will see how this principle also applies to digital forensics throughout the book.

Within the following quotation is found an oft-cited principle: "A criminal action of an individual cannot occur without leaving a mark," or, more succinctly, "Every contact leaves a trace." *Inman and Rudin* (2001, p. 44) more meaningfully assert that no one can act with the force that the criminal act requires without leaving behind numerous signs of it: either the wrongdoer has left signs at the scene of the crime or, on the other hand, has taken away with him — on his person or clothes — indications of where he has been or what he has done.

Although forensic analysis has developed considerably since the time of Bertillon and Locard, they introduced three core concepts that were major advancements in criminal justice and assist investigators — notably, crime scene documentation, suspect identification, and the discipline of trace analysis.

Unless there is some actual evidence, no hypothesis is of any use and it is as if there had been no crime. Unless a perpetrator may be identified through some valid process and placed at the crime scene via unadulterated evidence, the case cannot ultimately be solved. These principles are foremost in forensics and, of course, apply just as importantly to digital forensic examinations.

The evolution of fingerprint evidence

The next milestone in forensic science relates to fingerprint evidence. Fingerprints have been used on Chinese legal documents for centuries as a proof of identity and the authenticity of the documents. However, it was not until the end of the nineteenth century that Edward Henry devised a workable classification system and implemented it in India in 1897, publishing his book, *Classification and Uses of Fingerprints*, in 1900. The following year, Henry's classification was introduced to the London Metropolitan Police; later that year, it was fully functional at the Fingerprint Office at New Scotland Yard, with the first court conviction by fingerprint evidence being obtained in 1902.

However, the reliability of fingerprint evidence has recently been challenged in a number of jurisdictions, with concerns over the lack of valid standards for evaluating whether two prints match. No uniform process exists for determining a sound basis for confirming identification based on fingerprint examinations. Some examiners rely on counting the number of similar ridge characteristics on the prints, but there is no fixed requirement about the number of points of similarity, and this varies significantly in different jurisdictions. Some courts in the USA have gone as far as to state that fingerprint identification is not based on sound forensic science principles. Similar criticism about the lack of standardization and scientific research has been directed at digital forensics, a far newer discipline.

DNA evidence

Through recent scientific developments, **Deoxyribonucleic Acid (DNA)**, is used for determining the inherited characteristics of each person. DNA evidence can be extracted from a range of samples, such as saliva, used postage stamps and envelopes, dental floss, used razors, hair, clothing, and, more recently, fingerprints. This form of evidence has gained much publicity, with DNA samples recovered from a crime scene being compared with a sample from a suspect to establish a reliable and compelling match between the two. DNA evidence was first used to secure a conviction by matching samples recovered from the scene and obtained from the suspect in Oregon in 1987. Since then, it has brought to account many transgressors who might have otherwise remained beyond the reach of the law. It has also been used in "cold cases", proving the innocence of many wrongly convicted persons.

Because of the complexity of DNA evidence, juries were at first hesitant to accept DNA evidence as conclusive. As the discipline evolved, DNA evidence became more readily accepted in court. More recently, courts have been confronted with challenges to DNA evidence. Defense lawyers have claimed that DNA was planted at the scene to implicate the defendant or that the forensic collection or examination of the sample contaminated the evidence, rendering it inadmissible.

The probability of a sound match between the suspect and the crime scene sample has been questioned by the phenomenon of touch DNA, which are genetic markers left behind on many surfaces. It is common for the transfer of an innocent party's DNA involving a handshake with the offender's hand to be later inadvertently transferred to the murder weapon. Through this form of contamination, up to 85% of swabs have recovered traces of persons who never handled the weapons in question.

The onus is now squarely placed on the practitioner to determine the relevance of recovered samples and the history of how they got onto the artifacts recovered from the crime scene. It is also incumbent on practitioners to assist in determining the antecedents of recovered DNA to ensure the evidence does not implicate innocent parties. Evidence only tells part of the story. The fact that DNA is found at a location and/or on an implement only tells us that that is where DNA was found. It tells little else. It does not always tell when the person was there, nor does it guarantee that the person was there—only that their DNA was found to be there. It does not tell us what they were doing if it is established that they were in fact present. All too often, evidence is just evidence and *we* interpret the results to meet our expectations or achieve our desired outcomes. The problems created because of cross-contamination of evidence in the context of digital forensics is discussed in greater detail in *Chapter 4, Recovering and Preserving Digital Evidence*.

The basic stages of forensic examination

Some order is required when commencing any type of investigation, and forensic science has some key objectives that must be met. Preserving the crime scene is the primary objective because if the evidence is contaminated, lost, or simply not identified and overlooked, then all that follows may be of limited value to the investigators putting together the case evidence.

Recognizing the evidence and identifying where it is located and knowing just where to look can only enhance the outcome of an examination. This requires practitioner skills, knowledge, and experience. Once located, evidence needs to be collated and classified. This brings order to the examination and makes it easier for practitioners to ensure that nothing is overlooked and that the inclusion of recovered artifacts is correctly classified as relevant evidence.

Evidence cannot be viewed in isolation and should be compared with other evidence, and corroborating evidence should be identified. Then it should be described in scientific terms that can highlight the evidence with clarity so that a helpful reconstruction of the events may be presented.

Digital forensics is still in its infancy, and non-standardized processes are common in some civil and criminal investigation agencies. Standards, if they do exist, vary significantly in different jurisdictions. Various digital forensic investigation models are in use, showing slightly different stages in the examination process; however, there is no universal standard model used by practitioners.

Injustices based on faulty or mischievous forensic evidence are not a recent phenomenon. In the United Kingdom, during the past 30 years, for example, some high-profile injustices occurred, including the cases of the Birmingham Six, the Guildford Four, and the Sally Clark case, based on the ineptitude of the expert. Background information on the Clark case may be accessed at `http://netk.net.au/UK/SallyClark1.asp`.

These and similar cases that resulted in the conviction of innocent persons cast serious questions on the credibility and authority of forensic practitioners and their expert evidence. Forensic issues surrounding the Azaria Chamberlain case at Ayres Rock, more than 30 years ago, had profound implications on the quality of forensic practices here in Australia and had repercussions in other jurisdictions.

Defining digital forensics and its role

Digital evidence is progressively being used in legal proceedings and has been subject to scrutiny by the courts. This places an onerous burden on digital forensic practitioners to endeavor to present reliable evidence and sound analyses of their findings, which may also be useful to establish and test precedents for future court rulings. The dramatic increase in desktop computing and proliferation of cyber-based crime that exploits network systems has resulted in the need for enhanced information security management. It also requires practitioners to untangle the mess and try to bring to account the transgressors. Unrelenting attacks against computing devices and network servers are increasing and serve as the medium from which to exploit a wide range of victims, often based in another country. Computers and networks, however, are rich in information of evidentiary value that can assist practitioners in reconstructing transgressions.

Digital forensics emerged in response to the escalation of crimes committed by the use of computer systems as either an object of a crime, an instrument used to commit a crime, or a repository of evidence related to a crime. The requirements of investigating and examining digital evidence while at the same time ensuring that the integrity of original evidence remains unaltered were quickly identified as important functions.

Definitions of digital forensics

In the 1980s, it became apparent that similar to other developments such as DNA evidence and advances in molecular analysis, a new discipline was emerging: **digital forensics**. As computers became affordable, relatively easy to use, and were interconnected through local and wide area networks, computer crime emerged in tandem with the wonders offered by cyberspace.

Traditional laws became outdated, even by legal standards. Questions were raised, for example, as to how the theft of a computer device might be compared with the theft of intangible information copied from a computer and used without lawful authority. The information may remain on the computer although it has been copied without the owner's permission, yet the thief assumes permanent, albeit shared, ownership of the information.

Theft traditionally has a key element of transportability facilitating the permanent removal of tangible property. The file is there and then it is not, yet it is an intangible object stored on a computer. The copying process may well leave the original file information on the device, but it has been stolen from the point of view of its owner. Is copying theft or misuse of a computer? It is certainly a breach of privacy in most cases, and while there is a perception by an owner that their privacy has been breached, how does one claim so when the information is simply copied but yet to be disseminated? Does stalking a person in the street equate to stalking them online? The original legislation was intended to cover the former, and this raised serious questions as to whether established laws could be used to encompass new computer-based crimes.

Electronic and digital information is held or stored on devices and can be abused through such unauthorized activities. Computer crimes are a cyber version of well-established physical-world crimes. Extortion and threats are not new, but the use of computers to deliver the payload is. There was a call for new legislation to redefine computer-related crime, and largely, these recently introduced laws appear to serve the community well. However, confusion reigns in many jurisdictions as to the meaning of digital information tendered in court and an imprudent tendency of some practitioners and members of the legal fraternity to accept it at face value.

Digital forensics has yet to come of age according to many observers and practitioners and does require a scientific and impartial approach to analyzing digital information, sometimes in isolation if no other evidence is available. The evidence may be required in criminal or civil proceedings as well as in administrative and disciplinary cases. Courts and legal adjudicators expect that in line with more established forensic disciplines, scientific processes and tools will be used to preserve and assist in evidence analysis.

The stages of a digital forensic examination are geared toward the recovery and protection of evidence and a scientific approach to analyzing and interpreting the evidence, validating the evidence, and providing clear and precise forensic reports. *Chapter 4*, *Recovering and Preserving Digital Evidence,* and *Chapter 6*, *Selecting and Analyzing Digital Evidence*, describe these stages of digital forensic examination.

Looking at the history of digital forensics

Digital forensics is a relatively new phenomenon. Computers have been around for many decades and required a small number of staff to input data for processing and then receive the output in hardcopy form. They were regarded as secure information repositories as so few had the expertise and understanding to use the devices. Security was simply not a problem, and computer printouts were readily accepted by courts without issue. However, the advent of cheaper and easier-to-use desktop machines, combined with network systems, changed the security landscape of computing.

The early days

During the 1970s, computers were not readily available to all but large organizations, government departments, and, particularly, defense and intelligence communities using mainframe computers. What forensic activities surrounded these computers is not clear and is shrouded in secrecy.

The origins of digital forensics in the public domain emerged later and may be traced back to as early as 1984, when the FBI laboratory and other law enforcement agencies began developing programs to examine computer evidence. Andrew Rosen wrote the first purpose-built digital forensic tool, Desktop Mountie, for the Canadian police, which he followed up with versions of Expert Witness, Encase, and SMART. The rapid and almost worldwide acquisition of relatively cheap and easy-to-use desktop computers for personal and work use quickly attracted the attention of transgressors keen to exploit the new technology.

In response to mounting attacks on computers and networks, private organizations and governments began to develop and implement computer security policies and countermeasures. Digital forensics emerged in response to victims of cyberattacks and exploitation realizing that some structure was needed to deal with an escalating problem. Eventually, some established forensic processes emerged in the late eighties, but much of the research and development of digital forensic tools and software was vendor-driven or produced by enthusiastic law enforcement officers with some basic computer knowledge.

Some of the first government agencies with an overt and publicly visible requirement of carrying out forensics on external systems relating to criminal offences were taxation and revenue-collection agencies. It soon became apparent to those struggling to recover digital evidence that a level of specialist knowledge was needed to investigate this new technology.

A paucity of reliable digital forensic tools

Unfortunately for the digital forensic practitioner, no specific forensic tools existed in the eighties, which resulted in developers designing their own suites of forensic utilities based on **MS-DOS**. Many of these forensic software applications have been refined and updated, and persist in use to this day. Data-protection and recovery utility suites of that time that still exist include:

- Norton's Utilities
- Central Point Software
- PC Tools
- Mace Utilities

In 1990, there were 100,000 registered users of Mace Utilities, and Norton's Utilities became one the most popular utility suites available.

Initially, the only method of preserving evidence available to the forensic examiner was to take a logical backup of files from the evidence disk on magnetic tape. It was hoped that this process would be able to preserve vital file attributes and metadata and then be capable of restoring these files to another disk. This would then allow the practitioner to examine the recovered data manually using command-line file-management software such as these:

- Executive Systems, Inc.
- XTree Gold
- Norton Commander (NC)
- Appropriate file-viewing software, including the sector imaging method

The size of computer datasets at the time was in the megabyte range, but still sufficiently large to make the process of evidence retrieval a tedious and time-consuming task. There was a call for some forensic standards, guidelines, and definitions to assist digital forensics practitioners as well as an urgent call to revise existing legislation to ensure that newly forming cybercrimes were correctly defined. Sound legislation was overdue to recognize and be effective against old crimes now in a new format.

The legal fraternity's difficulty understanding digital evidence

In the mid-eighties, concerns were raised about the lack of understanding among various legal practitioners and lawmakers for failing to address the problems brought about by the increasing reliance of digital evidence in legal proceedings. This was a worldwide phenomenon caused by the dramatic upsurge in computer use and the advent of new devices, including digital mobile phones. Consequently, a coordinated approach to assist forensics and legal practitioners was mooted in the USA to assist them in overcoming difficulties encountered with tendering digital evidence.

By the turn of the century, the US and the European Union established a research corpus that would apply scientific processes to find solutions to forensic challenges driven by practitioner needs. Researchers at the time raised concerns about widespread misunderstanding as to the true nature of digital evidence. More worrying to them was the inefficiency and ineffectiveness of some forensic processes used in its recovery, analysis, and subsequent use in legal proceedings.

It was recognized that digital forensic examinations commenced with seeking answers about the identity of suspected transgressors, notably, establishing some digital link between the binary data and the suspect. Although mere possession of a digital computer was generally considered sufficient to link a transgressor to all the data the device contained, concerns were being raised as to the soundness of such assumptions. Would the assumption be valid in the future because of extensive computer networking? Would the data itself be capable of providing clues to the motive of a transgression?

In 1999, digital forensics designer Andrew Rosen appeared for the defense in Clarkson versus Clarkson (Circuit Court for Roanoke County, Virginia: case 3CH 01.00099), where it was eventually determined that the defendant's wife had placed child pornography on his computer and then tried to incriminate him so she could exit the marriage, maintain custody of the children, and marry her new lover. This case caused Rosen to be considered a "traitor" by law enforcement/prosecution-focused practitioners, who were evidently more interested in winning the case than seeking a just outcome.

This set the scene for a dangerous precedent, encouraging some practitioners to assume that the owner and chief user of a computer was the most likely transgressor. In my experience, in the handling of defense cases in criminal trials, the sound identification of other users, who are also potential suspects, has often been paid lip service to. This suggests suspect-driven and not evidence-led examinations, which is hardly an unbiased and scientific approach. This contradicts the concept that the practitioner is the "servant of the court". The nature and special properties of digital evidence are presented in *Chapter 3, The Nature and Special Properties of Digital Evidence*.

More recent developments in digital forensics

The years from 1999 to 2007 were considered the golden age for digital forensics, when the practitioner could see into the past through the recovery of deleted files and into the criminal mind through the recovery of e-mails and messages, thus enabling practitioners to freeze time and witness transgressions. Digital forensics was once a niche science that primarily supported criminal investigations. Nowadays, digital forensics is routinely incorporated in popular crime shows and novels. The dramatization of digital forensics and considerable exaggeration as to the technical prowess of practitioners and forensic tools is what is described as the **Crime Scene Investigation (CSI)** syndrome.

 In 1984, the FBI had established the **Computer Analysis and Response Team (CART)** to provide digital forensic support, but it did not become operational until 1991.

Research groups have since been formed to discuss computer forensic science as a discipline, including the need for a standardized approach to examinations. In the USA, these include the following:

- **Scientific Working Group on Digital Evidence (SWGDE)**
- **Technical Working Group on Digital Evidence (TWGDE)**
- **National Institute of Justice (NIJ)**

By 2005, digital forensics still lacked standardization and process, and was understandably heavily oriented toward Windows and, to a lesser extent, standard Linux systems. Even in 2010, while the basic phases involved in digital forensics examinations were well documented, a standardized or widely accepted formal digital forensic model was still considered by some researchers as being in its infancy. To those observers, it was clearly not in the same league as other physical forensic standards such as blood analysis.

In 2008, the **International Standard Organization's Joint Technical Committee (ISO/IEC JTC 1)** investigated the feasibility of an international standard on digital forensic governance, but to date, there are no ISO/IEC JTC1 standards that specifically address the issue. There exists, however, an international awareness of problems associated with the variations in the inter-jurisdictional transfer of information relating to legal proceedings (ISO 2009:4).

The digital forensics discipline developed rapidly but to date has very little international standardization regarding processes, procedures, or management, yet it does require governance similar to **Information Systems** and **Information Technology (IS and IT)** governance. Recently, some researchers have expressed concern over the intersection between the highly technical digital forensic discipline and the business approach of governance, making digital forensics a highly specialized discipline. There is a feeling of misgiving that few practitioners have sufficient interdisciplinary knowledge of computer, legal, and business aspects. That is perhaps unfair criticism of the majority of practitioners who do remarkable work with limited resources and support.

A conflicting view is that the emergence of organizations such as the **High Technology Criminal Investigators Association (HTCIA)** and the **International Association of Computer Investigative Specialists (IACIS)** did lend weight to the forensic process to ensure legal acceptance of digital evidence by ensuring the data is reliable, accurate, verifiable, and complete.

Studying criminal investigations and cybercrime

In line with more established forensic disciplines, digital forensics, a comparatively new field, also involves preserving the crime scene in a digital environment. Digital forensics practitioners examine evidence recovered from the complete range of digital devices and networks. This requires some understanding of computer technology, notwithstanding the advent of more automated forensic processes and tools.

 Many examinations do not necessarily end in a criminal case and may become part of civil legal action or internal disciplinary procedures. The reverse, of course, is also common, when a civil case can result in criminal prosecution.

Digital forensics falls into three broad categories:

- Public investigations: These are state initiated
- Private investigations: These are corporate
- Individual: These are often in the form of e-discovery

Personnel misconduct investigation requiring digital forensic examinations is an emerging category. Defense and intelligence forensic examinations are considered another category, but it is not covered in this book.

Evidence found on a computer may be presented in a court of law to support accusations of crime or civil action such as:

- Murder and acts of violence
- Fraud, money laundering, and theft
- Extortion
- Involvement with narcotics
- Sabotage and record destruction
- Pedophilia and cyberstalking
- Terrorism and bomb threats
- Family violence

Typically, criminal investigations and prosecutions involve government agencies that work within the framework of criminal law. Law enforcement officers are granted search and seizure powers under relevant criminal laws that enable them to locate and capture devices suspected of being used in crimes or to facilitate them.

Outlining civil investigations and the nature of e-discovery

Private organizations are not governed by criminal law per se and usually involve litigation disputes and disciplinary investigations involving computers and network systems, which are becoming more frequent. Civil investigations may escalate and become criminal cases. Civil cases rely on civil law, torts, and process, and information may be recovered from the opposing party through civil remedies, notably, "discovery" as well as powers of search and seizure, such as those provided by Anton Piller orders or search orders.

This book looks primarily at digital forensics and, to some extent, civil investigations. However, in my experience, there is no real distinction between criminal and civil examinations when using digital forensics. Each group is looking for the same sort of evidence but arguably to different standards. The e-discovery is almost entirely a civil matter as it involves disputes between different organizations, so the concept of evidence is slightly different. I contend that the approach used in the past for e-discovery typically involved a large number of machines, and it can be applied to digital forensics with some refinements as the only way to handle large data volumes. *Chapter 5, The Need for Enhanced Forensic Tools*, outlines some new software tools capable of processing large datasets, offering some long-overdue support to practitioners working in both environments.

The role of digital forensic practitioners and the challenges they face

Forensic practitioners not only recover and analyze evidence, but they also present and interpret its meaning to investigators, lawyers, and, ultimately, to the jury. Being a sound analyst is of course a fundamental requirement but practitioners must also be able to communicate with clarity their findings and professional opinion to the layperson. Evidence is blind and cannot speak for itself, so it needs an interpreter to explain what it does or might mean and why it is important to the case, among other things. I spend much time on casework explaining technical matters to the legal teams and juries to ensure that they have a clear understanding of the evidence—a rewarding task when the penny eventually drops!

The unique privilege of providing expert evidence and opinion

Under normal circumstances, hearsay evidence is not permitted in courts, and the opinion of witnesses is distinctly prohibited. Expert witnesses and scientific experts, however, may provide opinion based on their extensive practice and research, provided it is restricted to the evidence presented. These privileged witnesses may share with the court any inferences they have made from the evidence they have observed, provided that it is within their sphere of expertise.

Forensic experts are expected to provide information that may help the court form its conclusion, and the expert's subjective opinion may be included. However, it is the court's obligation to form its own opinion or conclusion as to the guilt or innocence of the defendant based on the testimony provided. The forensic practitioner, when acting as a forensic expert, should do no more than provide scientific opinion about the information to help the court form judgmental opinions.

Experts must avoid providing final opinions themselves since sometimes, expert knowledge is not completely certain. Across a range of legal jurisdictions, courts expect forensic practitioners to possess sound understanding of computer technology for their testimony to have any credibility.

The United Kingdom's Civil Procedure Rules (1998) require compliance by all expert witnesses, and Part 35 stipulates that the expert (practitioner) has an overriding duty to help the court and maintain strict impartiality and not to support the engaging party. The rules stipulate that:

- The facts used in the expert's report must be true

- The expert's opinions must be reasonable and based on current experience of the problem in question

- When there is a range of reasonable opinion, the expert is obligated to consider the extent of that range in the report and to acknowledge any matters that might adversely affect the validity of the opinion provided

- The expert is obligated to indicate the sources of all the information provided and not to include or exclude anything that has been suggested by others (particularly the instructing lawyers) without forming an independent view

- The expert must make it clear that the opinions expressed represent the practitioner's true and complete professional opinion

In 2008, the Council for the Regulation of Forensic Practitioners reiterated these stipulations and added further conditions expected of practitioners (*Carroll and Notley 2005*):

- They must disclose all material they have had access to

- They must express their range of opinion on the matter in question

- They must explain why they prefer their view to a different view

- They must provide the evidence based on which their opinion is offered

- They must not give evidence outside their field of expertise

The United Kingdom's guidance booklet for experts, *Disclosure: Experts' Evidence, Case Management and Unused Material*, published in 2010 by the Crown Prosecution Service, emphasized the need for practitioners to ensure that due regard be given to any information that points away from, as well as toward, the defendant. The booklet stresses that practitioners must not give expert opinion beyond their area of expertise. The booklet also addresses the independence of the practitioner as well as reiterating the requirement to examine and share exculpatory evidence with the court and other parties.

Case prosecutors in the USA are required to disclose materials in their possession to the defense based on the Brady Rule (Brady versus Maryland, 1963). Under the Brady Rule, the prosecutor is required to disclose any evidence to the defense, including any evidence favorable to the accused (exculpatory evidence), notably "evidence that goes toward negating a defendant's guilt, that would reduce a defendant's potential sentence, or evidence going to the credibility of a witness."

If it were shown that the prosecution failed to disclose such exculpatory evidence under this rule, and prejudice ensued as a result, the evidence would be rejected and suppressed by the court, irrespective of whether the prosecution knew the evidence was in its possession or whether the withholding of the evidence was intentional or inadvertent. However, the defendant would have to prove that the undisclosed evidence was material and show that there was a reasonable prospect that there would be a difference in the outcome of the trial if the prosecutor had shared the evidence.

This is something the digital forensic practitioner must constantly be aware of and comply with during case examination and evidence presentation. Known factors detrimental to the disclosure of digital evidence include the knowledge of exculpatory evidence that would challenge the evidence of an inculpatory or incriminating nature. Practitioners may be employed by the prosecution or defense, but ultimately, they have an overriding duty to the courts to present all relevant facts for or against their clients. It may be a poor legal strategy to disclose information that hurts your own case, but the courts do expect an open and honest exchange of evidence between the parties involved.

Experts must resist common pressure from courts to provide opinion on the probability of guilt or innocence and persist with the contention that their statements of opinion cannot substitute the opinions of the courts. It is common knowledge that jurors tend to be influenced by practitioners who exude confidence but whose testimony is sometimes biased and mistaken.

There is compelling reasoning to support an evidence-led approach to forensics and investigation. A suspect-led approach is judgmental and often biased to the detriment of those being investigated. Experienced investigators will let the evidence lead and avoid preoccupation with likely suspects cloud the impartiality of an investigation and affect their judgement unreasonably. The same stratagem must apply to forensic examiners. If for no other reason than to identify the weaknesses in a case, the examiner should always adopt this approach. If the analysis is flawed and reckless, it hardly serves the cause of justice. *Kaptein (2009, p. 3)* attributes United States Supreme Court Associate Justice A. Scalia from the Herrera versus Collins case (506 US 390, 1993) with the following statement: "*Mere factual innocence is no reason not to carry out a death sentence properly reached.*"

However, the late Judge Scalia has been somewhat misquoted here, and I urge you to find more about the meaning behind the statement attributed to him, as is provided at the following website:

```
http://news.lawreader.com/2008/08/30/barry-miller-widely-published-
scalia-quote-re-innocense-is-inaccurate-we-have-to-agree/.
```

Issues faced by practitioners due to inadequate forensics processes

On commencement of an examination, practitioners are usually confronted with determining the type of acquisition processes required, then locating the data required to complete the examination, and, most importantly, selecting the appropriate evidence analysis process. Careful planning of the examination is not always supported by existing processes and certainly not for practitioners faced with unfamiliar case types or unusually complex, large-scale cases. In such circumstances, practitioners need to be provided with the correct balance of case background information to assist them with filtering voluminous case information, which may otherwise prove overwhelming.

The examination of larger datasets may make it difficult to characterize the evidence of a crime and clearly define the scope and goals in the absence of tools, standards, or structured support processes. Regrettably, current forensics tools often fail to provide adequate investigatory support to practitioners and may be described as first generation without incorporating any decision support to aid the practitioner.

As early as 2001, the **Digital Forensics Research Workshop (DFRWS)** observed that practitioners were struggling to understand the daily challenges and dilemmas they faced, notably, missing or unconsidered steps in the investigative approach compared to proven investigative processes existing in more traditional forensic disciplines. The rapid pace of technological advancement together with the changeability of software applications and hardware have in effect compounded the challenges practitioners face.

The procedural inadequacies of digital forensics, in which practitioners were required to collect large volumes of data unprecedentedly in support of investigations, were further hampered by non-standardized analytical procedures and protocols lacking standard terminology. It was apparent then, and remains so to this day, that there was a need for forensic tools to be more carefully crafted to analysis processes. This would then meet the needs of the practitioner by providing more friendly user interfaces to address the problem of training and enhancing practitioner experience.

Better forensics processes were identified early on by researchers as urgently in need of being tested and put through trials in order to overcome the deficiencies in existing practitioner skill levels. Many researchers predicted this would inevitably become increasingly problematic. Their prediction was evidently well founded, as this now appears to be the norm.

Chapter 5, The Need for Enhanced Forensic Tools, emphasizes the redundancy of conventional forensic imaging and the indexing of increasingly larger datasets, and introduces new forensic processes and tools.

Inferior forensics tools confronting practitioners

Expert witnesses are often challenged by the opposing legal team and their expert, and this is very true in cases where digital evidence is being tendered. US courts are especially sensitive to expert testimony relating to digital evidence, and the much-publicized legal case in 1993 between Daubert and Merell Dow Pharmaceuticals set a precedent for forensic practitioners and the processes and tools they used to recover evidence. The ruling has set a standard of expectation by US courts based on case law where the initial ruling held sway. The Daubert Standard, which replaced earlier case law, requires practitioners to establish their personal expert qualifications and necessitates them validating the reliability and accuracy of the forensic processes and tools they use in recovering evidence.

Digital forensics tools are typically produced to obtain the "lowest-hanging fruit." In other words, they tend to encourage practitioners to look for the evidence that is easiest to identify and recover. Often, these tools do not have the capability to look for or even recognize other less obvious evidence. This issue is described in more detail in *Chapter 5, The Need for Enhanced Forensic Tools*.

Forensics software certification to confirm forensic soundness is not widely and formally tested. Vendor hype and practitioner willingness to accept untested, open source, and non-validated tools have created a miasma that the legal fraternity should, but cannot usually, see through. Researchers have advocated a structure to measure whether digital evidence meets specific criteria to address the need, applicability, and admissibility of digital forensics practitioners in a given situation, such as the one in the United States based on the Frye test, now replaced by the Daubert Standard.

The inadequate protection of digital information confronting practitioners

Forensic practitioners are often confronted with the inefficacy of conventional security processes embedded in computers and networks designed to preserve documents and network functionality; they aren't specifically designed to enhance digital evidence recovery. However, these processes can help in the identification of potential evidence and event reconstruction.

A common difficulty encountered by practitioners is a requirement for them to provide expert testimony to verify whether, for example, network systems provide and have maintained a sound protection of the stored data. Vendor hype used to secure the sale of a network system is not always reflected in them providing reassurance as to the accuracy and completeness of the data stores. Vendors often do not provide sufficient information about the software and networks' ability to protect the integrity of data. Consequently, practitioners are unable to validate the devices to the extent that they could survive legal challenge.

Because of the great number of inherent, technical complexities, it is often impractical for practitioners to determine fully the reliability of computer devices or network systems and provide assurances to the court about the soundness of the processes involved. An ordered process would be helpful for practitioners to ensure that no parts of the examination process were overlooked or were repetitive, thereby ensuring efficacious examinations through time saving and completeness.

The tedium of forensic analysis

During examinations, the practitioner may revisit portions of the evidence to determine its validity, which may require new lines of investigation and further verification of other evidence as circumstances dictate. It is often a tedious process, and frequently, an inordinate amount of time and resources is required to collect and analyze digital evidence. The sheer volume of the cases and the time required for investigation can negate the efficacy of practitioners to reconstruct and provide an accurate interpretation of the evidence.

However, from a pragmatic perspective, the amount of time and effort involved in the digital forensic process should pass the acceptable "reasonableness test", meaning that all possible effort shouldn't be put into finding all conceivable trace evidence and then seizing and analyzing it. This is especially becoming more challenging to practitioners as the volume of data to be analyzed becomes enormous and crosses over many networks. In my casework, it is evident that in practice, a gap exists between what is theoretically possible and what is necessary to complete an examination. While in theory there may be a desire to complete analysis of every byte of data, there is rarely any justification in doing so.

Qualities of the digital forensic practitioner

Digital forensics, also known as **cyber forensics** and **computer forensics**, is generally considered to consist of three roles in one: that of a cyber analyst familiar with the working of computer devices and networks, a detective with knowledge of investigating crime, and a lawyer with a sound understanding of the law and court procedures.

There is a growing cottage industry of self-claimed cyber forensic experts as well as a tendency for mediocrity in the industry. Self-qualified "experts" bamboozle the legal system and are not always challenged, and the truth of their evidence is seldom sought. However, there are basic standards of practitioner professionalism and experience required by computer and information security bodies, the courts, governments, and corporations

Forensic practitioners involved in the examination of digital crime scenes must assume command of the situation and identify all relevant digital evidence, which must be collated and compiled into a professional report for presentation to the lawyers and ultimately the courts. It is most important that to satisfy a court of law, a digital forensic examination must be legally well founded as well as convincing in the everyday sense. The practitioner must use sound and well-established processes for recovering data from computer storage media and processes that validate its accuracy and reliability.

Determining practitioner prerequisites

I am often asked by tertiary students wishing to enter the profession what skills and experience are required to get a head start. Well, saying you like reading books really does not mean you are suited to being a librarian and have all the considerable skills that librarianship entails. So it is with any profession. It really is important to pursue in life what really interests you rather than a passing fancy. What forensic team leaders look for in someone entering the profession without any forensic experience is a real desire to engage with the discipline. An interest in information technology through work or study and holding an information technology tertiary qualification or a BSc in ICT would certainly stand a prospective candidate in good stead.

For a law enforcement officer seeking to specialize in a forensic discipline, they would be expected to have the investigative skills and case experience; an understanding of the law would obviously be advantageous. As such, they would have much to bring to the role if they could also demonstrate some proficiency in and knowledge of computer systems.

It must be stressed that a forensic examiner and an investigator are interchangeable roles and they are often combined roles. Many practitioners will undertake forensic training courses and forensic tool competency training. Others will also publish blogs and even journal papers reflecting their research and involvement in important forensic matters.

Undergraduate courses, typically a three-year course of study, usually include some digital forensics but are predominantly oriented toward computer science and information security. Postgraduate diplomas and certificates based on theory and practical casework offer an effective entrée to the profession. They are cheaper, shorter in duration, and can be offered to graduates and those in law enforcement and investigation professions possessing the basic skills required to gain a position. The procurement of these certifications, provided they are based on sound theory and practical components, is highly recommended. Masters courses in digital forensics are another option but costlier and longer in duration.

I am currently preparing a four-unit graduate certificate course in digital forensics that includes e-discovery and multimedia forensics and can be completed online using virtual crime simulations. The certificate can be a foundation for a graduate diploma and masters in digital forensics. The offering is directed at law enforcement officers and **Information and Communications Technology (ICT)** graduates wishing to join the discipline and seek some basic theoretical and practical qualifications.

Some of my ablest students entered the profession lacking in field experience, but from the outset, their keen interest in digital forensics, competency in IT studies, and sound results in the experiential forensic training they completed made up for it to some extent. It gave them a solid foundation and cemented their interest in the discipline.

Case studies

The following examples highlight a small sample of previous cases that rely on digital evidence. *Chapter 3, The Nature and Special Properties of Digital Evidence,* will describe digital evidence in more detail.

The Aaron Caffrey case – United Kingdom, 2003

In 2003, Caffrey was acquitted of an offence: the unauthorized modification of computer material by sending data from his computer that shut down the Port of Houston computer servers. This was one of a few cases where a malware defense was accepted by the court without any proof of it controlling the computer. You can find details here:

```
http://digitalcommons.law.scu.edu/cgi/viewcontent.
cgi?article=1370&context=chtlj.
```

The Julie Amero case – Connecticut, 2007

School teacher Julie Amero had serious charges of the possession of indecent images, which were seen by her students; she was dismissed, thereby avoiding a lengthy jail sentence. The police examination was shown to be faulty, and malware on Amero's computer was thought responsible for the downloading of the indecent files. Refer to these links for details:

- `http://dfir.com.br/wp-content/uploads/2014/02/julieamerosummary.pdf`
- `https://reason.com/archives/2008/12/12/the-prosecution-of-julie-amero`

The Michael Fiola case – Massachusetts, 2008

A similar case was dismissed when the defendant was able to obtain confirmation from a practitioner that malware was probably responsible for the presence of the indecent files you will find details here:

```
http://truthinjustice.org/fiola.htm.
```

References

Carroll, R. and R. G. Notley. 2005. "Negligence of medical experts." *British Medical Journal* 330: 1024-1027.

Inman, K. and N. Rudin. 2001. "Principles and Practice of Criminalistics: The Profession of Forensic Science." *CRC Press*.

Kaptein, H. 2009. "Rigid anarchic principles of evidence and proof: Anomist panaceas against legal pathologies of proceduralism." in *Legal Evidence and Proof: Statistics, Stories, Logic.* Edited by H. Kapstein, H. Prakken, and B. Verheij. *Ashgate Publishing* [(1-3)].

Summary

This chapter outlined the nature of forensics, provided a potted history of the development of digital forensics, and defined its purpose in light of more established forensic disciplines. An outline was presented of its value in public and private investigations and the rise and nature of cybercrime. The role of digital forensic practitioners, the skills and experience required, and the challenges they face were provided along with some case studies of digital forensic crime scenes to highlight the topic. The chapter provided not only a brief insight into the challenges the discipline faces but also some solutions to better manage them through enhanced forensic processes and tools that are emerging. Finally, the chapter endeavored to share some basic ideas for those of you considering becoming a practitioner, which you will hopefully find insightful and constructive.

Digital evidence was presented in this chapter and will be described in detail in *Chapter 3, The Nature and Special Properties of Digital Evidence.* Understanding the qualities of digital evidence, and indeed its vagaries, is essential groundwork for practitioners. Digital evidence can provide a rich treasure chest of clues about a transgression. A clue may be considered a mistake by another name, and finding and interpreting them is what really adds to the excitement of a forensic examination. Analyzing digital evidence can be rewarding, disappointing, and often a frustrating process, but a greater understanding is always gained.

Chapter 2, Hardware and Software Environments, will outline the basic workings of computer hardware and operating systems and applications typically installed on them. It will describe how these environments are used to create, store, and transfer electronic data. An insight will be provided into the workings of computers and storage devices and the location of datasets where digital evidence may be located. This sets the scene for introducing digital evidence and the analytical approach to digital forensics.

2
Hardware and Software Environments

Before looking in any detail at digital evidence and the intriguing processes of its location, recovery, and analysis, it is helpful to understand the fundamentals of computer devices and how they store digital information. Doing so will provide a sound basis for understanding the nature of digital evidence and its value to the practitioner. The nature of digital evidence will be touched upon in this chapter but will be described in greater detail in *Chapter 3, The Nature and Special Properties of Digital Evidence.*

This chapter will describe and explain the basic workings of computer hardware and the operating systems and applications typically installed on them. It will describe how these environments are used to create, store, and transfer electronic data. An insight is provided into the workings of computers and storage devices and the location of datasets where digital evidence may be located.

The topics covered in this chapter will:

- Detail the wide variety of computers and storage devices and the nature of digital information they hold of potential evidentiary value

- Describe operating system software and applications used in the creation, transfer, and storage of electronic information

- Identify and explain filesystems and files that contain evidence of evidentiary value and where they are typically located on devices

- Explain password security and encryption used to protect information and conceal evidence

Describing computers and the nature of digital information

Digital evidence comprises digital information found on a broad range of electronic devices, and it is generally considered by practitioners to consist of only the information held in digital data format that is useful to the forensic examiner because of its value in various legal proceedings. Sources of potential evidence stored on digital devices include e-mails, audio and video files, electronic documents, spreadsheets, databases, system logs, and filesystem data.

Magnetic hard drives and tapes

Information containing potential evidence is located in files stored on hard drives, memory cards, access control devices such as smart cards, biometric scanners, answering machines, digital cameras, personal digital assistants, electronic organizers, printers, removable storage devices, and media such as CD-ROM and DVD discs, telephones, copiers, credit card skimmers, digital watches, facsimile machines, and global positioning systems.

The primary storage devices used for digital information until the beginning of the century were magnetic discs, floppy drives, and tape drives. Magnetic tapes and disks store digital data in binary form, that is, as 1s and 0s, as magnetic data on the surface of metal platters. Magnetic disks rotate these magnetized platters at high speed close to an electromagnetic read/write device, which enables selected portions of the surface to be read from or written to with a moveable arm. Magnetic tapes, on the other hand, can only be accessed in sequential order by playing the tape forward or backward. Both processes are still the predominant source of storage devices to date. For the time being, they are of paramount importance in reconstructing the activities of users relating to some transgression under investigation.

Hard disk drive technology emerged in the 1950s and was the predominant form of primary digital storage. The data is saved permanently and persists on the storage device unless later removed, destroyed, or lost through some physical deterioration of the device. This type of memory is termed **non-volatile memory**. The simple and consistent design of these devices has been advantageous to forensics practitioners using well-established processes such as dead analysis and forensic tools such as write blockers to recover evidence.

The last few decades have been a golden era for digital evidence, as evidence stored on magnetic hard discs is inconvenient to expunge permanently (*Bell and Boddington 2010*). However, the advent of **Solid-State Drives (SSDs)**, outlined shortly, is taking over control of the market, especially in relation to smaller data stores on handheld devices.

Optical media storage devices

CDs, DVDs, and Blu-ray discs are optical storage media that are relatively inexpensive and are capable of read-only bulk storage. These media rely on the physical interference of light waves reflecting off miniature dips and plateaus on the reflective surface of the disc. A laser burner is used to burn the disc surface, which is relatively slow and inconvenient. The disc surface may deteriorate, requiring some form of protection before use. The data embedded on these media is also non-volatile and, generally, what has been written to the media is recoverable in theory.

Random-access memory (RAM)

The central memory core of most computers, usually called **RAM**, is also a binary-based system that is stored and processed in the **Central Processing Unit** (**CPU**) on a large array of tiny, battery-like capacitors. These memory cells or capacitors are filled selectively with electric charges, using which data can be written and read back out again. The capacitors cannot store charge permanently or for long periods. By necessity, they have to be read out regularly and automatically and the memory recharged to prevent data loss.

Unlike the non-volatile data stored on hard drives, tape drives, and optical devices, such memory is termed volatile or dynamic RAM. It is not used for long-term storage of data because the constant refreshing process requires a continual source of electrical power. The instant the device is powered down, the memory stored in the RAM quickly dissipates.

Capturing RAM may be important as it provides details of the most recent use of the device and includes some keyboard activity. However, capturing the RAM's contents while the device is powered up might result in the practitioner overwriting and contaminating the memory in RAM as well as on the hard drive. Several forensic processes for capturing RAM will be described in *Chapter 4*, *Recovering and Preserving Digital Evidence*. Powering down a device such as a laptop or a mobile phone may make it impossible to regain access to the device if it is password protected and encrypted.

Forensics practitioners have well-established processes for examining magnetic disc storage devices such as IDE, SATA, and SCSI drives. However, new-technology storage systems based on complex, transistor-based devices are becoming increasingly common. For example, during the past 10 years, there has been a transition from portable magnetic floppy discs to USB transistor flash or thumb drives.

Solid-state drive (SSD) storage devices

SSDs are faster and more complex than conventional USB flash drives or thumb drives. The technology behind SSDs is as old as magnetic disks, but they have only recently emerged as faster, lighter, and physically more robust than magnetic drives. The popularity and demand for USB flash drives has resulted in cheaper and larger devices becoming available.

However, SSD technology, which is transistor-based, is slowly replacing magnetic hard drives, is complex, and stores data differently. These devices are expensive compared with magnetic drives and typically are available in sizes from 250 gigabytes up to 1 terabyte. They have generally been regarded as fast but with a shorter life span than magnetics, although new models are proving to be more reliable and longer lasting.

SSDs typically store data in 512-kilobyte blocks, subdivided into pages composed of large arrays of **Negative AND** (**NAND**) transistors, which are similar to the logic chips used to build computer processors mentioned previously. Because of the nature of SSDs, they do need to "house clean" their storage to maintain fast processing and reduce the overuse of transistors, which would significantly reduce the life of the drive. Consequently, they may erase deleted data automatically, thereby thwarting forensic recovery (*Bell and Boddington 2010*).

Network-stored data

In the case of data stored on computer network servers, access may be provided by connecting a device to the network and the practitioner being provided with authentication details. Less common is for external connections to the network to be used to access and image datasets for later analysis. This is a typical scenario for e-discovery and serious crimes such as fraud and network misuse.

It may often be desirable to make physical images of network servers rather than recovering the logical data provided by the operating system. An organization's ability to make the physical device available for acquiring the data makes this a challenging possibility in addition to the practical implications, such as ensuring that the effect on the organization's normal activities is minimized. This challenge is described in detail in *Chapter 5, The Need for Enhanced Forensic Tools*.

The cloud

Internet-based computing that shares resources and information has become a popular network feature used by individuals, organizations, and government agencies. Commonly referred to as the cloud, it is used for online communications and to store large amounts of data, much of it of a private or confidential nature. The next figure shows a typical cloud network: a convenient point of storage for employees working away from the office to access and store data for others to access and use. Finding evidence in larger datasets dispersed over networks is proving problematic for conventional recovery tools. *Chapter 5, The Need for Enhanced Forensic Tools*, describes solutions that offer better outcomes for practitioners:

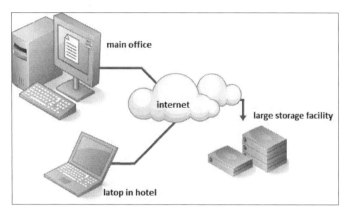

A typical cloud network

Acquiring evidence from the cloud is different and more challenging than recovering data from a network, because the data is stored on a device distinct from the device used to recover the data. Access to a cloud network is usually through the normal consumer access process to the resource, often owned by another entity. One of the challenges in recovering data is difficulty in identifying the path that the data takes from the cloud server to the storage device, which may not be a fixed route (*Adams 2013*).

Because the cloud consumers who own the data do not have physical control of the network servers storing the data, the process of obtaining a physical forensic image of the actual storage device is complicated; it is often unfeasible to do so. The network server may be located in one or more locations in different legal jurisdictions. This may often require travel and requests from the network operators to recover data, which is not always guaranteed (*Adams 2013*).

Another problem facing the practitioner arises when the network server running on the host resource is likely to be an instance of a virtual machine, which is also likely to be one of many on the same physical device. To acquire all the data, including deleted material and free space where non-erased information may be located, will require a copy of the virtual machine facilitated by someone with access to the server. This, too, raises problems with a third party being unwilling or having little incentive to assist in data recovery and possibly contaminating any evidence (*Adams 2013*).

Operating systems

An operating system is a set of programs controlling access between devices, including the keyboard, mouse, monitor, disk drive, and network devices, and application software programs such as word processors and browsers. You will be familiar with the range of Windows operating systems from Windows 1.0, released in 1985, through to the current version, Windows 10, released in 2015.

There are, of course, a range of other operating platforms that meet different user requirements, including Ubuntu, FreeBSD, Linux, iCloud, Palm OS, Blackberry OS, Xbox 360 OS, Android, and the Apple range of computers and handheld devices. This screenshot is from a typical Windows 10 operating system:

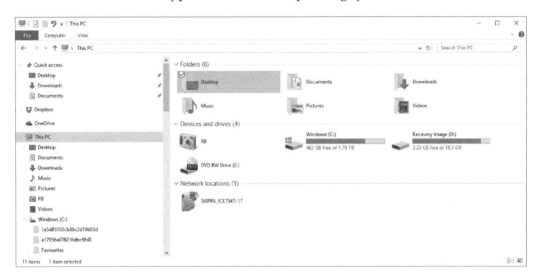

Windows 10 operating system

Connecting the software application to the operating system

To use a software application such as Paintshop requires it to be installed on a compatible operating system, such as Windows. By using the application, the user can create a picture and save it for further use, including modifying, deleting, and transferring the picture to another medium or through some communication process such as e-mailing it or uploading to the Internet. The following figure depicts the basic process of creating a picture image using Paintshop, in which the operating system allows the picture being created to be displayed on the computer monitor. The picture may be modified through the keyboard and other peripheral devices to be saved, transferred through the Internet, or printed:

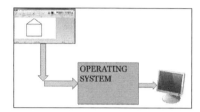

Producing a picture in Paintshop

The file is saved on the device in the creation, modification, and deletion processes, and it may later be recovered to see whether it could have some evidentiary value. The file leaves other records on the device, which, if recoverable, may also provide the practitioner with useful insight into its history.

Connecting the software application to the operating system and a device

If a device is connected to a computer device such as a scanner, special software must be installed to allow the device to connect to the operating system, which then facilitates the use of the device by the appropriate software application. This is achieved by device drivers—small programs used by an operating system to communicate with the attached device. The driver is designed to recognize a device's command language and characteristics.

Drivers are usually preinstalled on the device for convenient connection to peripheral devices such as monitors, keyboards, mice, and printers. A newer-model printer, for example, may prompt the device to download a new or updated driver through the Internet site associated with the printer or with software supplied with the printer. The following figure shows the use of a keyboard connected to a computer and enabled by the operating system to create a text document that may be viewed on a monitor:

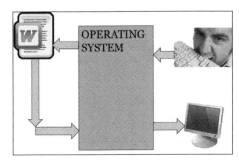

Word document creation

Describing filesystems that contain evidence

The way file information is stored varies among different operating systems. In the interest of clarity, they will be presented in the setting of the Windows filesystem environment, which is the most widely used operating system at present. However, *Chapter 7, Windows and Other Operating Systems as Sources of Evidence*, describes other operating systems in more detail and the files and filesystems they use. Files themselves may be looked at from different perspectives, and the way Windows catalogs them is a benefit to forensic examination.

Commands received from the operating system in order to read and write files are interpreted in a directory structure, incorporating a file index system that defines file naming protocols and the maximum size of the file. Microsoft operating systems manage these records in a **Master File Table** (**MFT**), where information is cataloged for every file and directory. The table is essentially a relational database table, containing various attributes about all the stored file records. For example, when an MS Word document is created and saved, it will be stored in a selected location, and timestamps will be created to record the process and the subsequent use of the file.

The value of timestamps and other file metadata will be highlighted in later chapters to demonstrate their importance in event reconstruction. This figure shows the process of storing data to a particular sector or sectors on a magnetic platter of a hard drive and its cataloging by the MFT:

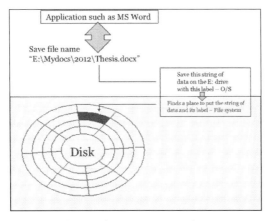

Storing data to a magnetic disc

Data is written to a file in the example in the next figure—a simplified representation of the process of writing four text documents to a hard drive platter:

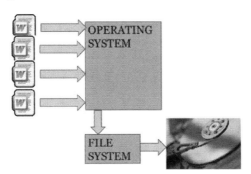

Writing files to a hard drive

The next figure represents the process of reading files from a hard drive. These files may be deleted and modified on the hard drive, which leaves metadata about these events of possible future value to the practitioner:

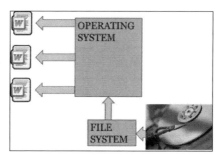

Data is read from the file stored on the platter

 Metadata is data about data; it describes various properties of a file, including the timestamp, location, creation date, date modified, last accessed date, and, sometimes, deletion dates.

The following sections describe the different categories Windows catalogs files into and outlines their value to the practitioner.

The filesystem category

The filesystem category records the general filesystem information, which, while following a general design, is a unique structure on each individual device. By cataloging this data, the filesystem category shows users where to find the data and files they are seeking as well as acting as a map for the filesystem (*Carrier 2005*). It brings order to chaos and allows sound storage and retrieval of files for users.

There is also a benefit of the filesystem, which is rich in file metadata, to practitioners. Filesystem metadata forms an essential part of practitioners' navigation and the examination of filesystem information. It can assist greatly in reconstructing events of relevance to a case (*Carrier 2005*).

However, if any of this data is corrupted or lost, then additional analysis is made more difficult because backup copies of the data and records will be required. Otherwise, the practitioner will need to guess what the original values were and guess the type of application that created the filesystem and the creation date of the file or folder.

The filename category

The filename category, sometimes referred to as the human interface category, catalogs data used to assign a name to each file. It consists of directory lists of filenames with the corresponding metadata address of each file. Deleted filenames and their corresponding metadata addresses are used to recover the file content using metadata-based recovery (*Carrier 2005*).

Being able to use filename listings is a fundamental part of forensic examinations as it allows the practitioner to identify the names of the files and parent directories and can be used for searching for evidence based on filename, path, or file extension. A file extension identifies the type of file, such as a system file or, in the case of an MS Word document, a file denoted by the `.docx` extension.

However, if the metadata address is cleared during file deletion, it may not be possible to locate further information. If only part of a filename is known, it is still possible to search using that part, such as in the case of the file extension or name being known, but not its full path. Metadata is stored in fixed-length tables with its own address. When a file is deleted, the metadata entry is changed to the unallocated state, and the operating system may wipe some of the file values. It should also be noted that file-wiping tools may delete filenames and metadata addresses or overwrite key values in the filename, showing that an entry existed before being invalidated (*Carrier 2005*).

The operating system stores all file data and metadata in binary form, which is translated to human-readable text or images through the application interface, often referred to as the **Graphical User Interface (GUI)**. This figure shows the filename data saved in binary form and the timestamp metadata:

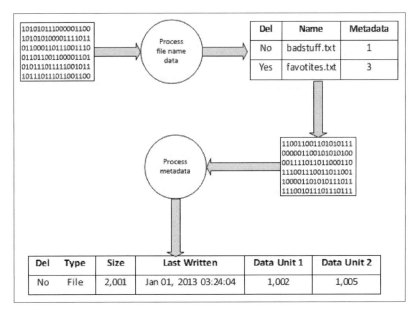

Filename information schema

The metadata category

The metadata category contains data that describes the properties or attributes of a file, displaying the file location and size. Most importantly, it provides a history of the file, providing timestamps for its creation, modification, and access. However, by itself, it does not record the contents of the file nor its name, unlike the file and content categories (*Carrier 2005*).

Analysis centers on finding more details about a specific file or searching for a file that meets certain requirements. The category contains much non-essential data and can be modified by the operating system, which can make changes to some of the metadata, such as file access times. This may provide some misleading metadata.

Metadata-based recovery may be required to look for that missing or elusive file and is used when metadata from the deleted file has not been erased. The file may have been relocated, such as being moved from one folder to another. This may prove problematic to detect as it is not uncommon when a file has been reallocated to recover two or more unallocated metadata entries that have the same file address.

Examination of metadata may assist when viewing file contents and searching for file values as well as locating deleted files. It is usually initiated when a filename points to a specific metadata structure and file examination is required (*Carrier 2005*).

The following figure shows metadata recovered from a thumbnail of a photographic image. The thumbnail database files keep a record of multimedia files stored in specific folders. Even after the original file has been removed from the folder, the small database file may remain, containing miniature versions of the original file and file metadata. In this example, the file metadata contains **Exchangeable Image File Format** (**EXIF**) data typical of photographs taken with a digital camera or device. This may provide additional details of the precise map reference where the image was taken for certain types of camera and, occasionally, the serial number of the camera.

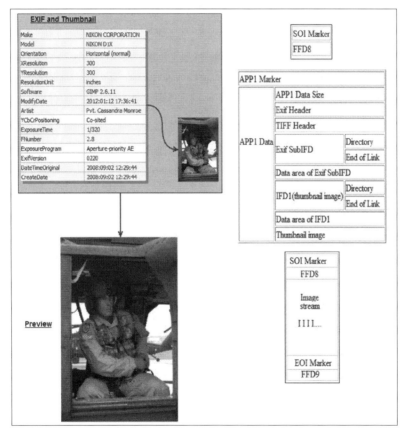

Metadata of a thumbnail file of a JPEG image

Different file types provide basic metadata and sometimes even versions of the file, as in MS Word documents. The file properties shown in the next screenshot provide details of the file creation, modification, and last accessed timestamps and the file location:

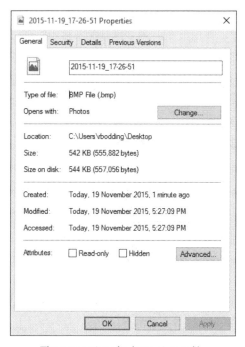

The properties of a .bmp picture file

Opening the file may recover the author of a text document and other advanced settings. However, without using some form of write protection, such action may contaminate the file metadata. Preserving the file in pristine condition to prevent unintentional modification to the file contents and metadata is an overriding requirement of sound forensic practice.

If, for example, no forensic protection was used to protect file integrity, the mere copying of the file from one location to another on the same computer will automatically alter the metadata. This contamination of the evidentiary state of the file can have serious implications for a legal case and is likely to attract a challenge by the opposing legal team. *Chapter 4, Recovering and Preserving Digital Evidence,* describes the importance of protecting digital evidence and highlights various processes and forensic tools used to prevent contamination of the evidence.

The content category

The content category consists of the contents of a file, such as the text written to a document file, figures added to a spreadsheet, or a picture inside an image file. If recovered from unallocated space, it may have no linked metadata or filename, and the only clues to its antecedents may be gleaned from the file signature and clues garnered from the contents, especially text documents.

Locating evidence in filesystems

The nature of the transgression to some extent dictates the type of relevant evidence that may be recovered. For example, in a homicide where the victim died of gunshot wounds, it would be helpful to determine the time, location, and cause of death. A search would commence for the weapon; discharged bullets or shot, spent cartridges; gunpowder residue; blood spatter; and projectile trajectory data. At a microscopic level, DNA analysis of samples from the spent cartridge, chemical analysis of the gunpowder residue, postmortem analysis to determine the cause of death, and so forth will be undertaken.

Locard's exchange principle, described in *Chapter 1*, *The Role of Digital Forensics and Its Environment*, is as relevant in a digital forensic examination as it is in the previous scenario. In a digital environment, we are also looking for the "smoking gun," which may take the form of a death threat sent to the victim by e-mail message. The e-mail itself has to be found, and the timestamp will help determine the time the message was sent. However, how do we know whether the date and time on the laptop were correct and which time zone was used? Can it be established that the message was created and actually sent from the seized laptop? Could a malicious user have created the message to cause mischief? Is there any other information that provides relevant background to the message or possible motivation? Who had access to the laptop if it was password protected?

One of the fundamental challenges practitioners face is determining with any certainty the link between a suspect and the data recovered from a computer. Without a human observer or perhaps a CCTV camera to place the suspect at the computer at the time of the transgression, it becomes a matter of an educated guess at best or speculation at worst. The practitioner must be guided by the evidence and if that proves inconclusive, he or she must look for more evidentiary clues to offer likely hypotheses as to what happened. The practitioner collects all relevant evidence that supports various hypotheses, but it is for others, such as juries, to decide whether the evidence helps determine guilt or innocence.

The challenge to practitioners is locating information or data of relevance to the case under investigation. Obviously, there has to be a reason for recovering data from devices—some transgression, offence, or activity that warrants the examination. The subject of the investigation tends to dictate the basic type of evidence that is being sought. However, finding the smoking gun may also mean looking for associated evidence that correlates with and corroborates the key evidence. It is also common for the examination to seek specific evidence in accordance with a legal brief, but during the examination, evidence of other transgressions may be recovered. Hence the need for vigilance and an open mind when trawling through digital cases.

In traditional forms of crime, investigators try to determine the means, opportunity, and motive for the transgressions being carried out. Some explanation as to how these three conditions apply in the digital environment would be helpful to consider before commencing a search for the evidence.

Determining the means of transgression

Investigators look for the means or suitable process a suspect used to carry out an illegal act, that is, determining how the transgression was carried out and by what process. The use of application software installed on a recovered device and linked to the transgression may record activities and may be useful for demonstrating how the transgression occurred. For example, the use of e-mail messaging to send a death threat or connecting to the Internet to download illegal pornography will leave an audit trail or event logs to allow a reconstruction of what happened and the processes involved. Reconstructing the transgression may be a relatively easy process, or it may be difficult to reconstruct because little record remains of the transgression and transgressors.

What appear to be simple concepts, such as sending a threatening e-mail, may require some proof that the message was created and sent from the seized device. On first inspection, this may appear to be so, but on further examination, it may become clear that while the e-mail account does record its dispatch, it does not necessarily establish that it was sent from the device. The process could have been completed by another person accessing the account remotely using a different computer. The practitioner would have to determine where the truth lay and undertake a thorough analysis of the e-mail message in relation to the computer being examined.

Another aspect of determining whether a suspect had the means to commission an offense is verifying whether the suspect had the computer skills to use the software involved, such as in the case of forging an electronic document or manipulating a photograph.

Determining opportunity to transgress

Having the opportunity to use a computer to do something illegal seems straightforward, but proving that the suspect alone had the opportunity through access to the computer may be problematic. It may be difficult, if not impossible, to link the time of the crime to a suspect's access to the computer or network in the absence of any corroboration. Audit logs recording the details of specific users accessing a computer or network often assume that the person who used the authorized user's logon details and password was the actual user. Often, that may be so, but if another person gained unauthorized access to the user details and logged on to the system, it may be difficult to prove unless there is some other evidence, such as a human observer or perhaps a CCTV recording, to clarify what occurred.

Audit and access user logs are not infallible and can be altered and falsified and are therefore not always reliable. Time and date stamps and file locations of key events help confirm the circumstances relating to a transgression. They may often help determine which user had the opportunity to transgress at a given time. Computer user access security may prohibit unauthorized access transgression and establish user identity. This would help narrow down the list of those users who may have been responsible for the transgression.

Ideally, determining who really had access to the device or network has to be established. Often, this is not conclusive and it is imprudent to assume the obvious. In criminal cases, much is made of assumptions as to who committed the offence, but it must be proven beyond reasonable doubt, and to a lesser extent in civil cases, where there is more of a balance of probability and a lower threshold. Yet, we still see a tendency to assume that the owner and custodian is usually the primary suspect for having carried out some unlawful activity. At least in the initial stages of an investigation, that seems logical. Further inquiry, though, can often show that others may have access to the computer or the network, so the circle of potential suspects widens. It follows that a thorough check of user access to the device must be completed. This is to show fairness in the examination to make sure that the list of potential users is determined.

Opportunity by a suspect may be discounted if a plausible and verifiable alibi can be offered to show that the suspect did not have the opportunity to commit the transgression. Many alibis are offered in computer-based crimes, including the fanciful and discredited alibi offered by Keith Griffin, sentenced to 12 years in jail in 2010 in the US for downloading child pornography onto his computer. Griffin blamed his cat for walking on the keyboard, resulting in the download of indecent photographs! (You can find more about the case at `http://newsfeed.time.com/2010/09/12/man-blames-cat-for-child-porn-on-his-computer/`.)

The issue of analyzing data to link events to specific users is described in more detail in *Chapter 9*, *Validating the Evidence*.

Determining the motive to transgress

It is not essential to prove motive, and it is often difficult to do so without perhaps some form of confession by the transgressor, for who knows what was in the mind of the transgressor at the time of the act? However, data may exist on a device that may offer some explanation to possible motivation or, for that matter, an absence of motive and criminal intent.

Motive may be determined by collecting evidence that links the user to some activities that confirm a degree of knowledge and control over the computer and relevant applications and files used in the transgression. Always be wary of the obvious. Speculation such as "it is the suspect's computer; therefore, the suspect is responsible" is highly inappropriate, even it if not voiced by the practitioner. As mentioned in *Chapter 1*, *The Role of Digital Forensics and Its Environment*, evidence-led investigations and forensic examinations are logical and more scientifically objective, but in cases dependent on digital evidence, it can be a vexatious process to unravel the truth.

False evidence, too, can relatively easily be generated by mischief-makers out to implicate an innocent party, which is demonstrated in the case study at the end of this chapter.

Deciding where to look for possible evidence

We have a transgression; somebody had the means, the opportunity, and the motive to commit it using a computing device. Records of the applications and files used and the operating system can provide some useful electronic fingerprints to help practitioners reconstruct what happened, when it happened, where on the device or in the system it occurred, how it happened, and, hopefully, why it happened — the often-hard-to-prove motive. So where should the practitioner start?

Computers and other devices store information in directory systems of varying sorts, similar to Windows Explorer. This screenshot shows part of a Windows directory structure viewed through the advanced forensic tool ILookIX:

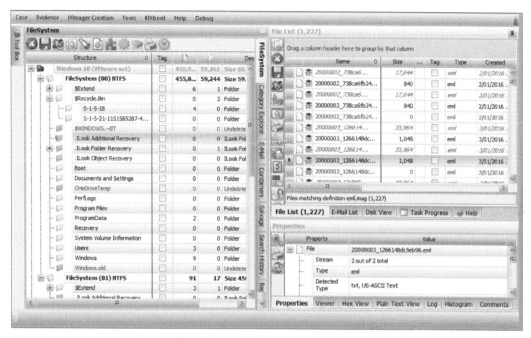

File directory structure under Windows 10

However, the number of files stored on a typical computer makes it impracticable because of time constraints and the fatigue of checking every file. Some are system files that will not normally be examined other than for specific checking. So, providing the practitioner with easy-to-review categories of files would be more helpful. If, for example, webpage files such as HTML and other categories were conveniently categorized, it would make locating and selecting evidence quicker and less tedious.

File categories can be divided into file signature and file type, as shown in ILookIX's **Category Explorer** panel in the next screenshot. File signatures recognize the internal structure and pattern of a file, while file types are based on the application software that uses the files, such as Microsoft Office using Word to open a file with the .docx file extension:

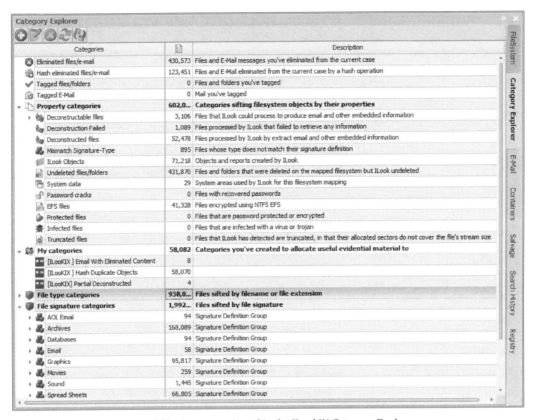

File types and file signatures viewed in the ILookIX Category Explorer pane

If e-mail messages or multimedia files were being sought, then these helpful catalogs would be a convenient start to a search. The main areas of interest may be cataloged and provide some useful starting points for a broad range of cases, as detailed in the examples set out in this table:

Category	Reason for search
Archive files	These include zipped and compressed files whose contents may be relevant to the investigation.
Audio	These files may record some Skype conversations or provide evidence of downloading music files in breach of copyright regulations.

Category	Reason for search
Databases	These include databases of thumbnail files (.db) and other records relating to user activities on the device.
E-mails	These are a rich source of information about human communications and sometimes contain incriminating evidence.
Event logs	These are records of various user and system activities retained by the device—useful for recreating timelines of events.
Internet browser files	These provide a record of browsing activities as well as a record of searches made that may relate to an investigation.
Link files	These files tell us about the files and applications most recently used and help reconstruct user activities and timelines of events.
Microsoft Office suite	This includes text and other documents relating to the activities of users and other respondents.
Recycler	Deleted files and folders are often a rich source of evidence.
Registry files	The registry records the state of various features available to users and has a record of various devices attached to the computer.
System files	Most of these may be irrelevant to an examination but some play an important role in reconstructing relevant events.
Video	These files may contain evidence of user activities of relevance to a case, or child exploitation material, for example.

Indexing and searching for files

Indexing and searching for files is another option and a more advanced process much favored by practitioners to locate information stored in large datasets, including desktop computers and laptops, with greater speed and convenience. It allows the data to be indexed based on file type and signature as well as filename, contents, metadata, time frame, size dimensions, and so on. So, for example, if looking for an e-mail death threat sent at an estimated time, the practitioner can search for all e-mails originating during that period and search for the content of the e-mail, such as details of the threat. The search could also be filtered to save time by looking for sender and receiver details that match known information.

Searches may be **index-based** or keyword searches. Index-based searches require the indexing of each file in the dataset that the practitioner decides may be relevant to the examination and can filter out extraneous files that would otherwise slow down the indexing and searching processes. Although indexing can take some time, it is machine-generated and will be described in more detail in *Chapter 5, The Need for Enhanced Forensic Tools*. Once the dataset is indexed, the time for a search is almost instantaneous, with quicker results of hits being provided to the practitioner. Keyword searches take longer but are also time savers.

The following screenshot shows a variety of search terms populating a configuration file created by the advanced ISeekDesigner program, which provides the practitioner with a rich selection of keyword search terms. In this process, the configuration file is used by the ISeekDiscovery automaton to search for the terms, which are later indexed for speedier analysis:

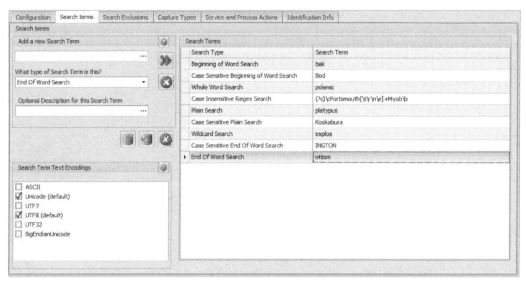

A variety of keyword search terms populating the ISeekDesigner configuration file

Search results are presented in a variety of formats, allowing the practitioner to examine a smaller and more manageable dataset, as highlighted in the following screenshot. It shows the result of a search of a large dataset consisting of more than two million files resulting in the identification of six files that assist the case reconstruction of this training crime simulation designed by me:

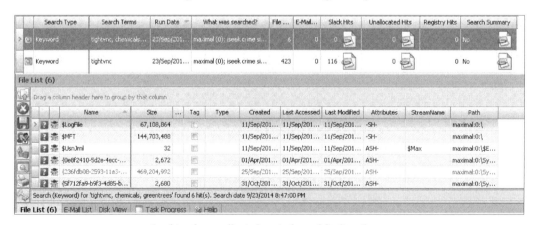

Looking for needles in haystacks and finding them

Unallocated data analysis

The area available to store data on a hard drive or storage drive depends on the size of the device and any installed components. For example, a newly acquired laptop may have on it the operating system and a range of basic software applications, system files, user data, and so forth. The remaining space, in pristine condition, is available to store data as required by the user, system, and software applications. This free space or unallocated space is initially empty but soon starts getting filled during normal usage.

Files may be recovered from allocated space, where they are maintained by the operating system in what is called a logical state. Most of the files here, unless they are hidden files, may be located and recovered during forensic recovery. The same may be said of deleted files that remain in the `trash` folder.

Eventually, the device can run out of space and crash the operating system or at least make its operation sluggish. Files are frequently deleted by users and held in the trash bin, from where they may be restored or removed back into unallocated space. There, the remnants of the file remain but will be further eroded and eventually completely overwritten by new files being written to and occupying the same space.

However, forensic tools allow the practitioner to recover these files or fragments of deleted files that may assist in reconstructing key events in a case. Deleted files may be readily recoverable by checking for deleted filenames held in file directories. However, it is not uncommon for the names of deleted files to be reused before any changes to the metadata are made. The files may have retained no filename, but the file metadata may still persist. Conversely, the filename and metadata may remain but not the file contents.

Consistency checking of unallocated blocks by an experienced practitioner may reveal deliberate attempts at data hiding or filesystem errors that have hidden data. Data wiping may be detected too by finding a zeroed or invalid entry between two valid entries. Data carving is the technique used to undertake the recovery of file fragments and can be done manually using a hex editor or automatically using advanced forensic tools. These tools and processes are described in more detail in *Chapter 5, The Need for Enhanced Forensic Tools*, and *Chapter 6, Selecting and Analyzing Digital Evidence*. However, unless access to the device can be gained, all these attempts at data recovery may be thwarted if the device is password protected and encrypted.

Explaining password security, encryption, and hidden files

The following sections describe password security and encryption and ways to protect information and conceal evidence from prying eyes. They outline the basic processes of managing the security of computer devices and networks as well as describing the reasons why digital information needs protection from a wide range of threats.

User access to computer devices

To protect data stored on a device from unauthorized access, user access controls offer some degree of protection. This applies to desktops, laptops, mobile phones and other handheld devices, home security systems, and a broad range of other electronic equipment. Not only is it essential to restrict direct human access to information to those who are authorized, but the information also needs protection from access by other programs, processes, or systems that may be connected to the device. For example, workers logged in to a network server should normally have no access to other workers' terminals (unless in a supervisory or support role). Otherwise, there would be no security of sensitive information, and it would be a chaotic situation at best.

So why is user access so important? Well, information has value in terms of its confidentiality, integrity, and availability, which are all at risk and need protection. These terms are described in the following subsections.

Understanding the importance of information confidentiality

Confidentiality or privacy is required to prevent unauthorized access to information. Even if the access is authorized, a user may use that information in an unauthorized way. For example, a coworker sees that a colleague has left the office but has left the computer running, thus permitting unauthorized access. The coworker accesses the computer and reads some confidential documents and puts knowledge of that information to improper (unauthorized) use. Later, the custodian of the information is investigated and there is no record of unauthorized access to his or her computer. The practitioner may be able to reconstruct the events and times of the unauthorized access, but it is unlikely that evidence of the intruder will be detected from the computer records.

Understanding the importance of information integrity

The integrity of information also requires protection: some sort of assurance or guarantee that the information has remained in pristine condition, is unaltered, and is uncontaminated. The creator and custodian of the information need some confidence that it has not been altered or corrupted by unauthorized action by human intervention or perhaps by a computer or system glitch.

Take, for example, a hacker gaining access to a victim's computer, such as a bank computer, and secretly changing the contents of important financial records as part of an online fraud. Such attacks not only alter the integrity of the records, but somebody gains and somebody loses. It also follows that bank personnel who have legitimate access to the records initially become the prime suspects.

The integrity of information requires some guarantee, then, that the information was not subject to unauthorized creation, modification, or manipulation and that all related transactions were genuine and proper.

Understanding the importance of information availability

Information availability means that information is accessible to those wishing to use it. However, a user may inadvertently deny themselves or others access to information, or a system process may render the information unavailable. Hackers and other malcontents use cyberattacks to deny users and organizations access to their own information. These attacks are termed **denial of availability attacks** and may also involve some form of extortion, demanding financial payment to ensure the information is made accessible once again to its rightful owners. A forensic examination of the networks and infected computer terminals may find the cause of the denial and allow the organization to restore access to continue normal business. An insight into new approaches of malware detection will be provided in *Chapter 5, The Need for Enhanced Forensic Tools*.

User access security controls

Protecting a computer, mobile phone, or network from unauthorized access is part of the security management of information resources. A day does not pass without there being some headline of cybersecurity breaches or us hearing of acquaintances whose computer or network has been attacked and compromised by an intruder. With the advances in technologies intended to improve the human condition comes a sinister downside threatening the privacy, integrity, and availability of information assets.

Protection against unauthorized access is done through strictly regulating who can access the data and what data can be accessed. User access management may be regarded as the first line of defense and is seldom infallible. It uses a range of protection processes based on an established security policy. For example, in its simplest form, when purchasing a new laptop computer, the user is usually granted administrator access—a higher level of management control of the device. As administrator, other users and guest users may be allowed to use the device by the creation of other user accounts, which may or may not be password protected.

For network systems, a more complex hierarchy of access control is used to channel a larger number of network users through tight access control points and levels. A list of users and details of their access rights or privileges is recorded, and an audit record of the date, time, and duration of each user's access would be recorded.

Passwords or passphrases are normally used in conjunction with the user's unique identification name. Biometric protection, such as fingerprint and iris detection, may be used, or some other form of security protection may be in place to deter and minimize the likelihood of unauthorized exploits.

Various applications provide some means of bypassing or unlocking hidden passwords so that access to the contents of a drive become readily available. Password-protected devices can present difficulties to practitioners seeking to examine a device, especially if the contents are encrypted, which is outlined more in the following subsection.

Encrypted devices and files

Encryption has been used for millennia to conceal information from unauthorized viewing; even when the message has been intercepted, encryption prevents, or at least hinders, unauthorized viewing of the contents of the message or container. In terms of protecting digital devices and messages, various forms of privacy security technologies are used to maintain the confidentiality of information. Encryption technologies are apparent on most digital devices, notably desktop computers, mobile phones and tablets, and server networks. They also include the secure encryption of e-mail and other telecommunication messages.

The Achilles heel of encryption, irrespective of its level of encryption, is the password or passphrase or other form of access control used to open the encrypted store. Without this access key, the data will remain unopened. Some simple forms of encryption, such as Word document protection, may be easily thwarted by the use of readily available programs on the Internet that will defeat the simple encryption protecting the documents. More advanced encryption applications may also be circumvented, but the robustness of the algorithm used to protect the information may make it a time-consuming process to open the store. Advanced encryption techniques used on more recent devices and, particularly, mobile phones with encrypted sectors and microchips are presently defeating experts seeking access with supposedly sophisticated forensic tools.

The problems facing practitioners confronted with locked and encrypted devices is becoming a serious challenge and will be discussed later in the book.

Case study – linking the evidence to the user

This case study relates to the examination of a forensic image of the defendant's laptop computer provided by law enforcement officers in 2006. A number of photographs and videos of underage sex were discovered on the defendant's laptop by a computer repairer, who reported the matter to the police, resulting in the seizure of the laptop and criminal charges being laid in 2008. The 2 year delay from arrest to trial may be assumed to be due to the heavy workload of the agency involved.

The defendant's apparent disbelief that he had downloaded illegal, pornographic files onto the laptop and the insistence of his innocence prompted the defense team's examination to measure the reliability of the relevant information, thereby assisting subsequent legal analysis. The offending material had been placed on the laptop during 2004 and 2005, and the laptop had been repaired by the same computer repairer during this period, who evidently did not notice and report sighting the material on the first occasion.

Examination by the defense team expert of the available information derived from the physical and logical restoration of the seized computer confirmed the police assertion that illegal movie files were most likely downloaded during the period between September and October 2004. It was evident that these files were most likely downloaded to the laptop through the use of the LimeWire program, with the remainder downloaded in January 2005 and probably viewed at that time on the device.

Both RealPlayer and Windows Media Player were installed on the computer, based on an examination of the relevant file-creation dates of the executable parts of the programs. These applications play movie, audio, and image files. Both applications have the ability to record the viewing of the most recently played files. According to the agency report, a number of the most recently played files had the same filenames as those identified as the movies of interest. Re-examination of the data confirmed that a number of the illegal files had been accessed several times by RealPlayer and only on one occasion by Windows Media Player.

The defendant's young teenage child had access to the laptop during the period, and two obscene image files were created on the computer and accessed. The last accessed dates of the movie and images were inadvertently altered by the virus-scanning program, obfuscating the dates and making reconstruction of the movie and image viewer applications incomplete. The agency's misreading of the unreliable last accessed date of the key files was tendered as evidence of the files being accessed by a user, thereby extending the period of possible criminal activity. In fact, the file metadata challenged the assertion and weakened the prosecution claim.

Taking the digital evidence at face value, at the point of seizure of the laptop, it may have seemed logical to assume that the defendant, the owner and custodian of the computer and whose house it was located in, was the likely suspect. However, others had access to the computer during the periods in which the movies were accessed and viewed between September 2005 to the date of seizure in 2006. Moreover, a young couple who lived at the residence from late June 2005 to early February 2006 also had unrestricted access. A number of other persons (friends of the couple) also had access to the laptop during the same period. Another person also lived at the residence between July 2005 and September 2005. It was common for the defendant to take the laptop to his place of work, where others were granted unrestricted access to it.

There was also evidence of the defendant being absent from his town during the time some of the illegal files were downloaded and played on the laptop. The defendant's teenage child was present and had a number of friends stay over at the home on a weekly basis, and they were believed to have used the laptop. Password security was basic, and the password known to whoever wished to use it.

Examination by the defense expert of the reconstructed usage timeline showed that an illegal movie file was modified and written to on 17 October 2005, when the laptop was believed to be in the possession of the computer repairer. This matter was not raised by the prosecution or disclosed to the defense team, yet it raised the likelihood of another potential suspect.

There was also some discrepancy over the actual number of illegal movies and duplicates of the same files located on the device. However, re-examination of the forensic image showed there to be six unique movies and nine copies of some of the files in contrast to a much large number claimed by the prosecution. The lack of precise recording of the files key to the prosecution's case raised doubts as to the professionalism of the prosecution expert.

The presence of malicious software in the form of a Trojan, `A0044827.exe Infected: Backdoor.Win32.Agent`, was evident on the computer. However, it was not shown that the malware had infected and facilitated control of the laptop rendering it vulnerable to unauthorized remote control. Again, checking of this malware's activity on the laptop was left to the defense expert to determine and at cost to the defendant!

Not surprisingly, the case against the defendant was dismissed.

This may well contribute to incomplete and biased analysis leading to a conviction using questionable evidence and faulty analysis. Great care must always be taken to ensure evidence-led investigation and not a suspect-led process, as appears to have occurred in this investigation.

References

Adams, R. 2013. "The emergence of cloud storage and the need for a new digital forensic process model." Cybercrime and Cloud Forensics: Applications for Investigation Processes: 79-104. Edited by K. Ruan. Hershey, USA: IGI Global.

Bell, G. B. and R. G. Boddington 2010. "Solid State Drives: The Beginning of the End for Current Practice in Digital Forensic Recovery?" Journal of Digital Forensics, Security and Law, 5(3): 1-20.

Carrier, B. 2005. File system forensic analysis. Upper Saddle River, New Jersey: Addison-Wesley.

Summary

This chapter described a variety of computers and storage devices and outlined the nature of digital information they hold of potential evidentiary value. The explanation of the functions and nature of operating system software and applications introduced the processes of file creation, file transfer, and the storage of electronic information. The chapter introduced and explained the nature of filesystems and outlined some typical files that contain evidence of evidentiary value and where they may be located on devices. A summary of password security and encryption has shown that digital devices are becoming more advanced and are using encryption as an effective security feature. This now poses some significant problems to practitioners attempting to look for concealed evidence.

Digital evidence as presented in this chapter is described in greater detail in *Chapter 3, The Nature and Special Properties of Digital Evidence*, which explains its nature and special attributes and really does dictate the forensic approach practitioners follow when engaged in case examinations. Digital evidence shares many of the characteristics of other types of evidence, but it does have unique properties of its own that make it both rewarding and challenging to explore and harness. *Chapter 3, The Nature and Special Properties of Digital Evidence*, highlights the technical complexities of digital evidence and the challenges they pose to practitioners in their analysis and explanation of the evidence to the courts. It defines the weight of admissibility and the requirements that digital forensics must meet for it to be considered admissible for use in legal cases.

3

The Nature and Special Properties of Digital Evidence

By the beginning of the twenty-first century, more than half of criminal cases involved a computing device of some description, and the trend has continued and is likely to rise. Its use in legal cases too has grown and shows no sign of diminishing. Digital evidence is derived from the examination of a wide range of digital devices and shares similar characteristics with other forms of evidence. There are some differences that enhance evidence recovery analysis, but, as will be seen in this book, there are characteristics that also make it challenging for practitioners.

This chapter defines and describes the special properties of digital evidence and its contribution to investigations. The topics specifically covered in this chapter will:

- Define digital evidence and its use

- Explain the special properties of digital evidence, including its time and location metadata and file characteristics

- Highlight the technical complexities of digital evidence and challenges to sound analysis

- Explain the requirements for determining the admissibility of digital evidence

- Provide a sample case study to illustrate the nature of digital evidence and its value in legal cases

Defining digital evidence

Digital evidence is information in digital form found on a wide range of computer devices; in fact, it is anything that has a microchip or has been processed by one and then stored on other media. Digital data is a numerical representation that is usually in binary form, as distinct from electronic data stored in analog form. It has been alleged that an Australian narcotics trafficker concealed a spreadsheet of his customers and transactions inside a microchip implanted in his pet dog. It was uncovered when a canny police officer queried the presence of a microchip implant gun, readily available online for a modest cost, in the suspect's premises. This discovery prompted minor surgery on the dog to remove the tag, which was later found to contain the incriminating information in the form of a spreadsheet containing a list of narcotics dealers and transactions.

Evidence tendered in legal cases, such as criminal trials, is classified as witness testimony or direct evidence, or indirect evidence in the form of an object, such as physical documents, the property owned by persons, and so forth. Evidence in electronic form, including digital and analog data, is defined as real evidence and sometimes as documentary evidence. It has also been referred to as IT evidence, electronic evidence, or computer evidence. Digital evidence includes e-mails, electronic documents, spreadsheets, databases, system logs, and audio, picture, and video files, amongst others. The most common form of evidence presented to courts is spoken word by practitioners when providing interpretations of digital evidence.

The use of digital evidence

Evidence in legal cases is used to prove (or refute) facts that are in dispute as well as proving the plausibility of disputed facts—most notably, circumstantial evidence or indirect evidence. Digital evidence, just like documentary evidence, provides inferences that may assist in proving some key fact of the case. It helps investigators and legal teams develop reliable hypotheses or theories as to the perpetrator of a crime. Its usefulness is apparent in establishing a link between a crime, the victim, and the perpetrator of that crime. The reliability of the evidence is paramount to supporting or refuting any hypothesis put forward as to the involvement of possible suspects. We will look at this more in *Chapter 6, Selecting and Analyzing Digital Evidence*.

Digital evidence can take many forms depending on the circumstances of each case and the devices from which the evidence is recovered. In the past, the most common recoveries have been from desktop and laptop computers and network servers. Digital evidence collected assists in both criminal and civil cases and, on occasion, may be the only evidence tendered. Recovery from desktop and laptop computers was generally performed by physically removing the hard drive from the source device and connecting it to the practitioner's computer. To prevent or minimize contamination of the suspect's source device, we can use a hardware device called a **write blocker** on the suspect's device so as to copy data potentially holding evidence. The use of hardware and software write-blocking tools and processes is described in detail in *Chapter 4, Recovering and Preserving Digital Evidence*.

The imaging process is intended to copy all blocks of data from the suspect's to the practitioner's target device. This is sometimes referred to as a physical copy of all data, as distinct from a logical copy, which will only copy what a user would normally see. Logical copies do not capture all the data, and the process will alter some file metadata to the extent that its forensic value is greatly diminished, resulting in possible legal challenge by the opposing legal team. Therefore, a full bit-for-bit copy is the preferred forensic process. The file created on the target device is called a **forensic image file** and various formats are available, including .AFF, .ASB, .E01, and .dd or raw image files, and virtual image formats such as .VMDK and .VDI.

The following screenshot shows a .ASB forensic image container produced by IXImager, which contains an encrypted log and an image file:

Name	Date modified	Type	Size
Suspect	26/11/2015 10:12 ...	Text Document	90 KB
Suspect001.asb	26/11/2015 10:12 ...	ASB File	154,327,10...

An ASB container and log file

The benefit of being able to make an exact copy of the data is that it can be copied and the original device can be returned to the owner or stored for trial without normally having to be examined repeatedly. This reduces the likelihood of drive failure or evidence contamination. The following screenshot shows part of the log file of an imaging process. This may be presented during legal proceedings to confirm the nature and circumstances of the imaging undertaken by the practitioner:

```
2015-11-26 11:58:26 syslogd started: BusyBox v1.16.2
2015-11-26 11:58:26 kernel: Initializing cgroup subsys cpuset
2015-11-26 11:58:26 kernel: Initializing cgroup subsys cpu
2015-11-26 11:58:26 kernel: Linux version 3.4.49-x86-erik (andersen@git.perlustro.com) (gcc version 4.7.2
(GCC) ) #1 SMP Fri Jun 14 17:06:52 MDT 2013

2015-11-26 11:58:27 root: System Information
2015-11-26 11:58:27 root:      Product Name: HP Compaq 4000 Pro SFF PC
2015-11-26 11:58:27 root:      Version:
2015-11-26 11:58:27 root:      UUID: XXXXXXXXXXXXXXXXXXXXXXXXXXXXXXXXXX
2015-11-26 11:58:27 root:      SKU Number: LE123PA#ABG
2015-11-26 11:58:27 root:      Family: 103C_53307F G=D
2015-11-26 11:58:27 root:      Manufacturer: Hewlett-Packard
2015-11-26 11:58:27 root:      Version: Not Specified
2015-11-26 11:58:27 root: Chassis Information
2015-11-26 11:58:27 root:      Manufacturer: Hewlett-Packard
2015-11-26 11:58:27 root:      Lock: Not Present
2015-11-26 11:58:27 root:      Serial Number: XXXXXXXX
2015-11-26 11:58:27 root:      Boot-up State: Safe
2015-11-26 11:58:27 root:      Power Supply State: Safe
2015-11-26 11:58:27 root:      Security Status: Unknown

2015-11-26 12:01:09 iimager: Making a Image of /dev/sda
2015-11-26 12:01:09 iimager: A 250.1 GB SAMSUNG HD256GJ Hard Drive
2015-11-26 12:01:09 iimager: Image will be stored on /dev/sdc
2015-11-26 12:01:09 iimager: A 2.000 TB Seagate Expansion Hard Drive
2015-11-26 12:01:09 iimager:    Output File Format: ILook Default Image Format
2015-11-26 12:01:09 iimager:      Output File Size: Unlimited
2015-11-26 12:01:09 iimager:           Compression: Enabled
2015-11-26 12:01:09 iimager:            Encryption: Disabled
2015-11-26 12:01:09 iimager: Case Number: XXXXXXXXXXXXX
2015-11-26 12:01:09 iimager: Agent Name: Richard Boddington
2015-11-26 12:01:09 iimager: Machine Owner: XXXXXXXX
2015-11-26 12:01:09 iimager: Seizure Address: XXXXXX Perth
2015-11-26 12:01:09 iimager: Known Passwords: XXXXXX
2015-11-26 12:01:14 iimager: User exited the Final Options Menu
2015-11-26 12:01:14 iimager: Beginning Image operation
2015-11-26 12:01:14 kernel: tntfs info: NTFS volume version 3.1 (cluster_size 32768, PAGE_CACHE_SIZE 4096).
2015-11-26 12:01:14 iimager: Opened output file '/ILookImager/ILook.001/XXXXXX001.asb'
2015-11-26 12:01:14 iimager: Calibrating '/dev/sdc2' for output, a 2.000 TB NTFS Filesystem on USB0
2015-11-26 12:01:16 iimager: Image is being stored to /ILook.001/ILook.001/XXXXXXX001.asb
2015-11-26 12:01:16 iimager: A 2.000 TB NTFS Filesystem on USB0
2015-11-26 12:01:16 iimager: Image is being stored to /ILook.001/XXXXXXX001.asb

2015-11-26 13:00:08 iimager: Image Complete
2015-11-26 13:00:08 iimager: Image was completed successfully.
2015-11-26 13:00:08 iimager: Read          :  250.1 GB (250059350016 bytes)
2015-11-26 13:00:08 iimager: Written       :  72.74 GB (72744460583 bytes)
2015-11-26 13:00:08 iimager: Total Processed:  250.1 GB (250059350016 bytes)
2015-11-26 13:00:08 iimager: Image Speed   :  70.80 MB/sec
2015-11-26 13:00:08 iimager: Elapsed Time  :  0h 58m 52s
2015-11-26 13:00:08 iimager: Compression   :  70.91 percent
2015-11-26 13:00:08 iimager: Bad Sectors   :  0
2015-11-26 13:00:08 iimager: Copying logfile to ILook.001/
2015-11-26 13:00:08 iimager: Clearing computer memory...
```

The log file shows the period of imaging of a 250-GB drive

Special forensics tools are required to open and examine the data held in an image, and they do so without altering the image and contaminating the evidence, in the tradition of sound forensic practice. Unlike an organic or physical exhibit, such as a corpse or an oil painting, where biopsies of tissue and samples of canvas and paint are excised and usually destroyed during testing, a forensic image preserves all the data in pristine condition. It allows files of importance to be extracted and displayed using the forensic software, but it does not change the composition and integrity of the image or the files and metadata it contains.

Being able to examine files and folders from an image to reconstruct events of relevance requires a user-friendly interface. Looking at system files, navigating file directories, and opening cache folders to view browsing history are now supported by enhanced forensic software. The following screenshot shows a text file being viewed using ILookIX so that the contents may be viewed while deciding whether the file is relevant to the investigation:

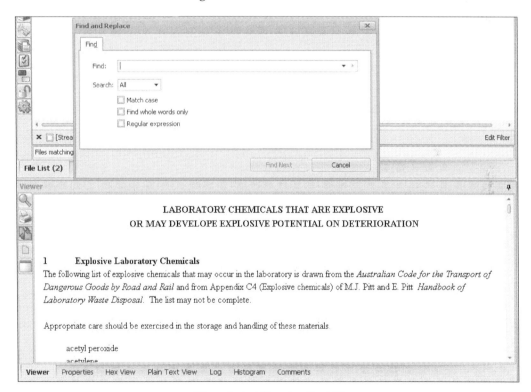

View of a text file using ILookIX

The exact view of a file is shown in the following screenshot, which displays the **Properties** sheet that provides a record of the file metadata, including timestamps and file location. This information may be useful in the reconstruction of a transgression or identifying a link to a perpetrator:

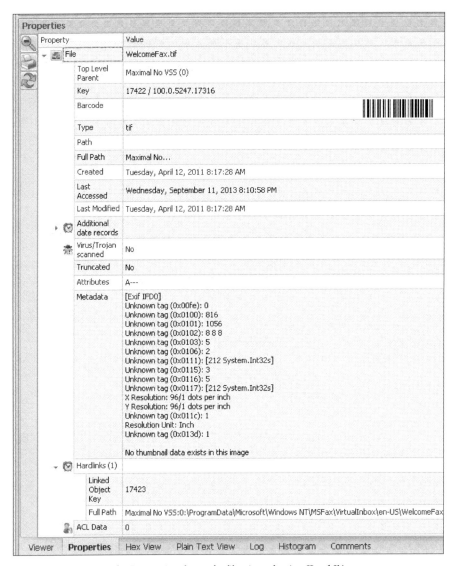

The Properties sheet of a file viewed using ILookIX

Similarly, recovering and viewing information from network server computers may be restricted because the organization may not want to stop its normal business, because each server or folder on a server may be imaged. To do so may be costly and time-consuming and not guaranteed to recover the sought-for evidence. The following figure shows a spreadsheet of search results of the ISeekDiscovery automaton deployed on a large dataset to recover files of potential value to an investigation without disrupting the functions of the network or contaminating the data:

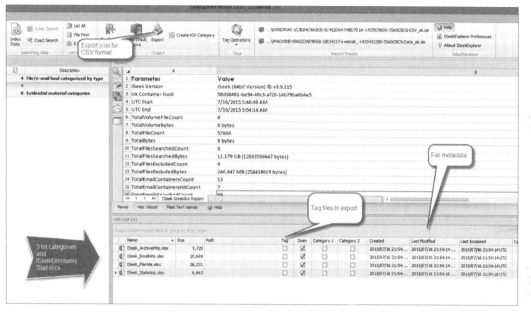

The ISeekDiscovery automaton: search term hit statistics and corresponding recovered files

The following screenshot shows files of interest that have been selected for further analysis. This can be shared with the investigator and legal team for them to see whether the information is useful and should then be extracted:

	Categories	▲		Description
	Available FileTypes		39,629	File/e-mail load categorized by type
	Case categories		0	Evidential material categories
	Search Results		3	Previous search results
	fraud: 26/06/2015 8:14:19 PM		566	fraud
	hutchens: 26/06/2015 7:24:...		67	hutchens
	hutchens: 26/06/2015 7:32:...		1,422	hutchens

ISeekExplorer Explorer

File categories based on search terms for later analysis

Mobile phones and other handheld devices are not imaged in the same way as desktops. The hardware and interface of external devices such as a forensic computer are different. Let's use the iPhone as a good example: unless the password is known, the device cannot be accessed. Apple uses a series of encrypted sectors located on microchips, making it difficult to access the raw data inside the phone. Special software has been developed for the recovery and analysis of data from mobile phones, **global positioning system** (**GPS**) devices, tablets, and remote phone modems.

This software connects the examiner's computer to the mobile device, which, through a series of user commands and some small changes to the settings on the device, allows the extraction of data. The software offers a logical extraction of the basic information on the device together with a record of the device characteristics and an extraction log. This enables a speedy triage of the data. Until recently, more detailed extraction of mobile phones was possible, permitting an extraction or a dump of much more of the device data in what was termed a physical extraction. The iPhone model 4S onward no longer enables physical extractions. More recent versions of Android devices similarly prevent more than a backup being taken of the device and no longer allow physical dumps to be recovered. The attached SIM card and any data-storage SD card can also be examined by these applications.

Leading software applications, such as Cellebrite and Microsystemation's XRY kits, create a proprietary evidence container of the device data that is recovered including extraction logs. The container can only be read by the software but does allow extractions and exports of files for further analysis. The software user interface is now refined and facilitates quicker analysis and report production, especially in larger investigations involving a greater number of devices.

The following screenshot shows an example of a physical extraction case summary in the XRY viewer screen. In this example, in an earlier Android version (2.3.4), it was possible to make a physical extraction of important evidence of browsing activities. This extra evidence provided the defendant the opportunity to prove his innocence of serious criminal charges. Recent testing by my fellow researchers shows that a considerable amount of data exists that is not captured by conventional extraction software:

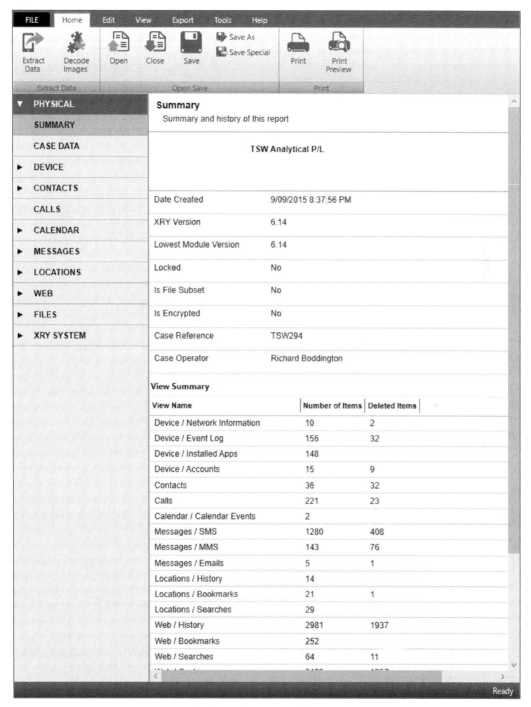

An XRY case summary view of a physical extraction of a Samsung GT-S7500l Galaxy Ace Plus

However, while connecting to the device, care must be taken to ensure that it does not connect to a mobile network, local Wi-Fi, or Bluetooth devices in the proximity. SIM cards are removed and may be examined separately to protect contamination to the phone by inadvertent local connections. There are numerous cases where mobile phones have been remotely reset to factory default mode, thereby wiping any data needed for examination. Remote-wiping applications, intended to allow phone owners to wipe private data on their phones in the event of theft or loss, are now used by those wishing to frustrate investigators from accessing potential evidence.

Unlike laptops and desktop computers, mobile phones are not fully write-block protected by forensic software and tools during data recovery. Small-sized programs are often installed on them to assist in the extraction process. This has the potential to contaminate and overwrite some space on the device, which, while not ideal, is unavoidable. *Chapter 8, Examining Browsers, E-mails, Messaging Systems, and Mobile Phones* will describe in more detail mobile phone forensics and the challenges it is presently posing to practitioners because of enhanced encryption.

The special characteristics of digital evidence

It will perhaps be useful for you to get some explanation as to what the courts consider to be acceptable and unacceptable evidence. There are different categories of evidence tendered in legal proceedings. The most common is **direct evidence**, sometimes called **witness** or **testimonial** evidence. This is evidence of events observed by the witness and depends on the credibility of the witness in terms of the reliability of the witness's memory, honesty, objectivity, and so on. Such witness testimony may be challenged and refuted, but it often goes a long way in establishing the truth of a matter before the court.

Human testimony must be based on human observation—an **eyewitness** account, as it is often called. It may be something the witness directly heard, felt, smelled, tasted, or touched, but it must not be **hearsay evidence** or layperson opinion. Hearsay evidence is any matter relevant to a case that a witness has not observed personally through the five senses.

Courts have strict rules regarding hearsay and normally will disallow evidence that has not been directly observed by the witness. For example, if a police officer is informed by a witness of an offense that has taken place and apprehends the perpetrator, the officer cannot provide evidence of what the witness observed and has made a claim about. Such evidence from the officer would be rejected as it would be considered unreliable. The witness may tell the court what was observed, not the officer. Courts do not consider hearsay to be credible, particularly as the courts are denied the ability to cross-examine for determining witness credibility.

There are exceptions to the rule, which are made by court practice, **legislation**, and **case law**. Opinion, for example, may be tendered as expert and scientific opinion, which will be discussed in greater detail in *Chapter 6, Selecting and Analyzing Digital Evidence*.

The circumstantial nature of digital evidence

Unlike evidence tendered by a human witness, which must be based on what was observed by the witness, **indirect evidence**, such as digital evidence, is considered to be hearsay. Indirect evidence, including digital evidence, is considered to be circumstantial evidence and may be categorized in the same way as, for example, a physical document such as ink on paper.

In theory, because the truthfulness of digital evidence is difficult to validate, it is inadmissible in a range of criminal cases in jurisdictions based on English law. Nowadays, however, its admission is discretionary in criminal cases. This has raised claims that such leniency runs contrary to the interests of justice.

Digital information stored in electronic databases and audit logs, for example, is computer-generated and does not always contain information generated by human users. Such information has been challenged in some earlier legal trials, but it has been successfully argued that these records may be admissible subject to certain assurances as to the reliability and accuracy of the computer that created and recorded the information. Courts also require some proof that the creation and storage of these records are part of the organization's business activities. The automated digital recording of speeding vehicles by radar detectors has been accepted as admissible evidence in courts for several decades, although its reliability has been challenged with some limited success.

Human testimony is not infallible and is sometimes found to be false, misleading, or just plain wrong. Circumstantial evidence has no voice and so inferences may be taken from it in an attempt to help prove some key fact. In this regard, inferences drawn from digital evidence are now commonly used to prove some key fact in a case, much in the same way as a knife found at a murder scene is tested for DNA and fingerprints to identify the suspect.

However, by its very nature, circumstantial evidence is probabilistic in nature, and that makes it challenging when trying to reconstruct a case. Digital evidence and documentary evidence are subject to the same degree of legal scrutiny. They are typically used as exhibits in a trial as supporting evidence in tandem with other evidence forming the combined testimony for the presenting party. Digital evidence is now more acceptable in courts because of its perceived similarity with physical documents.

The role of digital forensic practitioners is important as they explain the evidence and interpret its meaning through scientific explanation and opinion. They in effect interpret meaning from the evidence to assist the court in understanding the nature of the evidence and what inferences may be drawn from it. Ideally, documentary evidence is not submitted in isolation but corroborates or is corroborated by other related evidence that enhances its admissibility and reliability. The seasoned practitioner will look for extraneous evidence that assists in placing the evidence in the context of its creation and of those involved in events relating to the case.

It is interesting to note that the US Federal Rules of Evidence exclude statements of the state of mind or condition of witnesses from the hearsay rule. Rule 803(3) (`https://www.law.cornell.edu/rules/fre/rule_803`) provides for the admissibility of "a statement of the declarant's then existing state of mind, emotion, sensation, or physical condition (such as intent, plan, motive, design, mental feeling, pain, and bodily health), but not including a statement of memory or belief to prove the fact remembered or believed unless it relates to the execution, revocation, identification, or terms of declarant's will."

This important exception is useful in admitting e-mails and social networking websites, which, despite the apparent informality of their communication, often contain candid expressions of a writer's state of mind. It is a commonly accepted principle in other jurisdictions, although proving criminal intent must be undertaken in the context of proof beyond reasonable doubt and not 100-percent certainty.

File metadata and correlation with other evidence

Digital evidence is quite often easy to locate and process and may contain useful metadata that can provide important proof of past events. Many commentators consider it superior to other forms of evidence. Files recovered as digital evidence contain useful antecedents in the form of file content and metadata as to their history in terms of their creation, modification, and last accessed timestamps. The location and name of the file often remains on the computer, as does some information as to when it was last opened and viewed. Such information can be most helpful in reconstructing past events relevant to an investigation and is frequently present in digital evidence.

File metadata is stored in a broad range of applications. Windows Registry, for example, records standard peripheral devices attached to the computer, such as hard drives, monitors, keyboards, and printers. The following screenshot shows a record of a USB device attached to the computer and a record of the last modified timestamp and the type and serial number of the USB device:

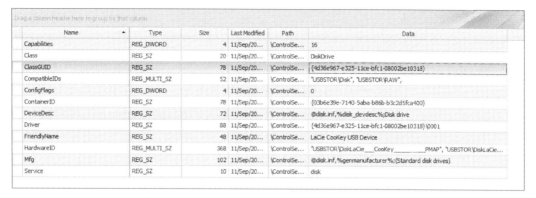

Windows Registry showing a record of an attached USB device

Link files showing details of recent files accessed by users are scattered around a computer. They are useful to see what applications were recently accessed and the identity of the file being accessed. This can be most useful information when reconstructing a time line of key events. Link files and jump lists are helpful in this regard and can provide file location and timestamp metadata, as shown in the following screenshot:

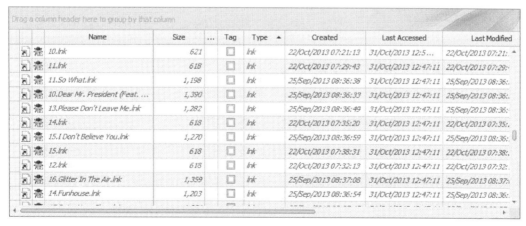

List of link files recovered

Knowing where a user has been browsing can also be insightful in crime reconstruction. Cookie files are commonly stored on computers. These are small text files that are created by each website visited by a user and are stored on the computer. A list of cookie files recovered from a computer is illustrated in the following screenshot:

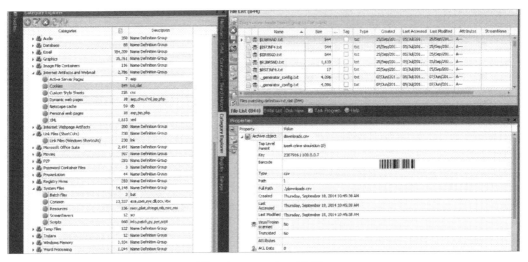

A list of recovered cookie files

Internet browsers typically store details of websites visited and these persist in cached files that may be recovered, as shown in the following screenshot. However, if the user has disabled browser history, this data may not be recorded:

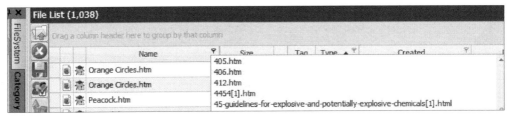

Recovered cached browser files

Even more helpful, the icing on the cake if you like, is information recovered from search history stores that show records of user searches made in browsers. This is shown in the following screenshot, which is rich in timestamps and search terms used. Remember that this information has been recovered from a forensic image and not through the process of booting up the computer to look through the browser history to view the information. That, of course, would probably contaminate the records and most likely only recover some of the data.

Other data may not be so easy to recover and would require a forensic tool to recover the additional datasets. It is possible to convert the forensic image to a bootable virtual drive to simulate the operation of the computer in logical or normal viewing or access mode and avoid contaminating the original image:

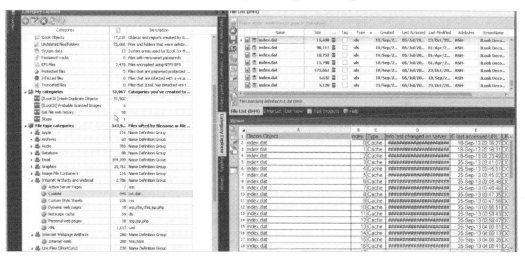

Recovered database files containing search term histories

Many software applications record data in their application logs. Multimedia players have this feature as a default setting, as shown in the following screenshot. These logs coupled with most recently viewed link files can be used to reproduce parts of a time line relevant to the investigation:

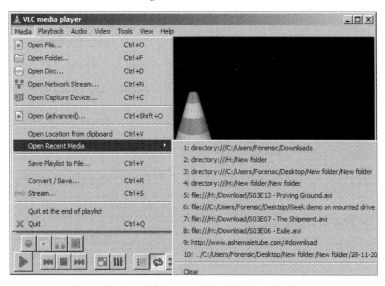

Recently viewed files recorded in VLC media player

Virtual machine applications such as TightVNC can be accessed through the `ProgramData` folder, as shown in the following diagram. The actual dates the program was accessed on and other user activity may be determined and recovered:

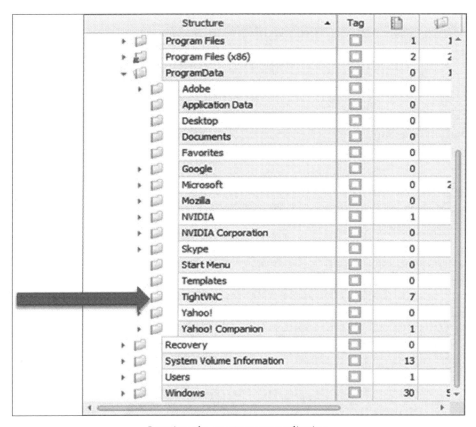

Location of a remote access application

File content information is invaluable to the practitioner, but metadata provides additional information, often of great value too. *Chapter 6, Selecting and Analyzing Digital Evidence* will provide more detail about file and metadata analysis.

The technical complexities of digital evidence

This section outlines the technical complexities of digital evidence and challenges to sound analysis. Like any form of indirect evidence, there are challenges to understanding more complex evidence artifacts recovered from a crime scene. Because of the technical complexity of digital evidence and its environment, some experience and specialized knowledge is required. Now that we have looked at examples of just how useful file and metadata information can be to the practitioner, understanding clearly and more fully the nature of digital information is vital. This section will introduce some challenges in using and analyzing digital evidence that show that digital forensics, which often provides such important material, is not a walk in the park.

Well before the emergence of electronic and digital data, it was difficult to forge and alter physical documents compared with digital data because of security measures protecting valuable documents and the special skills required to alter ink or pencil on paper. However, it should be noted that nowadays more than 90 percent of documents are stored in digital format. This creates significant difficulties in detecting any alteration to the data, requiring practitioners to link transgressors to initiating events or to some conclusive statement through an unambiguous trail of evidence. This sounds fine in theory, but often pieces of evidence are missing or erased and a complete chain of evidence is not always available. The file metadata may be present, but linking suspects to events through metadata that identifies the person who created the event is fraught with difficulty.

The most important requirement in any examination is to link the suspect to the events relating to, or associated with, a transgression. The lack of vigorous scientific processes for linking transgressors is further complicated by the rise in anonymous attacks on victims' computers and networks through various remote attacks. It can be a formidable prospect for practitioners to be aware of such exploitation, let alone trace the identities of transgressors. Even when the location of attackers is traced, they are often based in countries where the authorities provide a safe refuge for them. Extradition treaties, where they exist, do not always facilitate their speedy and economic apprehension.

The malleability of digital evidence

The relative ease with which digital evidence can be contaminated cannot be overstated, and this is highlighted in the case study at the end of this chapter. During any forensic recovery of potential evidence, great care must be taken to avoid contamination of the evidence and particularly the crime scene. Depending on the crime scene, different agents may be present that can destroy or at least alter evidence. Animal and insect scavengers, the elements, and earth disturbance can all affect the composition of a corpse. This may make it difficult to identify the body and estimate the time and cause of death.

Similarly, electronic data may be easily altered, damaged, or erased through improper handling, even by the well-intentioned. Switching on a digital device will launch the operating system and various applications linked to the startup system. Switching off a device will erase the RAM and, worse still, may make it impossible to regain later access if the device is password protected and encrypted. Forensic tools are required to connect and gain access to the data stored on the device. The tools must prevent, or at the very least minimize, contamination to stored data. *Chapter 4, Recovering and Preserving Digital Evidence*, describes in detail the processes and forensic tools used to minimize evidence contamination.

Digital evidence may be modified to remove all traces of its existence on computing devices, and evidence of such modification may not always be possible to identify. It requires considerable effort and expertise by an examiner and a high degree of luck or advanced data carving that may recover some filenames and content traces or metadata that show the previous existence of a file or software used to remove or modify it. As mentioned in *Chapter 2, Hardware and Software Environments*, thumbnail .db files are an example of this and show the previous existence of multimedia files on a computer.

Metadata should not be taken at face value

Metadata shows the various stages of the history of a file. Most commonly, it shows the creation date when the file came into existence in the folder on the device. In the case of a text document creation, the creation date, the date the file was modified, and the last accessed date would be identical, as shown in the following table:

Creation date	Last modified date	Last accessed date
10/10/2012 20:50:32	10/10/2012 20:50:32	10/10/2012 20:50:32

File metadata timestamps

However, if a user accessed the file at a later time, the last accessed date would reflect that later event, as shown in the following table:

Creation date	Last modified date	Last accessed date
10/10/2012 20:50:32	10/10/2012 20:50:32	15/10/2012 18:.03:49

Last accessed timestamp altered

In the event that a user accessed the file and modified the content, such as deleting part of a text document, that event would be reflected in a later timestamp to reflect the modification. The last accessed date would also change to reflect the occurrence, as shown in the following table:

Creation date	Last modified date	Last accessed date
10/10/2012 20:50:32	16/10/2012 11:50:59	16/10/2012 11:50:59

Last modified and accessed dates

It should be stressed that the metadata does not record all accesses and modifications that have taken place. A Word document may store previous versions, and this would require opening the file to see whether that provides additional information about the file antecedents and contents that may have been recorded. This feature is not a default setting for Word documents but is worth checking as a matter of procedure.

Last accessed dates should not be taken as the actual time the file was last accessed by a user, as antivirus scanners will access most files on a computer during a routine scan to detect malware, and that may change the last accessed date. This may be detected by reading the scan logs in the antivirus application.

In the following example, based on the case study in *Chapter 2*, *Hardware and Software Environments*, involving the use of a movie player to view movie files that formed an important part of a criminal case, close scrutiny of the file timestamps and user access logs was necessary. The prosecutor alleged that the movie was viewed from the time it was downloaded using the Kazaa file sharing application on **September 19, 2004** and moved from the `Shared Directory` folder to `My Documents` folder. This resulted in various versions being created of the same file. Various persons with user access were known to have used the laptop at the defendant's residence and place of work. The prosecution alleged that the movie had been viewed on **06 August, 2005**, its last known modified date. This did not show that the movie had been viewed, and the movie player log and link files did not correlate that actual viewing of the movie had occurred.

The prosecution alleged that the movie was last viewed on **02 December, 2005,** based on the last accessed date, the inference being that the movie depicting child exploitation footage had been viewed over a period of 15 months (adding to the gravity of the offense) and that it could be concluded that there was knowledge and control of the offensive material during this period.

The following table outlines user activity and file metadata for the movie file, an .mpeg video:

File activity	Date	User with access	Comment
File created	19 Sep 2004	Defendant	Same date.
File written			
File modified	06 Aug 2005	Defendant Guest User A Guest User B Guest User C Others	Other evidence corroborates user access.
File accessed	02 Dec 2005	Defendant Guest User B Guest User C Others	Unreliable data–virus checker contaminated.

Analysis of user access and anomalous movie file metadata

 The **Last Written** column displays the last date and time that a file was actually opened, edited, and then saved. If a file is opened and then closed but not altered, the last written date and time do not change.

The last accessed date of 02/12/05 was shown to have been modified by the computer virus scanner, as shown in the following screenshot, and not accessed by the user at this time. It shows the Symantec antivirus application log recording confirmation of a scan on 02/12/05 at 8:15:34 PM. This had the effect of reducing the potential viewing period to 12 months. This phenomenon was repeated in access instances to other movie files recovered from the laptop. It demonstrates that practitioners must always be wary of making premature conclusions about file metadata:

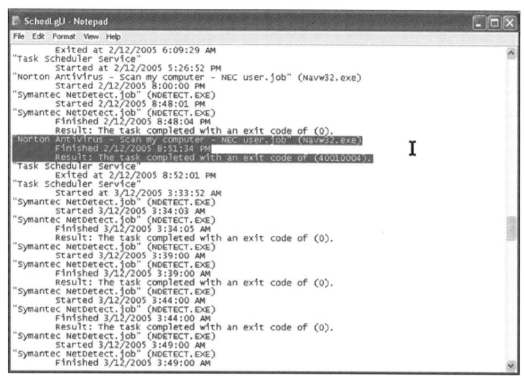

An antivirus application log showing confirmation of the scan on 02/12/05 at 8:15:34 PM

Last accessed dates should always be treated with some circumspection when viewed in isolation. For example, some applications and files may be sensitive to a mouse pointer hovering and touching the file, which may record it as having been accessed when it fact it was not. Access helps the practitioner analyze whether the file was opened or not. By verifying access to a file of importance during an investigation, that information may be used to infer knowledge and control of the file and its contents—most useful for courts to determine the likely guilt or innocence of a suspect.

Basic file timestamps also offer some confusing results, as is demonstrated in the following table. This example shows a last modified date that predates the creation date, which at first inspection looks like an error or contradiction of how files are stored. This is a common occurrence and reflects that in a previous form, the file was created on 09/09/2012 but was moved to or copied to another folder.

The original creation date becomes the new last modified date and a new creation date is based on the file's genesis as a new version of the file at its new folder. This phenomenon must be identified to avoid any misinterpretation of key dates:

Creation date	Last modified date	Last accessed date
16/10/2012 11:50:59	09/09/2012 07:01:13	16/10/2012 11:50:59

An example of the last modified date predating the file creation date.

Downloaded files, including image and video files, also demonstrate this phenomenon, sometimes with dates that are of seventeenth or nineteenth century in origin, well before the time of desktop computing. The `01/01/1801` timestamp is a common default time when time indexing is not initiated on the device.

Recovering files from unallocated space (data carving)

Chapter 2, Hardware and Software Environments described the process of file deletion and its degradation and eventual erasure through system operation. This results in many files being partly stored in the unallocated area of the hard drive. Traditionally, these fragments of files could only be located and carved out manually using a hex editor able to identify file headers, footers, and segments held in the image. The filesystem allocation information is not usually available to locate and examine these files, hence the need for a labor-intensive and challenging operation for the practitioner. However, file carving remains a vital process used in many cases where the recovery of suspected deleted files from an important part of an investigation is required.

Leading forensic tools such as ILookIX allow the practitioner to locate blocks and sectors on the hard drive thought to contain deleted information of importance. By manually looking at the disk through the **Disk View** component, as shown in the following screenshot, unallocated space can be viewed to see whether any data is stored there. In this view, the red blocks denote system files, the yellows show folder structures, greens indicate sectors allocated to a file, blues are free space, and greys (not shown) indicate unused space:

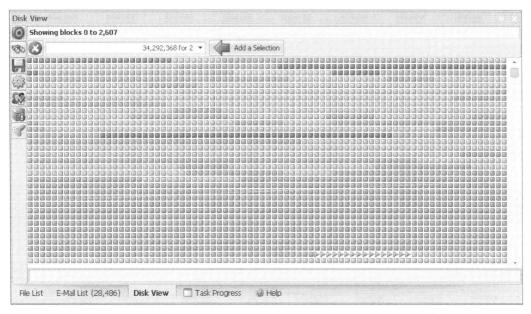

Disk View showing free space, unallocated space with data, and data-occupied space

The ILookIX hex editor allows the data on selected sectors to be viewed in hexadecimal and readable text as shown in the two columns in the following screenshot. Using this tool, the start and end of file segments can be selected and used in an attempt to reconstruct or partially rebuild the file:

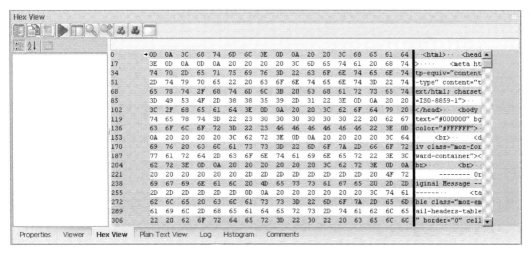

The ILookIX hex editor showing file data in hexadecimal and readable text

Obviously, this manual process is time-consuming as many filesystems contain millions of deleted files and file fragments, and automated systems have now replaced manual file carving to a large extent. ILookIX will recover and salvage deleted data, allowing the user to index this recovered data, as shown here:

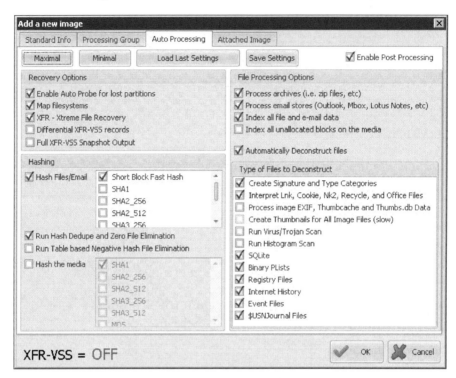

Indexing all unallocated blocks on a forensic image

This process will create an index of the data in all of the blocks not currently assigned to any file, facilitating near-instant searching of unallocated blocks. Indexing unallocated blocks can take a considerable amount of time to run and may not be useful for most cases. Indexing Mac OS unallocated blocks is not worth the time because of the compression the operating system uses. Like other search term queries for file, e-mail, and registry hits or traces, searching through unallocated space can be effected as shown in the following screenshot:

Results for search terms including unallocated space

Date and time problems

During any digital evidence analysis, the reliability of the file timestamps is critical in making a valid reconstruction of key events. The timestamps on all digital devices are an automated system that can often be adjusted manually. Laptop and desktop computers, for example, need to have the computer clock set when the device is first commissioned for use. Computer clocks are notoriously unreliable at sound timekeeping and require automatic synchronization with a reliable online service such as the **National Institute of Standards and Technology** (**NIST**). If the device has not been used for some time or there is no automatic synchronization, then it is more than likely that the computer clock has been running slow or fast. This discrepancy can increase exponentially and make the logs of file events unreliable. Some clocks may be running an hour faster or slower and, in some cases, this may be in terms of days or even years.

Users may also set the device to the local time zone, or the time zone may change in the instance of a traveler taking a laptop through various time zones where the device may have been subject to change. In Windows Registry, a record is kept as to whether automatic time synchronization is active or not and when the previous (last) time zone and clock settings were adjusted.

Some filesystems store all of the date/time information in **Coordinated Universal Time** (**UTC**). Others use the local time zone of the location wherein the mapped image originated. The origin time zone is the time zone used by the filesystem: it may be UTC or it may be another time zone. Even if the user has selected a specific time zone, Windows Registry will record the time zone as UTC or Zulu time or GMT+0. This must be acknowledged when interpreting timestamps in Registry as distinct from the general file folders shown in the Windows directory.

To emphasize the point, the view of Windows Registry shown in the following screenshot relates to a search for USB devices connected to the suspect's desktop computer. These timestamps were recorded as UTC and not UTC=8, the local time zone. This is just simply how Registry records information, and it can trap the unwary:

Name ↕	Type	Size	Last Modified	Path	Data
usb_vid_054c&pid...	REG_SZ	18	03 Jan 2016 04:52:51	\DriverDatabase\DriverPackages\v_mscdsc.i...	Sony DSC
usb_vid_054c&pid...	REG_SZ	40	03 Jan 2016 04:52:51	\DriverDatabase\DriverPackages\usbstor.inf...	Sony USB HiFD Drive
usb_vid_054c&pid...	REG_SZ	46	03 Jan 2016 04:52:51	\DriverDatabase\DriverPackages\usbstor.inf...	Sony USB CD-R/RW Drive
usb_vid_054c&pid...	REG_SZ	66	03 Jan 2016 04:52:51	\DriverDatabase\DriverPackages\usbstor.inf...	Sony Mavica Digital Still Camera
usb_vid_054c&pid...	REG_SZ	60	03 Jan 2016 04:52:51	\DriverDatabase\DriverPackages\usbstor.inf...	Sony USB Memory Stick Walkman
usb_vid_054c&pid...	REG_SZ	32	03 Jan 2016 04:52:51	\DriverDatabase\DriverPackages\usbstor.inf...	Sony USB Floppy
usb_vid_054c&pid...	REG_SZ	30	03 Jan 2016 04:52:51	\DriverDatabase\DriverPackages\v_mscdsc.i...	Sony Camcorder
usb_vid_054c&pid...	REG_SZ	64	03 Jan 2016 04:52:51	\DriverDatabase\DriverPackages\usbstor.inf...	Sony Memory Stick Reader/Writer
usb_vid_054c&pid...	REG_SZ	70	03 Jan 2016 04:52:51	\DriverDatabase\DriverPackages\usbstor.inf...	Sony MG Memory Stick Reader/Writer
usb_vid_054c&pid...	REG_SZ	50	03 Jan 2016 04:52:51	\DriverDatabase\DriverPackages\usbstor.inf...	Sony USB Network Walkman
usb_vid_054c&pid...	REG_SZ	70	03 Jan 2016 04:52:51	\DriverDatabase\DriverPackages\usbstor.inf...	Sony USB Memory Stick Hi-Fi System
usb_vid_054c&pid...	REG_SZ	70	03 Jan 2016 04:52:51	\DriverDatabase\DriverPackages\usbstor.inf...	Sony MG Memory Stick Reader/Writer
usb_vid_054c&pid...	REG_SZ	52	03 Jan 2016 04:52:51	\DriverDatabase\DriverPackages\usbstor.inf...	Sony MG Memory Stick CLIE
usb_vid_054c&pid...	REG_SZ	64	03 Jan 2016 04:52:51	\DriverDatabase\DriverPackages\usbstor.inf...	Sony Memory Stick Reader/Writer

Windows Registry timestamps showing UTC time

Later chapters will look at file analysis in much more detail. The next section looks at assessing the evidentiary worth and admissibility of digital evidence.

Determining the value and admissibility of digital evidence

If digital evidence is being contemplated for inclusion during legal hearings, it must meet a number of conditions and the high expectations of the court. It must have some probative value in that it adds to the chain of evidence that supports the criminal or civil case. Before the evidence tendering occurs, it must comply with some mandatory conditions as to its admissibility. If it fails any of these conditions, then it is likely to be deemed by the court as inadmissible and not admitted as evidence, preventing the judge or jury from examining and deliberating upon it.

In most jurisdictions, legislation and common law govern the admissibility of evidence. Some jurisdictions are far less prescriptive than others, such as the USA, relying heavily on magistrates or judges to analyze the circumstances surrounding the admissibility of digital evidence. Special forensic expertise is normally required to locate, analyze, and determine the admissibility of digital evidence, and it often goes unchallenged when it really should be scrutinized more thoroughly. Increasingly, courts have agonized over the admissibility of digital evidence, as legal disputes may arise that diminish its usefulness.

Inquisitorial systems are common in a number of different jurisdictions, such as France, Germany, and other European states; parts of Africa; South America; and a range of Asian countries. The inquisitorial system is based on earlier Catholic inquisitions and is constructed to seek the truth of the matter at hand by thorough investigation and examination of all evidence. It is an alternative model to the more recently adopted adversarial system used in common law countries such as the United Kingdom, Australasian countries, and North America. Critics of the adversarial system claim that it seeks the truth through competition between the prosecution and the defense to present the most compelling arguments, all of which can obscure the search for the actual truth. Both systems offer sound remedies for justice and now share many similar features, with the advent of hybrid justice systems combining features of each model appearing in recent decades.

The following subsections outline the value or evidentiary worth of evidence, its admissibility, and how legal conventions apply specifically to digital evidence.

Explaining the evidentiary weight of digital evidence

The value of evidence recovered from a crime scene is based on its relevance to other evidence available in support of some ultimate conclusion as to the identity and culpability of a suspect or suspects. The information considered of evidentiary value must be plausible and relevant to the matter at hand, that is, it is plausible and reasonable, has some bearing on the case, and adds to the collection of information from which inferences as to the guilt or complicity of suspects may be drawn.

It is the responsibility of judges and juries to evaluate the weight of the evidence to determine the defendant's guilt or innocence. It is explicitly not the role of the practitioner to comment on the defendant's culpability. However, the practitioner, who is probably the first to identify information that has some bearing on the case under investigation, must make a valued judgment as to the actual relevance of information located to the case. This is just as important in digital evidence examinations, where it is the practitioner who may initially be the only person to locate relevant evidence and understand its significance.

The practitioner may often be working to a specific brief to locate evidence, such as in a fraud investigation, and would have some idea of the nature of the offense and the type of evidence that supports a prosecution. Legal argument and debate may occur over the strength of the inferences that may be drawn from the evidence. Challenges will normally ensue when it appears the evidence may be misinterpreted or is unreliable.

To strengthen the weight of a case, sufficient evidence is required to prove or disprove the elements of the matter. Obviously, any evidence rendered inadmissible will degrade the overall stature of the case and could lead to its collapse. Many cases do not go to trial because the weight of the evidence is tenuous and lacking corroboration and any certain proof of linkage to the suspect may be uncertain.

Issues with the admissibility of the evidence may also prevent many guilty suspects from facing their day in court. However, before the weight of the evidence may be deduced by the court, it has to be admissible. We will look at this in some in detail in the next subsection.

Understanding the admissibility of digital evidence

Disputes over whether evidence is admissible are not uncommon; yet, in cases where digital evidence is tendered, there seems to be an unwillingness to contest digital exhibits when in fact there may well be strong grounds for doing so. This may be due to the newness of digital evidence and the legal fraternity's uncertainty in handling cases of a technical nature. A lack of understanding by lawyers of digital evidence, especially when viewing exhibits that may be technically complex, may also contribute to them failing to understand whether this new type of evidence is admissible or not. In practice, it is the judge's right to evaluate the admissibility of a digital document; however, this may sometimes be passed on to the jury to deliberate during the actual trial.

It is the role of the practitioner to advise the investigative or legal teams as to the admissibility of digital evidence. Because of the increasing complexity of technical evidence and the length of time it takes to run these costly court cases involving this type of evidence, there may occur a trial within a trial in the presence of a judge and absence of the jury. The hearings consist of the experts from opposing sides in the case presenting technical evidence and expert opinion. These trials are called **voir dire** hearings, sometime jokingly called **hot-tubbing** hearings. It allows the court to hear arguments from both sides and make a ruling as to the admissibility of the evidence without confusing and possibly creating bias in the mind of jurors.

The weight of evidence is normally not defined by legislation, but the admissibility is, and evidence must meet court guidelines and practices in various legal jurisdictions. Admissibility of evidence requires that the evidence be acquired lawfully, be relevant in that it proves or disproves some part of a case, and be reliable.

Defining the lawful acquisition of digital evidence

The first rule requires the party presenting the evidence to provide assurance that it was obtained lawfully. Now, this may simply be a matter of the owner or custodian of the evidence having provided free and unhindered access to the evidence and permitted it to be taken, or imaged in the case of digital evidence, for use in legal proceedings. Some written authority from the owner to that effect would normally be acquired.

Lawful acquisition may be covered under relevant legislation, empowering law enforcement officers to gain access to premises and seize computer devices suspected of containing evidence. This could be a customs officer at an airport examining a computer and having some reason to suspect that there is incriminating evidence stored on the device. The powers of seizure of suspected objects are provided by the specific legislation governing the agency, and no search warrant is required.

A search and seizure warrant issued by a magistrate or judge is the other option law enforcement agencies have. A warrant specifies the reason for its issue, the place where it may be served, the persons to whom it relates, and the type of objects that may be seized.

Practitioners must have a sound understanding of the legal issues involved regarding what constitutes legal seizure of computing devices, including mobile phones, as well as the data that may become evidence located on the devices and on computer networks. Practitioners should always consider that the evidence may well be required for legal hearings in the future, notwithstanding the original circumstances and purpose of the acquisition of digital evidence, which may not originally have been intended for use in legal proceedings. Consequently, practitioners' understanding and compliance with legislation covering the acquisition of the evidence is important.

The seizure of mobile phones during the arrest of suspects and searches of their homes and vehicles has recently presented some problems for law enforcement officers in the United States. Recent US Supreme Court rulings impose requirements, irrespective of whether the phones were seized during a general search warrant or under an agency's seizure powers, requiring that a separate search warrant be obtained to examine the seized phone. A 30-day stipulation may also be imposed, requiring the agency to provide evidence obtained within that period. This has caused some concerns that mobile phones, which in themselves are becoming increasingly difficult to obtain forensic images from, and the backlog in criminal cases stretching police resources may make it untenable in the future to examine mobile phones unless in exceptional cases and emergencies.

While this may frustrate investigations and displease practitioners, it does require them to have sufficient training, policy, and technology for the proper handling of mobile-device evidence. Sound professional development that enhances the effectiveness of law enforcement agencies in digital evidence collecting can only enhance the admissibility of digital evidence in criminal proceedings.

If, in the execution of a warrant, action by the officers goes beyond what has been stipulated, or the warrant was obtained after the seizure of evidence artifacts, many jurisdictions will suppress the evidence, thereby rendering it inadmissible under normal circumstances. However, in some jurisdictions, such as in the United States, if other untainted evidence exists supporting the case, the defendant may be convicted on the strength of the suppressed evidence.

Emphasizing the importance of relevance in terms of digital evidence

While varying somewhat in different jurisdictions, the relevance of digital evidence is assessed by courts in the same way as other forms of circumstantial evidence. Various court standards and case law generally expect that evidence be relevant, not be hearsay, and not be overly prejudicial. Accordingly, courts may require practitioners to explain the complexity of the creation and storage of digital evidence in terms of the relevance of the evidence presented.

Relevance as well as the plausibility of the evidence is also a matter for the jury to deliberate upon in terms of the weight that may be inferred from each evidence exhibit. Because of the technical complexity of digital evidence, judges have difficulty in determining whether to admit the evidence based on what they believe its relevance is. It is not uncommon for an overzealous or inexperienced practitioner to misinterpret or overinterpret evidence to suit the particular argument or hypothesis.

The evidence must pass some form of logical relevance test, which is not overly onerous, as a court's determination of logical relevance is reviewed under a test applied to digital evidence, in much the same way as it would apply to more traditional evidence forms. The relevance test of digital evidence is intuitive and dismisses the view that digital evidence possesses some fundamentally mystic logical relevance.

Outlining the reliability of digital evidence

In attempting to define the reliability of digital evidence, a number of adjectives spring to mind as there is no universally acceptable definition. Authenticity, accuracy, and fidelity are often offered to explain the definition, rather than taking the word "reliable" at face value, which has a multitude of different interpretations in different contexts. While the definition varies among jurisdictions, it is generally agreed that the evidence is considered to be what it purports to be and has not been tainted or contaminated in some way. It is helpful to define the reliability of digital evidence in terms of the protection of its integrity with respect to:

- The reliability of forensic tools used in its collection and preservation
- The efficacy of the recovery and protection process
- The absence of human or machine contamination of the digital evidence
- The adequacy of device and network security to protect the digital evidence

The importance of the reliability of forensic tools and processes

Practitioners use a variety of forensic tools to search large datasets and complex computer file structures to recover files relevant to a case for further analysis. When acquiring and processing digital evidence, evidence may easily be contaminated and ruin other potential evidence stored on a device. It is normal practice for practitioners to make forensic images of each device, thereby facilitating the identification of further evidence through further analysis. There is a problem if the acquisition tools and forensic processes fail to preserve and lead to the contamination of evidence. Data may be overwritten or lost, and false information could be retrieved if some software program has been set as a booby trap to conceal or destroy evidence, for example.

Courts have questioned the admissibility of digital evidence because of concerns of contamination during recovery and have denied evidence from being admitted because of suspected contamination. The Daubert Test, mentioned in *Chapter 2, Hardware and Software Environments*, is used extensively in the United States to evaluate the validity of tools and recovery processes, but it is regrettably yet to be widely used in other jurisdictions.

Courts have recognized that with the pervasiveness and increasing significance of digital evidence, there is a concomitant increase of risk of evidence being tampered with. Many courts recognize that digital evidence presents more complicated variations of the authentication problem than do paper documents. In the case of digital evidence, some forensic expertise may be required to verify that the evidence is trustworthy. Evidence considered untrustworthy may be considered inadmissible in legal proceedings and becomes irrelevant to the case and, of course, detrimental to one of the contending parties.

Chapter 4, Recovering and Preserving Digital Evidence, will look in greater detail at digital evidence preservation, and *Chapter 5, The Need for Enhanced Forensic Tools*, will present the need for more advanced recovery and analysis tools.

Evaluating computer/network evidence preservation

Information is a critical resource for most organizations, which are progressively becoming more reliant on computer-based systems to store and manage their information records. These management systems incorporated in computer databases are often linked through electronic networks to a range of internal and external users who need to access and use the information.

While an efficient and convenient system for managing information, these databases are vulnerable to a range of threats capable of degrading the overall reliability of the records they hold. When connected through a networked system, these computer databases face even greater risks, being vulnerable to a variety of threats that may jeopardize their admissibility as reliable evidence.

Increasingly, networked database system administrators and users are confronted by security problems from a wide range of threats. System security is not showing any signs of real improvement, and some argue that it may be getting worse. The problem of network database security, attributed to the rapid development of information technology during the past 40 years, appears to be further exacerbated by it developing at different rates, in different locations, and in different industries.

Although some courts have imposed stringent requirements to verify the authenticity and accuracy of digital records, it has been more often the case that more courts have been less demanding in accepting assurances as to the authenticity of such evidence. Fraud trials, for example, frequently involve altered paper documentation, which, through various techniques, can easily be altered, and while defendants challenge the authenticity of the evidence, courts will not support such claims based on the unsubstantiated supposition of alteration or fabrication.

However, there is a view that because of the different characteristics of digital evidence, it requires closer scrutiny to verify that sufficient evidence of authenticity and relevance is present to be considered admissible. Often, the circumstances of the preservation of a paper document are paramount, not the circumstances of its creation, so as to assure that evidence being tendered is what it purports to be. Digital evidence is of a different format and poses more complicated authentication problems than does paper records.

English courts have long adopted the "best evidence rule" in determining the admissibility of evidence on the grounds that they will attribute more credence to the best evidence available, notably original documents and oral testimony. This rule also applies to network-stored data, although the retention of original digital information will require some degree of authentication and assurances as to the integrity of the network security.

Corroborating digital evidence

As in traditional legal cases, it is always desirable to corroborate digital evidence wherever possible. Windows Registry, for example, retains records of the operating and application systems' environment and can be used to corroborate and explain other located evidence. But it too may need to be corroborated with other information stored on the computer rather than being taken at face value. Such corroboration might include consulting application log files and `.lnk` files.

As mentioned previously, computer clocks are inherently unreliable timekeepers with a propensity to change time almost imperceptibly. Over time, this can result in inaccurate timekeeping that may adversely affect the validity of timelines. There have been cases of network terminals being more than a year slow because of failure to synchronize with a reliable timekeeping service.

Proving the authenticity and correctness of digital evidence is a constant requirement in legal cases to determine its evidentiary worth. Taken at face value, there is a danger that digital evidence has sufficient evidentiary weight, and some form of corroboration helps add to its value. For example, the operating system may create some instability that may skew evidence, such as the accuracy of file timestamps or identifying user access, leaving it to be misinterpreted.

Documentary evidence may also provide corroboration in support of specific digital evidence. For example, the evidence of an incriminating document being created on a work computer and then printed may show which user account created the document because of a microdot identifier on the printed document. This would be especially helpful if the electronic records of the printer and the computer were unclear as to the history of the document, printer spool records often being overwritten and difficult to interpret conclusively. Such processes, including microprinting, are commonly used to prevent and detect forgery of computer-created documents. The following site provides some recent developments in such security protection:

`http://www.xerox.com/innovation/news-stories/microtext/enus.html`

Corroboration may be enhanced by the use of human testimony. A witness can testify that the suspect was at the keyboard at the time of the offense. Conversely, a true alibi may be provided by a witness who confirms that the suspect was not present at the computer at the alleged time. This is highlighted in the following real-life case study.

Case study – linking the evidence to the user

Consider a recent case where a departing employee contrived to forge a $50,000 separation bonus assisted by the company accountant. The employee e-mailed the accountant to seek the CEO's approval requesting that the bonus be backdated to a time prior to the takeover of the company by a new owner. The letter of approval tendered to obtain payment was backdated but not received and paid to the employee until after the takeover by the new owner, who believed that it was a pre-takeover arrangement. What later attracted the attention of the new owner was the large amount of the bonus. Further inquiry revealed that the e-mail records between the employee and the accountant were deleted from the employee's computer, in itself thought a highly suspicious act by the new owners.

Fortunately, the e-mails were recovered from the e-mail server, but no record of the creation of the letter approving the bonus was located on the accountant's or CEO's computers. Using forensic tools, the e-mails were partially recovered from the employee's computer and the bonus attachment was recovered from a deleted e-mail backup file (`.OST`). Staff members who had tried to piece together the e-mails on the two computers did so without any formal forensic knowledge and altered several related documents that had been attached to the incriminating e-mails. The last accessed and modified dates had been inadvertently altered, preventing a fuller reconstruction of user access to the documents.

Potentially, allegations by a defense lawyer recognizing that there had been access to the files after the computers had been returned by the employees could be made to suggest that the e-mails could have been altered or falsified by these staff members. It was possible to determine the document metadata from server records. However, the timestamps on the e-mails and documents, so crucial to prove a conspiracy to falsify the bonus claim and approval, were now compromised.

Examination of the bonus approval document showed that it had been scanned from an original signed document and saved in PDF format. This document had retained its creation date but no authorship details. It appeared that the CEO's electronic signature had appeared on the original document, which was not recovered. The dates appended to the signature were handwritten and pre-dated the sale of the company. The CEO's electronic signature was present on a number of other documents found in the accountant's e-mail files and could possibly have been added to the original text document prior to it being scanned.

However, the PDF metadata showed that the document had most likely been created post-takeover and was confirmed to be a scanned document by virtue of its content and identification by the ILookIX scan-detection tool. The tool was able to open up volume shadow snapshots that recovered and deconstructed the e-mail backup file containing various deleted e-mails. These e-mails, corroborated by the more reliable records stored on the server, assisted in reconstructing the case antecedents, which could then be used in subsequent legal proceedings.

This case exemplifies the value of file content and metadata, but it also demonstrates the vulnerability of the data to deliberate and unintentional human action resulting in evidence contamination. Had the fraudster had the wit and opportunity to delete e-mails while still synchronized to the e-mail server, those records too would have been erased and not necessarily recovered. This also shows the need to ensure that e-mail servers keep a full record of all e-mail messages, even those deleted by users. A backup of the e-mail stores for defined periods is often a legislative requirement of government organizations. In many countries, this is mandatory for public companies, as enacted in the US under the far-reaching provisions of the Sarbannes-Oxley Act of 2002.

References

Frieden, J. D. and Murray, L. M. 2007. "The admissibility of electronic evidence under the federal rules of evidence." *Richmond Journal of Law and Technology* 14(2): 1-39.

Summary

This chapter defined digital evidence and explained its evidentiary value and the conditions it must satisfy to be admissible in legal proceedings. The special characteristics of digital evidence were described, showing its great value but also the problems in using it because of its often-complex technical characteristics. The special role of the practitioner to analyze and explain digital evidence to the layperson and the legal fraternity was emphasized.

The reliability of digital evidence in terms of its integrity and use as best evidence was introduced, and in *Chapter 4, Recovering and Preserving Digital Evidence*, we will look more deeply at the tools and processes for its recovery and preservation. *Chapter 4, Recovering and Preserving Digital Evidence*, will cover innovative technology that helps practitioners preserve evidence in better and unique ways to avoid contamination as well as making their work a little less arduous.

4
Recovering and Preserving Digital Evidence

The importance of recovering and preserving digital evidence collected from a broad range of devices and the processes used to do so are looked at in this chapter. The chapter explains the importance of preserving digital evidence in line with legal expectations. It describes the forensic processes and tools used to acquire digital evidence without undue contamination. The topics covered in this chapter are as follows:

- The concept of the chain of custody in relation to the preservation of evidence from its collection up to its tendering in legal proceedings
- The acquisition and safe custody of digital devices and data
- The recovery of digital evidence through forensic imaging processes, also known as **dead recovery**
- The acquisition of digital evidence through **live recovery** processes
- The efficacy of existing forensic tools and the emergence of enhanced tools
- Case studies that highlight the processes and pitfalls of recovering and preserving digital evidence recovered from a crime scene

A digital forensic examination requires a systematic, formalized, and legal compliance approach to enhance the admissibility of the evidence, the need for which was introduced and emphasized in *Chapter 3*, *The Nature and Special Properties of Digital Evidence*. It is always important to assume that any forensic examination will be critically scrutinized. Courts need to satisfy themselves as to the reliability of the evidence and the integrity of the forensic processes and tools used to procure, secure, and analyze the evidence throughout the entire forensic process.

The digital crime scene is integrated with the physical crime scene in that the digital evidence is located in a physical artifact, notably, some form of computing device such as a desktop computer, a mobile phone, or a digital storage medium, including flash drives and external storage drives. A physical crime scene observes the laws of a physical nature, which dictate the appropriate recovery of physical evidence, whereas the analysis of stored digital data is used to find digital evidence.

Courts will generally accept that a chain of responsible and legitimate custody of an exhibit acts as an assurance of the integrity of evidence unless proven to be otherwise. Any break in the history of what is commonly referred to as the chain of custody potentially degrades the admissibility of digital evidence as well as its evidentiary value. It is the maintenance of the integrity of the evidence from seizure until the time the practitioner or custodian of the exhibit produces it in court.

The next section describes the chain of custody and its importance in preserving evidence exhibits that will later be used in legal proceedings, criminal as well as civil.

Understanding the chain of custody

Whenever possible, great care must be taken when collecting and taking lawful possession of any physical objects that may potentially be used as evidence in legal cases. There are a number of important reasons why collected evidence must be safeguarded from contamination. Preventing any intentional or unintentional tampering of the evidence is paramount. If the evidence is not maintained in pristine condition, some inconvenient and probing challenge from the opposing legal team may well be anticipated.

If the evidence is seen to be tainted in some way, then its admissibility is questionable. Not unreasonably, it should, as a matter of course, be challenged because it is possibly unreliable and its authenticity is in serious doubt. In criminal cases, where there is doubt about evidence, the jury would clearly be placed in a difficult position trying to unravel the truth and determine the reliability of a questionable exhibit. In such circumstances, the judge may well direct that the benefit of the doubt be given to the defendant. The value of the exhibit is therefore diminished and the judge may have it struck out as being inadmissible. This is highlighted in the case studies later in this chapter.

Assurances that sound protection processes and adherence to court conventions and standards have been observed must be demonstrated to the court. Courts expect that reasonable steps are taken to ensure exhibits were protected at all times. It is critical to observe the rules of collection and the chain of custody of the evidence by ensuring that the recovered evidence was not contaminated. This includes ensuring that the evidence was not altered between its acquisition and its presentation in legal proceedings and even before its acquisition by the practitioner. If it was altered for some reason, then this must be disclosed to the court and other parties to the trial; some explanation and justification should also be provided.

The rules of collection for a typical digital forensic recovery include the following:

- Some assertion that the devices and evidence acquired were done so under lawful authority.

- A complete record describing the computer devices and peripheral equipment such as modems, monitors, and printers and their location in the premises where the devices were seized or accessed — a sketch map is essential.

- Photographic and video recordings of the previous two points.

- The handling of each seized exhibit using antistatic and sterile gloves and tagged with a firmly affixed label that describes the exhibit and may be cross-referenced to the evidence register.

- Noting the powered state of each device and recording whether the devices were powered down and the nature of access if a live recovery was attempted.

- A description of the forensics tools used, including hardware and software write blockers used, the model or version of each device or piece of software that was used, and confirmation that the tools were tested and up to date.

- A record of the personnel who seized and handled the devices and a complete record of access to each device and the evidence storage device from the point of seizure to court presentation.

- A report of any alteration to the evidence recovered and an explanation and justification of such alteration. For example, during the recovery of data from mobile phones, it is normal to switch on the device and install a small executable file to allow extraction. In theory, this might cause a loss of data from the phone but it is an unavoidable process and self-justifying, provided the practitioner can explain this if required to do so.

The complete history of the custody of the exhibit must be fully documented to account for its location and custodianship between seizure and presentation. This includes confirmation of its safe custody until the expiration of possible appeal periods. The court must also be satisfied that there is a complete record of any test and examination of the exhibit, in particular, whether the exhibit was altered in any way, such as in the case of sample tissue removed for toxicology and other analysis. The court also requires some proof that the exhibit was protected from physical damage while being transported from the crime scene to the place of safekeeping and laboratories.

Obviously, the case can collapse if it can be shown or there is some suspicion that there has been a break in the chain of custody. On occasion, the judge may direct that the evidence is inadmissible, but alternatively may also permit the jury to make a decision on its admissibility while considering its evidentiary value. Therefore, it is important to show that the chain of custody is unbroken; otherwise, the court may disallow it if it were to be challenged by the opposing legal team. The completeness and accuracy of the evidence logging of the chain of custody enhances the court's willingness to accept assurances as to the authenticity of digital evidence. Consequently, it is crucial that the chain of custody adhere to approved legal standards.

Describing the physical acquisition and safekeeping of digital evidence

The process of handling digital evidence is especially vulnerable to errors. Just like blood samples or fingerprints, which may easily be contaminated at the crime scene, digital evidence may also be damaged during collection and extraction unless strict procedures are followed. The storage and safekeeping of physical records, such as witness statements, crime scene photographs, facsimiles of manuscripts, and so forth, require prudent record-keeping and safe custody, thus facilitating their production as evidence. It must be reiterated that the courts expect that digital evidence can be shown to be unaltered or contaminated from its point of seizure to the time it is tendered in legal proceedings.

This is no different from crime scene preservation, which requires preservation of the evidence in pristine condition. In traditional crime scenes, it is not uncommon for the scene to be disturbed by those who make discovery of it. Disturbance by extreme weather conditions, such as fire, heat, wind, rain, and water, as well as animals, insects, and bacteria can also alter the state of the evidence. This leaves the forensics examiner with the challenge of trying to preserve the remains and other exhibits, such as a corpse or the murder weapon, from further deterioration. Consequently, it makes reconstructing the events of the crime difficult.

So it is with a digital crime scene, which must also be protected from contamination and further interference. It is common that information stored on a computer suggesting some form of offense or impropriety is discovered by an organization's personnel, such as a supervisor of administrator. Their well-intentioned efforts to preview and collect what they consider to be vital evidence may in effect contaminate and render such evidence inadmissible at worse and altered so as to diminish the weight of the evidence at best. Without some sound forensic training in evidence recovery and initial management of suspected transgressions, this will remain a problem to practitioners left with the task of reconstructing the chain of key events.

You can refer to just such an occurrence mentioned in the case study in *Chapter 3, The Nature and Special Properties of Digital Evidence*.

Explaining the chain of custody of digital evidence

The recovery of digital evidence is often a complicated process requiring great care to ensure that evidence is not inadvertently contaminated, destroyed, or lost (refer to the case studies at the end of this chapter). Common pitfalls are often encountered during the recovery and preservation stage, and it is easy for an overzealous and inexperienced examiner to alter the evidence unintentionally when examining the crime scene or back in the forensic laboratory. Recall from *Chapter 3, The Nature and Special Properties of Digital Evidence*, how easy it is to alter digital metadata. For example, the last accessed timestamp may be inadvertently deleted or overwritten by an inept practitioner or custodian of the computer prior to or at its point of seizure.

Simply seizing an exhibit and locking it in a secure container until it is required in court will not suffice. A formal record cataloging the history of the exhibit is required. The courts expect exactly the same assurances that apply to other forms of evidence as to the safe care of digital evidence throughout its possession. Documented careful handling of the evidence by practitioners enables courts to reconstruct the events surrounding the creation of digital evidence as well as what occurred on a computer system in the past. This will substantially enhance confidence in the genuineness of the evidence.

The chain of custody is important. Each exhibit acquired and every forensic image made of the data recovered from the devices must be recorded in detail. When taking possession of an exhibit, a record of the acquisition must be recorded. This should include a full description of the exhibit, case reference, the custodian details, and signatures of all parties involved, as shown in the following screenshot:

TSW Analytical Pty Ltd

Unit 2, 27 Clark Court
Bibra Lake
WA 6163

TRANSFER OF EVIDENCE DOCUMENT
TRANSFERRING INTO THE CUSTODY OF TSW ANALYTICAL

TSW Reference No: ____________

At ________ (time) on the ________ (date) day of ________ (month) ________ (year),
________________ of ________________ transferred the analytical samples as listed below into the possession of ________________ of TSW Analytical Pty Ltd.

Details of Samples:

____

Signatures of all parties:

Name: ____________
Title: ____________ Signature: ____________
Date: ____________

Name: ____________
Title: ____________ Signature: ____________
Date: ____________

Name: ____________
Title: ____________ Signature: ____________
Date: ____________

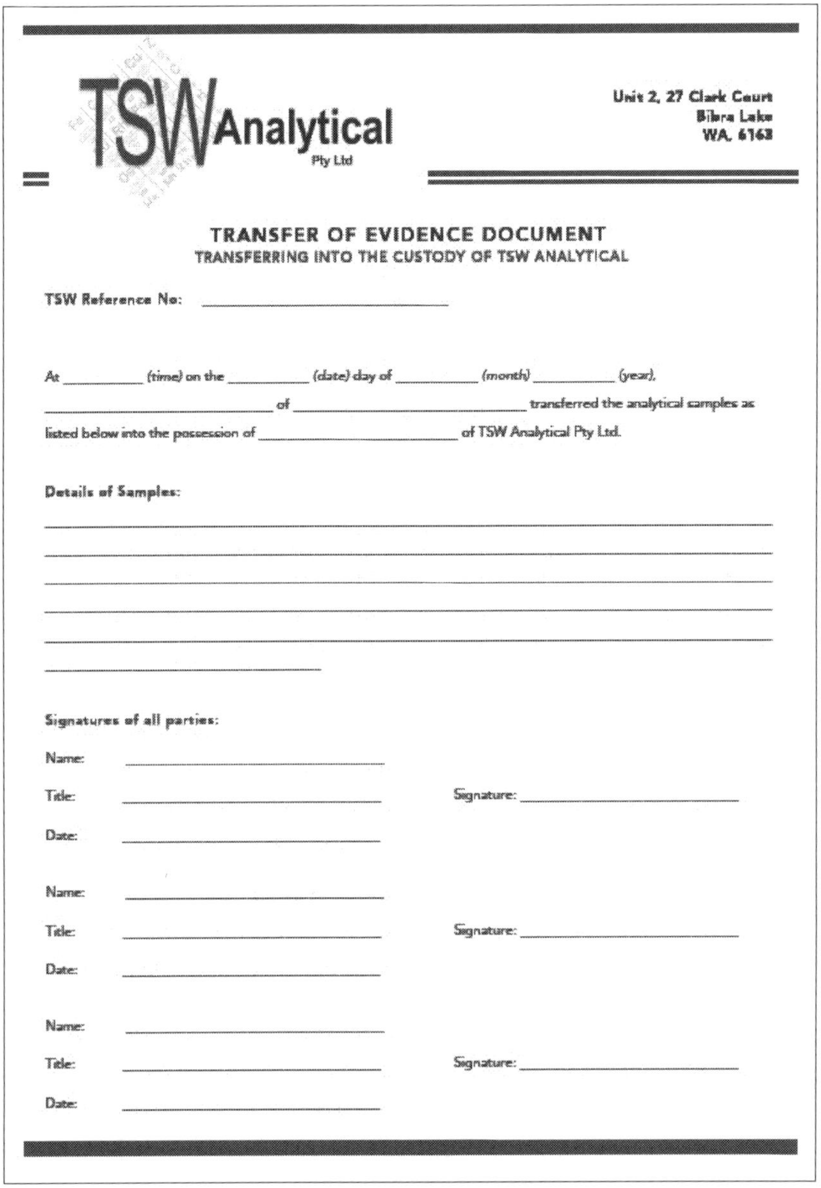

An acquisition of evidence exhibit

When the custodianship is passed to another party, such as the forensic examiner or an external examiner, or is released back to the original owner, the transfer details must be recorded in the chain of custody register. An example of such a form is shown in the following screenshot:

TSW Analytical Pty Ltd

Unit 2, 27 Clark Court
Bibra Lake
WA, 6163

TRANSFER OF EVIDENCE DOCUMENT
LEAVING THE CUSTODY OF TSW ANALYTICAL

TSW Reference No: ____________________

At ________ *(time)* on the ________ *(date)* day of ________ *(month)* ________ *(year)*,
____________________ of TSW Analytical Pty Ltd transferred into the possession of
________________ of ________________ the analytical samples as listed below.

Details of Samples:

Signatures of all parties:

Name: ____________________
Title: ____________________ Signature: ____________________
Date: ____________________

Name: ____________________
Title: ____________________ Signature: ____________________
Date: ____________________

Name: ____________________
Title: ____________________ Signature: ____________________
Date: ____________________

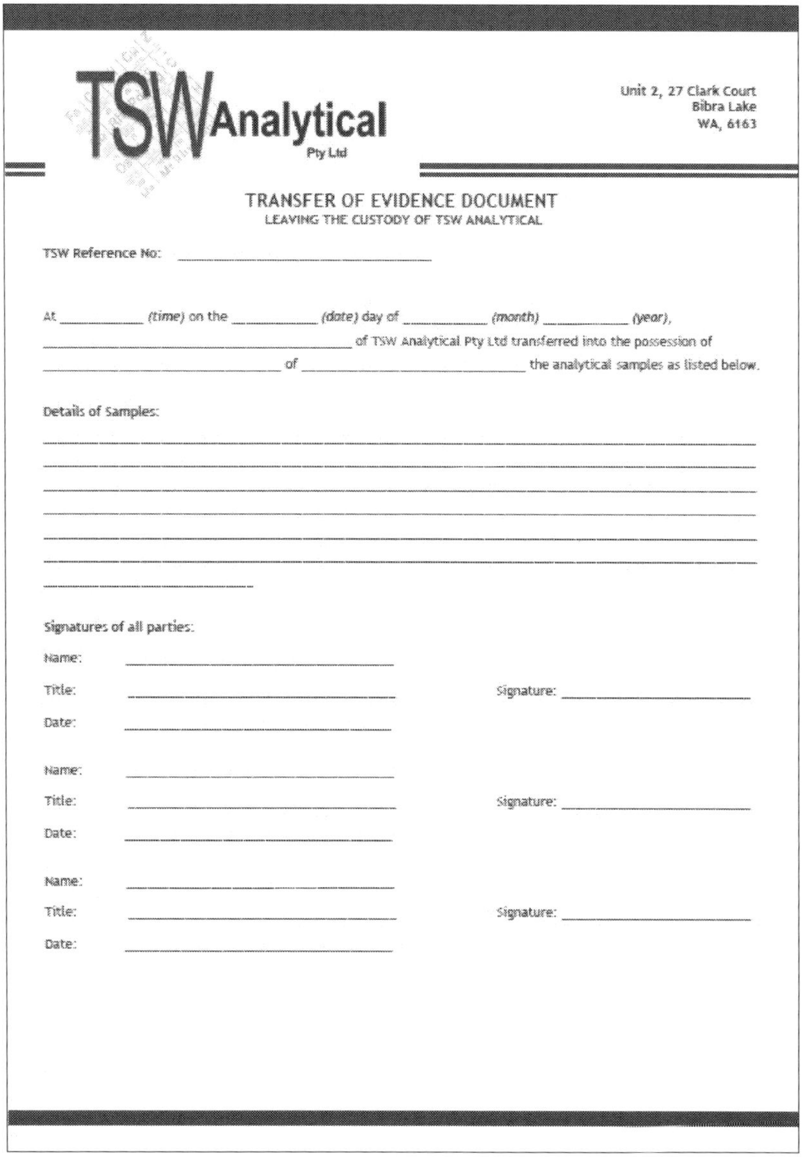

The transfer of an evidence exhibit to another party

Outlining the seizure and initial inspection of digital devices

In conventional crime scene examinations, each item of physical evidence is a single and often independent component of the case. The inadmissibility of a physical exhibit may not seriously weaken the strength of the case and the prosecution may well succeed without it. In contrast, a digital evidence artifact is often highly interconnected with other evidence and, if it is deemed inadmissible, may occasionally be more damaging to the case. It is so important when reconstructing a timeline of key events to support any hypothesis or counter-argument as to the nature of a transgression that, wherever possible, the practitioner should try to corroborate each evidence object against other information or at least show some correlation between two events. If there is any indication that the evidence has been tampered with before, during, or even after the recovery process, this may alter data and metadata such as relevant timestamps, which would diminish its value. Consequently, the practitioner needs to preserve the integrity of evidence contained in seized devices.

When making a forensic image of a device, it has been traditionally necessary to remove the hard drive from the device, which, if it is not immediately returned to the device, should be removed with great care to avoid physical damage to the drive. The use of sterile antistatic gloves should be used to avoid creating a short circuit to the drive, which might make it inoperable. The drive and the drive to which the image is being copied should be tagged and placed in an anti-static exhibit bag recording the date and time of the imaging process, the case identifying details, the details of the parent computer and drive serial number, make and model, and the name of the person filling out the tag.

The record of this exhibit identification process is duplicated and cross-referenced in the chain of custody register. This should record the date, time, and location of the acquisition and the forensic process and tools used in the recovery of digital information. We will now look at samples of evidence collection forms, starting with the following screenshot:

TSWAnalytical
Pty Ltd

Evidence Collection Form

Forensic Examiner:	
Job Number:	
Date & Time:	

Location			
Address/Name of Building		Site Number:	
Room Name/Reference		Room Number:	

Scene Photos:	☐ Yes	☐ No	Scene Sketch:	☐ Yes	☐ No

Evidence Description/Identification			
Owner/User:			

	☐ Desktop ☐ Tower ☐ Laptop ☐ Server ☐ PDA ☐ Mobile Device ☐ Other		
Computer	Make:		Model:
	Serial Number:		Asset/Other Reference Number:
	Is the drive encrypted?		If yes, encrypt tool and version.
	Encryption key held with?		Key Obtained?
	Is system on?	☐ Yes ☐ No. If yes, powered down at: *(sys date/time)*	
	Type of Operating System:		System password:
	Time check/BIOS:		Time check /External source:

	Make/Model:		Memory Size:
HDD1	Serial Number		IDE / SATA / SCSI

	Make/Model:		Memory Size:
HDD2	Serial Number		IDE / SATA / SCSI

	Make/Model:		Memory Size:
HDD3	Serial Number		IDE / SATA / SCSI

Other:	

Image Acquisition		
Image Description:		
DTT HDD used:		DTT Image Ref:
Writeblocker:		Writeblocker model/version
Imaging tool:		Imaging tool version:
Hash Value (SHA1) after imaging		
Signature	Date and time	Description of imaging process

A sample evidence collection form

The following screenshot shows an example of a sketch plan to show the connectivity of devices and their location at the crime scene:

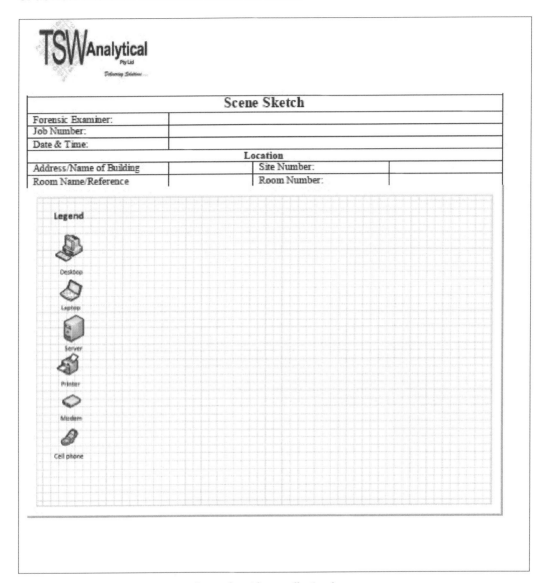

A sample evidence collection form

The following screenshot shows the details of the seized exhibits:

EVIDENCE CHAIN OF CUSTODY TRACKING FORM For Digital Evidence

Matter Number : _____Client Number : _____

Original Submitting Person (Name/position)

_____

Employee or Representative For Respondent:

_____

Employee or Representative For Plaintiff:

_____

Date/Time Acquired : _____
Address Acquired_____
GPS location Acquired _____

Description of Evidence		
Item #	Quantity	Description of Item (Model, Serial #, Condition) Photographs as Evidence attached ___

Chain of Custody				
Item #	Date/Time	Released by (Signature & ID#)	Received by (Signature & ID#)	Comments/Location

A sample chain of custody form

The following screenshot shows an example of the exhibit tracking form and final disposal certificate:

Chain of Custody				
Item #	Date/Time	Released by (Signature & ID#)	Received by (Signature & ID#)	Comments/Location

Final Disposal Authority

Authorization for Disposal

Item(s) #: _____ on this document pertaining to matter): _____
is(are) no longer needed as evidence and is/are authorized for disposal by (check appropriate disposal method)

☐ Return to Owner   ☐ Destroy/Divert

Name of Authorizing person: _____ Signature: _____ Date: _____

Witness to Destruction of Evidence

Item(s) #: _____ on this document were destroyed by Evidence Custodian _____ ID#: _____
in my presence on (date) _____.
Name & ID# of Witness to destruction: _____ Signature: _____
Date: _____

Release to Lawful Owner

Item #: _____ on this document was/were released by Evidence Custodian
_____ ID#: _____ to
Name _____
Address: _____ City: _____ State: _____ Zip Code: _____
_____
Telephone Number: (____) _____
Under penalty of law, I certify that I am the lawful owner of the above item(s).

Signature: _____ Date: _____

Copy of Government-issued photo identification is attached. ☐ Yes ☐ No

This Evidence Chain-of-Custody form is to be retained as a permanent record

A sample chain of custody form

Attached to the collection form should be a further exhibit: the imaging log report that confirms the identity of the device imaged, the date and time of the imaging, the name of the practitioner, and a hash of the device. A sample taken of an imaging log from a self-authenticating `.ASB` file (an IXImager digital forensic evidence container described later in this chapter) is shown in the following screenshot:

```
2015-11-26 11:58:26 syslogd started: BusyBox v1.16.2
2015-11-26 11:58:26 kernel: Initializing cgroup subsys cpuset
2015-11-26 11:58:26 kernel: Initializing cgroup subsys cpu
2015-11-26 11:58:26 kernel: Linux version 3.4.49-x86-erik (andersen@git.perlustro.com) (gcc version
4.7.2 (GCC) ) #1 SMP Fri Jun 14 17:06:52 MDT 2013

2015-11-26 11:58:27 root: System Information
2015-11-26 11:58:27 root:        Product Name: HP Compaq 4000 Pro SFF PC
2015-11-26 11:58:27 root:        Version:
2015-11-26 11:58:27 root:        UUID: XXXXXXXXXXXXXXXXXXXXXXXXXXXXXXXXXX
2015-11-26 11:58:27 root:        SKU Number: LE123PA#ABG
2015-11-26 11:58:27 root:        Family: 103C_53307F G=D
2015-11-26 11:58:27 root:        Manufacturer: Hewlett-Packard
2015-11-26 11:58:27 root:        Version: Not Specified
2015-11-26 11:58:27 root: Chassis Information
2015-11-26 11:58:27 root:        Manufacturer: Hewlett-Packard
2015-11-26 11:58:27 root:        Lock: Not Present
2015-11-26 11:58:27 root:        Serial Number: XXXXXXXX
2015-11-26 11:58:27 root:        Boot-up State: Safe
2015-11-26 11:58:27 root:        Power Supply State: Safe
2015-11-26 11:58:27 root:        Security Status: Unknown

2015-11-26 12:01:09 iimager: Making a Image of /dev/sda
2015-11-26 12:01:09 iimager: A 250.1 GB SAMSUNG HD256GJ Hard Drive
2015-11-26 12:01:09 iimager: Image will be stored on /dev/sdc
2015-11-26 12:01:09 iimager: A 2.000 TB Seagate Expansion Hard Drive
2015-11-26 12:01:09 iimager:   Output File Format: ILook Default Image Format
2015-11-26 12:01:09 iimager:     Output File Size: Unlimited
2015-11-26 12:01:09 iimager:          Compression: Enabled
2015-11-26 12:01:09 iimager:           Encryption: Disabled
2015-11-26 12:01:09 iimager: Case Number: XXXXXXXXXXXXX
2015-11-26 12:01:09 iimager: Agent Name: Richard Boddington
2015-11-26 12:01:09 iimager: Machine Owner: XXXXXXXX
2015-11-26 12:01:09 iimager: Seizure Address: XXXXXX Perth
2015-11-26 12:01:09 iimager: Known Passwords: XXXXXX
2015-11-26 12:01:14 iimager: User exited the Final Options Menu
2015-11-26 12:01:14 iimager: Beginning Image operation
2015-11-26 12:01:14 kernel: tntfs info: NTFS volume version 3.1 (cluster_size 32768, PAGE_CACHE_SIZE
4096).
2015-11-26 12:01:14 iimager: Opened output file '/ILookImager/ILook.001/XXXXXXX001.asb'
2015-11-26 12:01:14 iimager: Calibrating '/dev/sdc2' for output, a 2.000 TB NTFS Filesystem on USB0
2015-11-26 12:01:16 iimager: Image is being stored to /ILook.001/ILook.001/XXXXXXX001.asb
2015-11-26 12:01:16 iimager: A 2.000 TB NTFS Filesystem on USB0
2015-11-26 12:01:16 iimager: Image is being stored to /ILook.001/XXXXXXX001.asb

2015-11-26 13:00:08 iimager: Image Complete
2015-11-26 13:00:08 iimager: Image was completed successfully.
2015-11-26 13:00:08 iimager: Read          : 250.1 GB (250059350016 bytes)
2015-11-26 13:00:08 iimager: Written       : 72.74 GB (72744460583 bytes)
2015-11-26 13:00:08 iimager: Total Processed: 250.1 GB (250059350016 bytes)
2015-11-26 13:00:08 iimager: Image Speed   : 70.80 MB/sec
2015-11-26 13:00:08 iimager: Elapsed Time  : 0h 58m 52s
2015-11-26 13:00:08 iimager: Compression   : 70.91 percent
2015-11-26 13:00:08 iimager: Bad Sectors   : 0
2015-11-26 13:00:08 iimager: Copying logfile to ILook.001/
2015-11-26 13:00:08 iimager: Clearing computer memory...
```

An extract from a .ASB forensic image log

There is a legal expectation that the custodian of the exhibit be able to demonstrate some documentary proof of an unbroken chain of custody from the creation of the record to the tendering of the exhibit in court. Obviously, practitioners should handle the computer holding the potential evidence as little as possible to ensure that an authenticated copy of the data preserved in a forensic image or container is not altered. If it has been altered, the practitioner must be able to account for and describe any alterations that occurred.

The recovery and preservation phases of digital evidence acquisition attempt to stabilize the digital crime scene, thereby preventing, or at least minimizing, the loss or alteration of data being extracted. It will require isolating the system from any cable and active Wi-Fi network connections. Ideally, the means to recover potentially important volatile data such as RAM, which would be lost when the system is turned off, should be considered by practitioners beforehand.

Standard procedure is to take photographs and record video footage of the crime scene, including the computer monitor and any image that is displayed on the screen. Taking notes associated with each exhibit, such as its position at the crime scene, any cabling connected, and its powered state, should be a routine procedure.

When removing hard drives or opening a device, antistatic forensic gloves should be worn, or at least an antistatic band worn on the practitioner's wrist and be earthed appropriately. This will minimize any damage by static electric discharge to the circuitry of sensitive electronic equipment that may render it inoperable.

The practitioner should also consider identifying any suspicious processes running on live devices. Furthermore, the use of telecommunication equipment and Bluetooth transmitters, such as those embedded in mobile phones and tablets, may interfere with the devices being seized. If practicable, these telecommunication devices, and any equipment that emits strong magnetic waves, should be disconnected. The use of portable Faraday cages to transport and examine mobile phones should be considered if it is necessary to prevent nearby external telecommunications interfering with the devices.

The transportation of the physical artifacts to a suitable location for later examination may typically involve the physical transfer of seized computer devices to a safe location. Less commonly, it may involve network transmission of data. It is important to ensure that during transportation, the evidence is protected from physical harm or electronic interference. Exhibits also need to be protected from heat, moisture, dust, and physical shocks. Some form of protective packing is desirable, as well as an identity tag to clearly describe the artifact to avoid it becoming misplaced or misidentified. Isolating the device, especially if it has some form of telephony or Wi-Fi connectivity, is essential, and this certainly needs to be considered in the event that the device, such as a mobile phone, is switched on when accessing stored data on the device.

The collected evidence will, in most cases, need to be stored securely because examination cannot usually take place immediately. Care should be taken to identify and tag physical evidence such as a computer, which will often link stored digital evidence through the device to a potential suspect. The digital crime scene may be considered a secondary crime scene to the physical crime scene. Recall *Locard's exchange principle* too: it may be necessary to take samples of DNA and fingerprints to determine who had access to the keyboard and device.

If the forensic examination leads to a court case, the practitioner needs to explain how and why forensic tools and processes were used. The practitioner must be prepared to vouch for and be able to verify the integrity of all these aspects of examination if called upon to do so. This would include describing the collection processes and confirming that the collection process caused no contamination, and that the evidence remained uncontaminated after it was collected and during its examination.

The practitioner may sometimes be called upon to verify that the evidence was unaltered in any way by later comparing the forensic image made with the state on the original computer. This is usually achieved by comparing the hash signature of the device and the image, which should be identical. This process is discussed in more detail in the subsection called *The reliability of forensic imaging tools to recover and protect digital evidence* later in this chapter. The opposing legal team and the court can insist that the digital evidence presented be able to be confirmed by independent analysis.

Digital information suspected of containing evidence is normally preserved by storing it on another computer, external storage device, or DVDs. Before this copying process is undertaken, sound forensic processes must be adhered to that require strict compliance with the chain of custody. Forensic imaging is part of the chain of custody and is presented in the following section.

Recovering digital evidence through forensic imaging processes

The practitioner takes possession of the physical exhibits that contain digital evidence, which are kept in secure storage in exactly the same way as other exhibits. As discussed in *Chapter 3*, *The Nature and Special Properties of Digital Evidence*, the courts recognize the increased risk of evidence tampering and authentication problems with digital evidence. Tampering of digital evidence is relatively easy and has, in the past, created great uncertainty about its soundness. The use of reliable forensic tools minimizes the risk of evidence contamination during formal recovery of digital data. Regrettably, the immature status of digital forensics as a scientific discipline continues to cause disagreement over defining helpful and broadly accepted standards and processes.

A practitioner has the option of undertaking a dead recovery or a live recovery of data from a computer believed to hold evidence of value. However, the practitioner will need to examine the data and has several options to do so. It has been the usual and preferred practice to make a forensic image of the drive or drives contained inside the device. This form of recovery is often referred to as a dead analysis and allows the imaging of drives without activating the operating system. This is intended to avoid evidence contamination and copying errors. Poor practices at this stage may put the admissibility of the evidence at risk if contamination occurs.

Dead analysis evidence recovery

A **dead recovery** occurs when data from a computer is being forensically copied without using the computer's operating system. The term "dead" refers to the state of the operating system and uses the computer's hardware booted from a trusted CD or external device or copies data from an extracted hard drive using a hardware write blocker.

Dead analysis recovery may be achieved by powering down the device and either removing the drive and making a duplicate copy of the drive by imaging it separately or by powering on the device to copy the drive in situ. A dead recovery occurs after the system has been shut down and then trusted forensic applications and hardware tools recover the data. For some time now, it has become progressively impractical to seize anything more than actual computer terminals. In both cases, the drive is not fully booted, and in the latter case, the device is accessed by a CD or USB thumb drive, which prevents the operating system from being mounted but allows the practitioner to view and select the file partitions for imaging.

Write-blocking hardware

In effect, dead recovery ensures that all operating system processes are terminated by turning the system off in the event that the device is active at the point of seizure. Write-blocker hardware and software is normally used to prevent evidence from being overwritten. Dead recovery ensures that later analysis of the forensic image may be undertaken using reliable forensic hardware and software in a trusted operating environment to find evidence. This process continues after data has been imaged to ensure that the image is not altered in any way, because it is essential to preserve the data for future analysis.

One benefit of making forensic images is that they can be copied and the duplicates used as backup copies, handed to other examiners for analysis, or handed to the other legal team for independent evidence inspection. However, logic would dictate that it is only necessary to collect data that is needed. Here, I part company from the die-hards in the discipline preoccupied with the need to make a forensic image of "anything that moves". The discipline has created some bad habits, and indiscriminately imaging entire hard drives is one of them.

It is entirely possible that data may be written to the device containing evidence unintentionally during the forensic recovery and examination stages. Naturally, such an eventuality may lead to the inadmissibility of the digital evidence during legal proceedings. It requires the practitioner to take measures to avoid contamination of the evidence.

Normal computer operation involves writing data to or reading data stored on the device by specific commands and transmitting these commands to the storage device, such as a hard drive, thereby contaminating the device from a forensic perspective. An effective way to avoid such contamination is using write-blocker software or hardware to allow data recovery from a device without writing to it.

[The use of a write blocker prevents the sourced computer from writing to its hard drive's interface and onto the hard drive, which would otherwise overwrite or contaminate the data.]

Here is an image of a hardware write blocker that may be used to access a SATA drive:

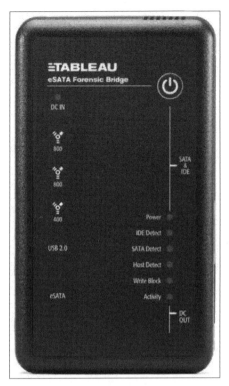

The Tableau write blocker

The following image shows a laptop connected to a SATA hard drive through a hardware write blocker:

A laptop connected to a SATA hard drive through a hardware write blocker

With live recovery, where the device is not powered down, there is a high risk of recovering false and incomplete evidence because the operating and application software may be untrustworthy or may conceal or falsify data. However, cutting off the power supply too quickly may lead to information being cleared from memory. Moreover, by powering down abruptly, there is a possibility that it may not be possible to power the device back on. Damage to the device hardware may eventuate as well as an inevitable loss of some running services and filesystems. For desktop and laptop computers, which will maintain some log activity of these processes and some information on the hard drive in RAM slack, swap, and page files, they may be partially recoverable.

There is a range of disk editing programs, including Norton Diskedit, that can read and recover the contents of RAM, which may hold login passwords. More recently, RAM contents are required for malware analysis to more easily locate encrypted or obfuscated malware, which has been decrypted in RAM and is normally difficult to decrypt and analyze otherwise. However, these capture processes require the system to be operating and the programs to be installed prior to shutdown, which may itself contaminate data. When recovering data from networked systems that store large datasets, shutting down the system before collecting volatile data may result in some evidence loss.

The overriding need for the preservation of the operating system files and all other stored data must be considered prior to the recovery process, which may alter the source device. Preservation processes must be incorporated with data recovery processes to minimize, and ideally prevent, contamination and preserve the data in pristine condition. Dead recovery may be inappropriate on an organization's network as it may result in a loss of functionality for an extended time. This may occur if the network is not mirrored or duplicated for deployment to avoid a disruption to normal business.

Write-blocking software

Using write-blocking software offers advantages of using hardware write blockers that require the removal of hard drives, as described in the following process.

During the process of booting and then suspending the computer with the hard drive still in situ, the imager USB dongle (or CD) is inserted and the *F12* key pressed to allow booting to take place from the USB dongle (or CD). The imaging prompt screen, in this case, IXImager (shown in the following screenshot), appears on the monitor, allowing keyboard instructions to be keyed in to access and use various features of the software application that contains a write blocker:

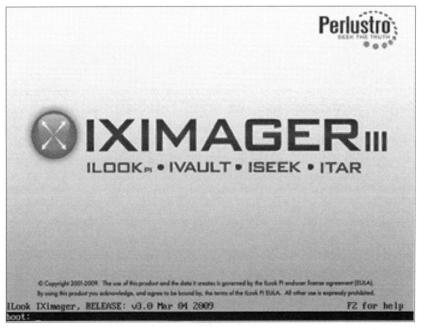

A forensic imaging program's splash screen

Further prompts allow the devices held in the computer to be copied or cloned to an attached external drive. The imaging application shown in the following screenshot prompts the practitioner to compare the **basic input/output system (BIOS)** date and time with external reliable time and enter a separate date and time to record any difference between the actual time and the computer clock, which usually runs slow or fast:

IXImager: reading the computer clock and adding a record of the actual time for comparison during analysis

The following screenshot shows the various options for selecting various hard drives and partitions:

IXImager: selecting a drive to image

Once the device to be copied and the target device where it will be stored have been selected, the imaging process takes place, as shown in the following screenshot. Depending on the size of the data stored, the speed of the source drive in the computer, the computer speed, and the speed of its USB cable port, this process can take considerable time.

In the example shown in the following screenshot, a relatively small 123-GB drive was selected. The larger the drive and stored data, the longer the imaging process takes:

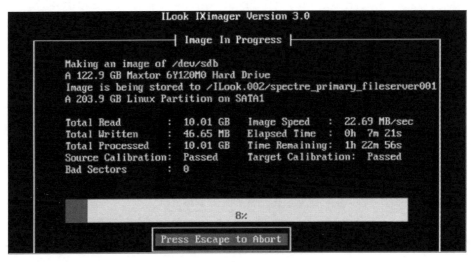

The imaging process commences

In the example shown in the following screenshot, an even smaller device was copied and 130 MB of data was copied to the image file. The panel shows the unique hash value as an **SHA-1 Value**. In this instance, the image was compressed but not encrypted. The hashing process can considerably increase the duration of the process.

Confirmation of the completion and status of the imaging process

It should be noted that IXImager is independent of a physical hardware write blocker, as it relies on blocking software embedded in its program code.

Viewing the data inside the image is facilitated by a variety of different forensic applications. The example shown in the following screenshot shows the directory structure and file viewing and property panels for the practitioner to study files of interest:

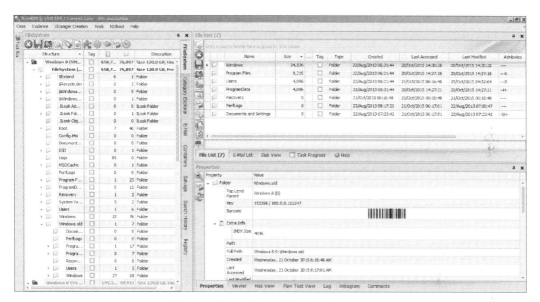

Viewing data inside an ASB forensic image

Viewing the data captured in a forensic image may also be done in a virtual environment such as VMware and VirtualBox, provided the image can be mounted. Forensic images may be mounted through such forensic tools as ILookIX. While this does not amount to a live recovery, the operating system and applications can be used as if a live analysis were taking place, and it may be of supplementary value to the practitioner and often a shortcut to identifying the location and contents of application logs and other files relevant to an investigation. As the forensic image is a copy and in non-writable mode, evidence contamination is avoided as the original data remains on the sourced device.

Enhancing data preservation during recovery

It is standard forensic practice to ensure that forensic tools are calibrated to meet the manufacturers' specifications and that any firmware updates are installed. This will reduce the likelihood of errors and inaccuracies occurring in the recovery process, such as during forensic imaging of devices. It is also important to calibrate digital storage devices such as external hard drives used to store forensic images and other media. These devices should be zeroed, hashed, and checked to ensure there are no bad sectors or errors that may affect the imaging process and the composition of the image. Failure to configure the destination device may result in residual data from previous events or from the manufacturing process remaining on the device mixing with the recovered data to cause contamination.

Effective preservation processes are typically recorded by acquisition logs and hashes that permit the attribution of events and data to the users of the device and prohibit future claims that they were manipulated by the practitioner imaging a device. The promptness with which data is forensically acquired minimizes the effect of future claims of deliberate or accidental contamination.

Hashing comprises taking an input of any length of data, performing complex mathematical calculations, and creating a fixed-length string that is unique.

The modification of the input data produces an altered output that is detectable by comparison of the two inputs. In theory, two identical inputs produce identical hashes, providing a repeatable process of verifying that two files are identical.

In practice, hashing the same drive with the same forensic software a second time does not always produce the same hash. Hashing is a time-consuming process and really only of value in forensic imaging, which in itself may eventually become obsolete—perhaps an outrageous prediction in the mind of less forward-thinking observers. The declining importance of forensic imaging is discussed in the *Outlining the efficacy of existing forensic tools and the emergence of enhanced processes and tools* section, which discusses emerging technologies that herald a paradigm shift in the way digital evidence is garnered.

Recovering remnants of deleted memory

While dead recovery may deny the practitioner access to volatile memory, remnants of it are often left in what is termed file slack, which may facilitate some memory recovery. This is a phenomenon of Windows operating systems, which dictate the length of each file saved on a hard drive. Because most files vary in size and a percentage of clusters in each allocated cluster or file space is not occupied by the file, the sector is filled with clusters called **RAM slack**. The computer may pack this free space with a random series of data from the computer memory, which may be recoverable and provide some useful evidence from recent and old RAM events. In the event that more drive sectors are needed during file storage, drive slack is used and is padded with remnants of deleted data. Both drive and RAM slack may hold remnants of memory, providing logon names and passwords as well as other potentially useful information. Recovering this may include advanced data carving during analysis of the forensic image. Live recovery may be able to more easily recover volatile memory, and this is discussed in the following section.

Acquiring digital evidence through live recovery processes

The process of recovering digital evidence by extracting live system data before powering down a computer involves capturing and at the same time preserving volatile memory, system processes, and network information that would otherwise not be recoverable with the traditional dead recovery process. Live recovery occurs when the computer operating system is still running. Until recently, it has been widespread practice to undertake dead recovery, with the recommendation that computers should be turned off to prevent accidental deletion and contamination of evidence.

The comparatively small size of datasets made it feasible but still time-consuming to image hard drives as a matter of convention. There was also the belief that the courts expected the best evidence to be produced and accepted that forensic images of hard drives were acceptable and certainly assisted the recovery and analysis of evidence while safeguarding the data.

Practitioners felt that there was a risk in using live recovery because the very examination could lead to data being overwritten and erased. Furthermore, there were well-justified concerns that the operating system and software applications may have been modified to delete vital information or produce false readings and information during the recovery process.

In exceptional circumstances, practitioners have found it expedient to access original data through the live recovery process. To undertake live recovery, practitioners must be competent to do so and to give evidence explaining the relevance, justification, and implications of their actions. A full report of all the processes used in the recovery must be recorded and made available for examination if later required.

The benefits of live recovery

One of the objectives of live recovery is the preservation and collection of the computer's volatile data to the best extent possible, preserving the state of the computer operating system and data. It is not uncommon for practitioners to undertake some form of triage, especially during an incident-response scenario, where it is important to determine whether a significant event occurred. This approach has the benefit of securing a sound data collection for a full forensic analysis if justified as a result of a triage. This seems to be quite common practice in mobile phone recovery using field kits.

Live recovery does not create a bit-for-bit image of the target drive, but it takes a snapshot of the targeted part of the system, which is not always reproducible later as the target drive may have been in subsequent use and earlier data may have been modified. While courts have questioned the admissibility of evidence acquired during live recovery because of concerns over some loss of data during the recovery process, this is now becoming less of an issue. However, this is provided the practitioner is able to explain the recovery process involved and assure the court that any small data loss would not adversely affect the remaining evidence presented. This concern is described in more detail in *Chapter 5, The Need for Enhanced Forensic Tools.*

The challenges of live recovery

Practitioners are still reluctant to use live recovery, not considering it to be a sound and straightforward forensic process. However, others consider the process will only have minor effects on the operating system and data. If undertaken, the practitioner should be able to predict the effects of the recovery on the system and data and explain and justify the process. Interestingly, much case law supports the preference to use whichever method best preserves all the data on computer media.

To reiterate, it is normal practice for practitioners to take forensically sound images of all bytes of data contained within each media device, thereby facilitating the identification of further evidence. To date, practitioners prefer dead recovery to capture and preserve digital evidence for fear of modifying it, and have shut down computers to do so. As pointed out previously, there is a concern that by closing down a device, there will be a loss of some metadata. Timestamps, for example, may be altered, thereby frustrating and confusing later event reconstruction. Moreover, it may not be possible to access the hard drive if it has been password protected and encrypted. RAM data will also be lost.

An emerging problem for practitioners examining local and computer networks is determining the authenticity and reliability of digital evidence because of the use of anti-forensic toolkits. These toolkits can obfuscate the reconstruction of events and may well obstruct recovery from live network sources. Slurred images can also occur as a result of the live recovery of a filesystem modified by a running program, thereby modifying and altering the metadata during acquisition, affecting correlation with file data.

In extreme cases, anti-forensic tactics may booby-trap a device so that when it is booted up, a previously installed program deletes or alters the data held on the device. Other anti-forensic ruses, such as the Metasploit Project, target and prevent forensic tools from recovering evidence. In other instances, explosives have been wired to computers in the hope that while powering it up, the investigators will be killed by the explosion.

The loss or tainting of digital evidence during its handling by practitioners is commonplace and potentially affects its admissibility. This has forced courts, notably those in the USA, to consider one of two existing standards: the court may pass a judgment on incomplete or missing evidence, or the court operates under the "good faith of the prosecution". However, some commentators believe that these practices could condemn a potentially innocent person or allow a guilty defendant to walk free. Until now, reliable forensic tools to undertake live recovery were not available. These are presented in *Chapter 5, The Need for Enhanced Forensic Tools*, relating to the emergence of enhanced forensic tools.

The benefits of volatile memory recovery

One of the advantages of live recovery is the ability to recover volatile and non-volatile data. Volatile data, such as that stored in RAM, is information that may be lost if power to the machine is disconnected, which would not be available if using dead recovery.

However, and most helpfully, IXImager can reboot fast enough to enable capture of the system's RAM, effectively allowing the capture of running programs, passwords, and so on. This may be undertaken by inserting a forensic USB drive, CD, or even an SD card into the computer, rebooting the computer and commencing the imaging process, and imaging the RAM captured in the device folder. It would be prudent, though, to determine which function key (often *F12*) needs to be pressed on the respective device to prevent the normal startup process and ensure that the imaging process is successful.

Live recovery also facilitates the recovery of non-volatile data. The recovery of volatile data may assist in reconstructing a timeline of events to determine the identity of the suspect, the possible motive for a transgression, and other useful records of events. The type of volatile data that may be of value would include:

- The system date and time
- Current network connections
- Open **Transmission Control Protocol (TCP)** and **User Datagram Protocol (UDP)** ports and the executables that are opening these ports
- Users currently logged on
- The internal routing table
- Running processes
- Scheduled jobs
- Open files
- Process memory dumps

Live recovery can help correlate information between the computer being examined and other network-linked computers. Volatile data can be located and saved during live recovery. The order of volatility ranges from memory RAM, which is erased rapidly, through to raw disk blocks that are more persistent and will normally remain on a drive after it is switched off. The range of volatility, from most volatile to least volatile, is as follows:

- Memory
- Swap file
- Network processes
- System processes
- Filesystem
- Information
- Raw disk blocks

Isolating the device from external exploits

The threat from external sources to the integrity of data held in a computer is an ever-present problem. This is especially so when attempting a live recovery of evidence. It is prudent to isolate the device from unpredictable data on the device. Data located on a system that may have been booby-trapped to prevent forensic examination will most likely contain executable files that may, for example, delete all files on the device.

It may also be programmed to communicate with a remote system and warn others of the live recovery taking place. There may also be unintentional consequences of opening files, such as an HTML file, causing the installed browser to execute scripts and download files from a remote site. Isolation from the external environment is important to prevent any tampering from occurring to the suspect system by hostile parties. This will also prevent unintentional transmissions being sent out that may compromise a forensic examination.

When undertaking a live recovery, the practitioner needs to identify and suspend any suspect processes that may contaminate data. If there is a network connection that should be physically unplugged or the device may be connected to an empty hub, then care should be taken to prevent a log message about the network disconnection being sent to any external parties connected to the device. The risk of remote access to the device has to be prevented, and this may be achieved by applying network filters, thereby preventing any remote access.

The possibility always exists that a remote attacker can be linked to the computer server being examined during a live recovery. Moreover, it is possible that a brute-force attack may be taking place from the server and directed against other networked computers. It is standard practice to check a computer's network connections for active connections and identify legitimate ports from those that may indicate a hacker attack. For the inexperienced practitioner facing this form of recovery, they will often be confronted with a significant number of unidentified open ports, which may be legitimate or can be exploited as a backdoor attack. Therefore, it would be prudent to determine what executables are present on the computer that may exploit these open ports.

Live recovery recognizes the value of preserving volatile data that may be lost, but it may result in some effect on the system and data. Many feel this is an acceptable tradeoff given the value of the data that can be collected from a running system with minimal impact to other evidence. Some practitioners have commented that changing the evidence admissibility regimen to demonstrate that live recovery has not or cannot materially modify or introduce new information will empower practitioners to undertake more efficacious examinations. This may facilitate more digital evidence to be tendered in court proceedings. If one file is critical to prove a case, it must show that it has not been altered from its original state, as the process of evidence identification and file recovery becomes less of an issue.

Another argument often proposed by practitioners claims that live recovery should be a last resort until the use of the process is endorsed by case law and court rulings. Perhaps, rather than awaiting a response from the courts to make a change, practitioners should move the debate in a new direction. This may require some sound experience and training to undertake live recovery so as to be able to present and explain the processes involved to the court. In effect, many practitioners are already undertaking live recovery using new forensic tools designed for that purpose—tools that have adapted to the inefficiency of forensic imaging in the light of large and dispersed datasets.

Until recently, the discipline seemed preoccupied with heavy caseloads, large datasets, and tools that seemed to fall short of delivering sounder outcomes for practitioners to meet these new demands. The next section discusses the limitations of existing tools and processes.

Outlining the efficacy of existing forensic tools and the emergence of enhanced processes and tools

There has always been a need to validate forensic processes and tools as well as determining the trustworthiness of the digital evidence they recover and analyze. The processes and tools must present verifiable results as to how they produce evidence that is complete, authentic, and accurate, and has integrity and accuracy. While there has been a call from within the discipline emphasizing a scientific review of tools and processes, there have been complaints about the reliability of the tools. Questions have been raised as to their capability to gather data and the susceptibility of the imaged data to forgery.

Reports emerge from time to time of the apparent malfunction of some types of forensic hardware during data recovery, raising doubts as to the effectiveness of the imaging and hashing process. There have been earlier complaints from practitioners of forensic tools being incapable of detecting and recovering hidden data stored in the **Host Protected Sectors (HPA)** and the **Device Configuration Overlay (DCO)**, thus raising doubts as to the effectiveness of the tool's imaging capabilities. My co-research developers have identified shortcomings in mobile phone tools to recover all that is recoverable from many of these devices.

Other observers have been disappointed with the paucity of academic research being successfully transitioned to practitioners, further compounded by forensic tool vendors being relatively uninformed about academic forensic research. Practitioners are in the hands of the vendors, who may find little profitability in continuing to invest much time and money in selling tools to a relatively small market of cash-strapped law enforcement officers. Banality also rules supreme in the commonplace acceptance of a generally low standard of tools.

The courts have a not unreasonable expectation that practitioners and the tools they use are eminently suitable for the job. Court and legislative standards exist, but whether they have any positive effect on raising the quality of forensic tools is questionable. While standards do exist, they appear to be seldom adhered to in many jurisdictions and paid little real heed by vendors designing and trialing new tools or versions. A preoccupation with profit-seeking by vendors, their apparent lack of understanding of the real needs of practitioners, and lack of first-hand forensic experience may well have contributed to the low quality of forensic tools available today.

The following subsections discuss the standards for digital forensic tools, their reliability to recover and protect digital evidence, and the emergence of new tools that overcome some of the major challenges in evidence recovery.

Standards for digital forensic tools

Various software packages assist practitioners in searching large datasets for suspected evidence. These tools filter and reduce large amounts of data into more manageable collations. They also assist in carving out deleted files and locating hidden data. Tools such as ILookIX, using **Xtreme File Recovery (XFR)**, designed and field tested by **information and communications technology (ICT)** experts and practitioners, will identify and open folders and files and can also salvage data that other tools simply do not notice and which remain undetected and unused. Consequently, the tedium is now being removed from wading through the large, disorganized data output conventional tools produce. This means quicker resolution of case analysis through more automated, intelligent filesystem analysis.

The standards governing information security are outlined in ISO/IEC 27041/2015, which sets guidelines for validating forensic tools. This is intended to ensure that tools are suitable for use in forensic recovery and analysis. Many commentators say that these standards lack depth and sufficient detail for anyone to understand what they mean and they encourage designers to apply them ad hoc into the design of new forensic tools and applications. The rapid and ongoing changes to digital technology hardly lend themselves to being absorbed into some form of regulatory guideline without some concerted effort being made by those who set the standards.

The **National Institute of Standards and Technology (NIST)**, based in the United States, manages the Computer Forensics Tool Testing initiative, which attempts to ensure that forensic tools meet the expectations of courts. In particular, the initiative is intended to make sure the tools are reliable, provide accurate recovery, and minimize any data contamination during imaging and analysis.

In 2014, the United Kingdom's Forensic Science Regulator released a draft guideline called **Digital Forensics Method Validation**, focusing on the validation of processes used to recover digital evidence. The proposed guidelines require that all recovery processes produce reliable evidence and that adequate documentation detailing the steps followed to validate their processes be created and retained. However, similar to the **National Institute of Standards and Technology (NIST)** guidelines, no specific criterion is provided regarding "the integrity of the case files and chain of custody, despite them being an important part of digital forensics processes." (*McCutcheon, 2014*)

The **International Organization on Computer Evidence (IOCE)** stipulates that forensic software tools, including imaging packages, require independent assessment of the validity or some assurance from the software provider that it would support the validity of its product in court hearings if required. Most digital forensic tools are commercial software applications and hardware and are not independently validated, and some may be customized by the user. The IOCE has identified the impracticality and prohibitive expense of the independent validation of all tools, relying on a more pragmatic solution to validation-checking through greater cooperation between law enforcement agencies to identify suitable and reliable tools and then sharing the results of trials, testing any deficiencies identified with the tools.

It should be recalled that the Daubert Test benchmarks the validity of forensic processes and tools. This sometimes requires the manufacturers of these tools to explain and verify the efficacy of their tools so that courts may determine their suitability. Most of these digital forensics tools have been accepted in a wide range of jurisdictions with little or no challenge as to their soundness and accuracy. In the United States, the Daubert Test and court conventions are less likely to accept the soundness of a tool based on any unqualified claim by the manufacturer or practitioner without some form of formal and scientific assurances.

To some extent, there has been a lackluster approach to sharing information about the development of better-quality forensic tools that meet practitioners' needs, further aggravated by a lack of standards for tools and any form of real compliance requirement in many jurisdictions.

This has resulted in a duplication of efforts to address the same problems and the denying of efficacious research and gains to produce valid forensic tools. For some 10 years or more, it has been recognized that future analyses of large datasets will become increasingly time-consuming, further aggravated by requirements to produce timely results for stakeholders. Moreover, predominantly human involvement in analyzing large datasets has been unavoidable because of the absence of sophisticated, automated recovery and analysis techniques. Such time restrictions and manual intervention hinders the practitioner, who is also expected to provide expert witness testimony in addition to producing the recovered evidence.

The reliability of forensic imaging tools to recover and protect digital evidence

The IOCE has asserted, perhaps with a lack of full investigation into the matter, that the forensic imaging of hard drives is a straightforward process dependent on having its accuracy confirmed by a reliable verification tool.

Forensic images must be verifiable as authentic copies for them to be admissible. This is typically achieved through a hashing process, which is the current standard for proving the integrity of forensic images and is used to prove the identical nature of two files or images. These hashes, often stored as unprotected text files, must be protected as they may vulnerable to tampering or alteration difficult to detect. This protection requires completing complex mathematical operations on the image during acquisition and recording the results for future comparison.

Hash reports are linked to digital evidence files and are constructs that store the files from the source device and store logs, hashes, and other information describing the acquisition process, but in reality, these processes fail to increase the security or integrity of the image file, as they may be deliberately modified. A transgressor could simply recalculate the hashes with altered input. An encrypted image file could be modified by those with access to the decryption key. This is a position an honest practitioner would not wish to be in and a dishonest one not overly concerned with, as any interference might be unlikely to be detected even if it were suspected.

Digital evidence image files are most commonly preserved in the E01 and Advanced Forensic formats, which claim to preserve and protect data recovered from computer devices. The images may be hashed to later verify that the evidence is the same as that copied from the original device and has not been altered in any way. Until recently, it had been assumed that when these image files had been password protected and encrypted, they could not be manipulated without detection. File image acquisition logs were intended to be inviolable, but those created by popular forensic imagers such as FTK Imager and EnCase are now known to be vulnerable to exploitation.

However, McCutcheon (*2014, p. 49-52*) has demonstrated that the E01 forensic image format, which dominates some 90 percent of the forensic imaging environment, is not contamination proof: McCutcheon demonstrated that with unsophisticated editing tools, E01 images can be tampered with without being detected or practitioners having the ability to authenticate the forensic image. This revelation has attracted little or no response to seek for better imaging such as that offered by the .ASB image container, which is no stranger to the discipline.

Experimentation by McCutcheon unequivocally demonstrated that the metadata contained within an E01 image could be manipulated using open source third-party libraries, raising doubts as to the effectiveness of commonly used software processes to check the validity of forensic images. These findings show that file data and metadata could be altered as well as the image acquisition logs and, with a modicum of skill, be camouflaged to prevent detection by tools such as **Forensic Toolkit (FTK)** and **EnCase**. At the time of writing this, these tools were simply unable to authenticate the integrity of the image files. This means that such evidence can be challenged if the opposing team believed there was a suggestion of any impropriety on the part of the practitioner during the imaging process or there were doubts as to the integrity of the data recovered and imaged.

The following link will provide you with more information regarding this experiment:

http://researchrepository.murdoch.edu.au/24962/

My field and laboratory testing of the IXImager .ASB evidence container confirmed claims that it does securely store a forensic image inside a protected evidence container. It offers a solution to the concerns about evidence authentication raised by McCutcheon in 2014. These experiments, completed in 2015, provided some significant and encouraging results, as follows:

- Unlike EnCase Forensic Imager, which records null data relating to the altered data, IXImager self-authenticates an altered image and repairs it by writing zeros to the altered space, making it possible to detect the adulterated sectors, thereby alerting the practitioner to those specific sectors of the image that have been subject to alteration.

- When opened with the imaging application IXImager, the application verifies that the image had been modified and is no longer authentic. The application provides a report detailing the specific modification of the image. Such occurrences are made known to the practitioner during checking of the evidence container.

- Embedded and encrypted in the evidence container is the log of acquisition and a secret, duplicate log for verification, which is inviolable and provides the practitioner with a true record of the circumstances of the original acquisition.

The .ASB evidence containers have for some time provided practitioners, when challenged during court hearings, the means to provide validation of digital evidence, yet the majority of practitioners are unaware of or seem uninterested in the problem. Most continue to use E01 files that do not self-authenticate and are unable to provide tamper-proof acquisition logs. NIST has, at the time of writing this, not looked at this practice, which potentially diminishes the value of forensic images. However, IXImager, which creates the .ASB container, is the only 100-percent NIST-certified imaging software (*NIST, 2013*). This situation has not altered at the time of writing this chapter in 2016.

IXImager is loaded through a CD or USB thumb drive when booting the device and provides a safe harbor for the forensic image and the embedded imaging log sheet. Furthermore, its write-blocking software avoids the use of expensive hardware write blockers and multiple dongles. Tests on the speed of data imaging also put this software ahead of its competitors.

There have been concerns expressed that digital forensic tools are inappropriate for use on networked computers, being oriented to imaging and analyzing single computers removed from networks. Recovery requirements would stipulate online local or remote analysis of networked systems that does not contaminate evidence during the imaging and recovery processes. *Chapter 5, The Need for Enhanced Forensic Tools*, looks at a solution to this problem in some detail.

The next section presents two Australian case studies that stress the importance of maintaining the highest professional standards when recovering digital evidence and emphasizes the importance of evidence preservation. They beg the question as to why law enforcement agencies over-rely on specialist digital forensic units rather than providing some sound basic digital para-forensic training and more effective tools for rank-and-file officers, for it is they who are often the first respondents at crime scenes that are increasingly involving computing devices of some form or other.

Case studies – linking the evidence to the user

Sometimes, when challenges to admissibility occur during legal proceedings, digital evidence may be inappropriately passed to the jury for it to adjudicate because of a failure of the judge to understand the nature of the evidence and the argument on which the challenge is based. This was epitomized in the case of indecent possession of child pornography in the jury trial of Mowday versus the State of Western Australia (2007). The case illustrated the failure of the trial judge to reject digital evidence where serious doubts on the antecedents about its safekeeping were raised by the defense lawyer at the commencement of the trial. Consequently, during the appeal proceedings, the digital evidence in the Mowday case was rejected as being invalid and specific convictions were reversed. You can read about the case here:

```
https://jade.io/article/12808
```

In a 2008 child pornography case in Australia, child pornography videos and picture files were located on the defendant's laptop by a computer technician tasked previously by the defendant to upgrade the device and remove suspected malware. In the process of upgrading the computer with new memory chips, the operating system was deleted and the defendant's personal data was saved to the technician's backup computer. After defragmenting the hard drive, the operating system was reinstalled on the laptop and the defendant's personal data was copied on to the laptop. No special forensic tools were used to copy, remove, and later restore this personal data to the laptop.

During the copying process, the technician opened some video files that appeared to depict child pornography. Local police were notified of a possible offence, visited the workshop, and directed the technician to copy the data to a DVD, which was duly handed to the police officers. On police instructions, personal data was restored to the laptop and it was then returned to the defendant for later seizure. Subsequently, the police officers lost the DVD.

The laptop was held on a shelf in the technician's office for several weeks while awaiting the arrival of the correct memory chip. Other technicians had access to the room where the laptop was casually stored, yet no attempt was made by the police team to seize the laptop and preserve the evidence. This very fact led to the case being challenged on the grounds that no chain of custody was in place prior to the laptop being seized some considerable time later during a raid on the defendant's residence by a specialist computer team.

Two mistrials occurred. A third retrial eventuated in some of the digital evidence being determined by the judge as being unreliable because of anomalous file metadata—hardly surprising when the drive had been wiped and then more data placed on it. A comparison of the restored data and the original data deleted from the laptop could not be provided. There remained the possibility that the restored data may have differed from the original data or had been manipulated.

However, the jury convicted the defendant on the remaining possession charges despite the defense counsel making repeated and vigorous challenges to the absence of a reliable chain of custody that would prevent tampering of the evidence.

A subsequent appeal by the defendant was disallowed and the appeal court noted that the defendant had made some verbal admissions to the possession of child pornography on the laptop. Despite the appalling lack of any duty of care of the data contained on the defendant's laptop and the loss of the copy of the DVD, the evidence was allowed to be presented to the jury.

The onus was on the prosecution to verify that the digital evidence was in pristine condition, when it clearly was not. In drug trafficking and child pornography possession cases, there is a reversal of the presumption of proof of innocence, leaving defendants having to prove that they were not aware of possession of illegal or offensive material. It seems incredulous that the evidence was regarded as admissible when in fact its authenticity seemed in doubt—a view shared by the prosecution lawyer! What may have influenced the jury in reaching its guilty verdict was a partial admission of guilt by the defendant during a video interview.

Such lack of professionalism in digital forensic investigations is regrettably not uncommon. Information that is intended to form part of court proceedings or information that could conceivably be used as evidence must be handled carefully and protected. There is no room for a casual and lackadaisical approach. So, dear reader, if you are contemplating becoming part of the discipline, be disciplined when it comes to evidence handling.

References

Grossman, M. R. and Gordon. V.Cormack. 2011. *Technology-assisted review in e-discovery can be more effective and more efficient than exhaustive manual review.* Richmond Journal of Law and Technology (17): 11-16.

Mowday versus the State of Western Australia. 2007. WASCA 165.

NIST. 2013. *IXImager v3.0.Nov.12.12: Test results for digital data acquisition tool.* Department of Homeland Security Science and Technology. Ref: http://www.dhs.gov/cyber-research.

Summary

This chapter looked at evidence recovery and preservation in a general sense and then focused on how these two interlinked requirements relate to digital evidence. From the physical safekeeping of the exhibits that hold digital information to the recovery of it in its digital form, the chapter outlined the responsibilities of practitioners as well as the challenges that confront them in evidence handling.

Dead and live evidence recovery processes have been described, although these well-established processes are now facing a paradigm shift heralded by enhanced technologies. New and sounder ways of recovering and preserving evidence were presented as was a more reliable and efficient way of forensic imaging.

Chapter 5, The Need for Enhanced Forensic Tools, will look at new processes and technologies that address and overcome some of the disadvantages of live recovery by introducing some "disruptive technology" that has arrived just in time to give practitioners the edge in forensic examinations. This will enable you to build on the knowledge gained from this chapter and provide an exciting look into the newly emerging environment of digital evidence recovery and handling.

The chapter will also highlight the rapidly changing forensic environment, where conventional forensic imaging and indexing of increasingly larger datasets is becoming unviable. It will introduce new forensic processes and tools to assist in sounder evidence recovery and better use of resources. This "disruptive technology" is already challenging the established digital forensic response and overreliance on forensic specialists, who are themselves becoming swamped with increased caseloads and an inability to process larger and disparate datasets.

5

The Need for Enhanced Forensic Tools

This chapter highlights the rapidly changing forensic environment, where conventional forensic imaging and indexing of increasingly larger datasets is becoming unviable. It introduces new forensic processes and tools to assist in more sound recovery of evidence and better use of resources. The chapter introduces the advent of **disruptive technology** that is challenging the established digital forensic response and overreliance on forensic specialists, who are themselves becoming swamped with heavier caseloads and limited ability to process larger and disparate datasets.

The topics specifically covered in this chapter will look at:

- Emerging problems confronting forensic laboratories and practitioners in recovering evidence from increasingly large and widely dispersed datasets

- Processes and forensic tools to assist practitioners to deal more effectively with these challenges

- Empowering non-specialist law enforcement personnel and other stakeholders, such as IT administrators, forensic auditors, and security officers, to become first respondents at a digital crime scene

- A case study to illustrate the challenges of interrogating large datasets

Digital forensics laboratories

During the past decade, digital forensic training and education has accelerated in the government and private sectors to meet the growing demand for qualified practitioners. Many of these entrants to the discipline gain employment with forensic laboratories now undertaking digital forensic examinations. More recently, budgetary constraints are affecting many digital forensics laboratories, which have seriously restricted staffing numbers and specialist training. At the same time, the dramatic increase of laboratories' caseloads can have a detrimental effect on the soundness of the work output. Simply put, forensic laboratories are expensive in terms of equipment, personnel, and buildings.

However, knowledge sharing within the digital forensic community has resulted in significant progress in mapping and creating solutions to assist with forensic analysis. A broad range of digital forensic laboratories, especially those in the law enforcement environment, are using this shared body of knowledge to develop guidelines to enhance analysis that will lead to the automation and speeding up of otherwise tedious and time-consuming tasks to process larger datasets.

The recent demise of many businesses in many parts of the world has sometimes involved a degree of dishonesty by managers and employees seeking to exploit a failing business for some form of financial gain. These transgressions involve the theft of business and client assets that require the expertise of forensic auditors to investigate, who in turn require the expertise of practitioners to locate and analyze relevant digital evidence. This has placed an extra burden of increased caseloads on private laboratories, which also require additional staffing by experienced and qualified practitioners.

The purpose of digital forensics laboratories

Few organizations have digital forensic capability, and not all government departments have digital forensic laboratories, for they are expensive and require experienced personnel who are not always readily available. It is more common for organizations to integrate digital forensics as a part of security-incident response programs. Digital forensic examinations can be costly in terms of time and manpower, as are the laboratories that provide these services. Law enforcement agencies, defense and intelligence agencies, larger financial institutions, and international accounting firms, such as Deloitte Touche Tohmatsu, Ernst & Young, KPMG, and PricewaterhouseCoopers, have well-established laboratories.

Smaller organizations may use the services of established private practitioners or forensic personnel from large and medium-sized accounting practices. The cost of hiring forensic experts is always high and no different from defense legal teams seeking an independent review of the digital evidence recovered by the prosecution experts. Regrettably, it is not always affordable for many defendants to hire consultant practitioners, unless they are well funded or receiving some form of legal aid.

Well-designed and functioning laboratories provide essential support and coordination for practitioners and for the organizations they serve. Such laboratories enhance and raise the standard of forensic examinations to that expected of courts and offer efficiency in processing cases and better management of resources. The design of an effective laboratory will vary among various organizations, but there are some common requirements. Without some formally established forensic body attuned to and compliant with the evidentiary rules of the relevant legal jurisdiction, digital forensic examinations would be poorly coordinated, piecemeal, and ineffectual.

The following sections outline the essential components of a digital forensic laboratory and look at the significant challenges they face.

Acceptance of, consensus on, and uptake of digital forensics standards

It should be recalled that the previous strength of DNA evidence was challenged in the OJ Simpson case, which was well funded to assist the defense team to successfully refute forensic evidence by claiming it was contaminated in the laboratory, resulting in his eventual acquittal of the murder charge:

```
http://abcnews.go.com/US/oj-simpson-trial-now/story?id=17377772.
```

There have been many similar instances worldwide, where poor laboratory practice has resulted in miscarriages of justice. In Australia, the highly publicized disappearance of the young baby Azaria Chamberlain and her presumed murder at Ayers Rock uncovered sloppy forensic practice and misinterpretation of the evidence, still resonating in Australia to this day:

```
http://www.abc.net.au/news/2012-06-13/eastley-a-dingo-did-steal-her-
baby/4068026.
```

Accurate and valid examination results are critical to ensuring that justice is served well. Faulty and incompetent forensic examinations may well result in a wrongful conviction, or at least an unsafe trial. Consequently, accreditation of digital forensic laboratories sets higher standards, from which the court may have greater confidence in the forensic analysis and handling of exhibits. Although several jurisdictions require the formal accreditation of forensic laboratories, most do not, notwithstanding repeated calls for accreditation as well as forensic practitioner certification. Such calls insist that forensic practitioners require certification that includes proficiency testing that qualifies them to practice and provide expert testimony.

However, it seems unlikely that any general agreement on such accreditation is going to be accepted in most jurisdictions, and even less likely that any international accreditation agreement will ever be reached. What is more likely is that practitioners will be required to establish their professional credentials with courts and employees to show that they merit acceptance as a professionally qualified practitioner.

Recall from *Chapter 3, The Nature and Special Properties of Digital Evidence*, the use of the Daubert Test to measure the competence of digital forensic tools and the qualifications of forensic practitioners, common in the United States, yet still not adopted in other jurisdictions to any major significance. The United States tends to show the way in testing and validating digital forensic practice, which has been driven to a large extent by case law and legal precedent.

There is also an expectation that digital forensics laboratories be accredited to ISO 17025 or the US equivalent **American Society of Crime Laboratory Directors/ Laboratory Accreditation Board (ASCLD/LAB)** international requirements. ASCLD/ LAB international accredited laboratories must conform to some 360 standards of ISO 17025 but a significantly lower number for digital forensics laboratories.

Although the regulation does not define digital evidence, it requires some guarantees from laboratories as to the:

- Appropriate safe custody of physical exhibits
- Validation of the forensic processes and tools used
- Adherence to forensic best practices
- Forensic computers being in effective working order
- Verifiable calibration of forensic tools

Under this regime, evidence preservation and handling and physical security policies and processes must be geared to preserve evidence. The "tagging and bagging" of physical exhibits such as computer and storage devices is addressed clearly but in terms of the definition of digital evidence and a digital evidence container, they are not defined at all. This raises some concerns as to whether the computer or its hard drive is the actual evidence and the computer case its container. Regrettably, no definition is provided to clarify whether digital data stored on the hard drive or other storage media is the evidence container.

These may be considered semantic issues, but the lack of clarity has raised challenges as to the nature of digitized copies of the original evidence, such as videotapes generated during examination and exported for court presentation being called **original evidence**. However, legislators and courts have taken a pragmatic approach to digital evidence and consider that any data recording on a computer that may be printed, duplicated, or copied is the best evidence and may be admissible, provided its authenticity is verified.

The adoption of standards has been driven by the United States and the European Union. Unfortunately, these standards tend to cover only general requirements and are not geared specifically towards digital forensics, leaving digital forensics laboratories resorting to expensive piecemeal efforts to try to meet the expectations of the courts. While ISO 17025 has a sound track record in establishing quality management systems for the more established forensics disciplines, it has shown to be time and resource intensive and ineffective in digital forensics laboratories. This is because the standard was designed for traditional disciplines. Those implementing the design are often traditional forensics managers with limited understanding of digital forensics and best practices.

Best practices for digital forensics laboratories

Best practice manuals, regulations, and governance are an essential part of any forensic laboratory, ensuring that case management runs as smoothly and professionally as possible. Best practice includes the management of examinations and a report overview to ensure that the examinations of devices and forensic analyses have conformed to best practice and that the practitioners' findings have been cross-checked for soundness and completeness as well as for any errors and anomalies.

The protection of all digital evidence and devices relating to each case must be properly recorded and accounted for in a custody of evidence register, which records all movements of the exhibits and those personnel who have examined or tested them. The appropriate tagging and cross-referencing to the evidence register of computer devices and storage media submitted for analysis must be promulgated in the regulations governing best practice in the laboratory.

Proficiency testing of all forensic software applications and technical tools must be undertaken prior to their use in examinations. Imaging and copying of digital media onto a forensic computer and copying of other digital media should be in compliance with the laboratory custody of evidence register and evidence analysis and reporting protocols.

Archives of digital evidence, computing devices, and storage media may often require cataloging and storing for future referral at appeal trials, cold case reviews, and other investigations. Some material may require disposal or destruction after a designated period of time under government evidence, archiving, and record-keeping legislation.

The physical security of digital forensic laboratories

Physical security is paramount to controlling and protecting evidence and technical equipment from unauthorized contamination and tampering. It also protects personnel from potential attackers or hostile parties. Evidence must be secured and its chain of custody carefully maintained, managed, and coordinated. Digital evidence and the containers and original hard drives or tapes should be stored in security-grade lockers, cabinets, or safes—preferably secured with combination and keyed locks.

However, the nature of preparing forensic images and drives for analysis may require the forensic equipment to operate for extended periods, including out-of-office hours. Therefore, the workspace allocated for the evidence processing must itself be guarded from unauthorized internal or external access. Ideally, this may require strict access control of each practitioner's workstation, requiring its isolation from physical access with controlled entry and some form of security alarm system to notify of unauthorized access attempts. Access to the laboratories and evidence exhibits must be strictly controlled. The supervision of all visitors in order to prevent unauthorized access to and tampering with evidence and related devices is important.

In addition to physical security protecting the perimeter of the laboratory and some degree of internal segregation of workstations, computer monitors should not be viewable from outside through the laboratory windows to prevent any privacy compromise.

Network and electronic requirements of digital forensic laboratories

Reliable and approved electrical infrastructure is an essential requirement for protecting sensitive equipment from damaging peaks and troughs in the power charge. Ideally, each computer circuit should be limited to two terminals and peripheral equipment to avoid power drains and outages. Isolating each computer system from other systems reduces power issues and enhances the security of the data being examined.

Each practitioner/examiner requires a separate workstation and storage space for exhibits being currently examined. Ideally, the size of the workstation for each practitioner should be a minimum of 6 square meters and include a workbench for disassembling computing devices as well as one for undertaking analysis of recovered data. Network access should also be available to practitioners as they may often need Internet access to check information recovered during analysis. However, there are some inherent risks in doing so, especially if other users with access to the network connection gain information about the examination. Some measure to protect against such interception and conceal the research activity must be in place.

The electrical cabling should be designed to reduce the harmonics typical in computer networks that shorten the life of other equipment such as monitors. Surge protectors for all sensitive equipment, uninterrupted power supply to prevent data loss in the event of power outages, and simplified cable management at each workstation are essential enhancements.

Electromagnetic interference can potentially contaminate digital data stored on a range of devices that have Wi-Fi communication installed or attached to the device. Mobile phones are one such example, as are many other devices, including computers equipped with Bluetooth and other forms of Wi-Fi communication hardware. Digital forensics examinations of such devices would require that they be disarmed and unable to communicate with local communication networks.

It is standard procedure when commencing data recovery from mobile devices to remove SIM cards from mobile devices and switch the devices to flight mode to prevent them from communicating with external communication points. This prevents new data being downloaded to the device or existing data being modified or deleted, which would deny the practitioner the recovery of all potential evidence. It is far better to shield the device prior to it being powered on.

Such testing is carried out in screened rooms that are sealed with several layers of fine metal mesh or perforated metal. The metal layers are grounded to dissipate any electric currents generated from external or internal electromagnetic fields in order to block a large amount of the electromagnetic interference that may damage devices being examined and alter data stored in them. These rooms may be substituted by forensic (*Michael Faraday*) bags that are portable and can be taken to a crime scene to protect and examine a mobile device. They are in effect Faraday cages capable of blocking electrical interference to protect electronic equipment from the potentially damaging effects of external radio frequency interference.

Air conditioning and dust-minimizing (antistatic) carpeting for personnel well-being and maintaining the correct room temperature for servers and computer equipment is also essential. Acoustic soundproofing should also be installed because of the confidential nature of examinations to ensure there is no violation of case privacy.

Dilemmas presently confronting digital forensics laboratories

The proliferation of cybercrime-related offences is now significantly higher than conventional forms of crime. Cybercrimes cover a broad range of offences and most notably include credit card fraud, identity theft, phishing attempts, extortion, and unauthorized access to e-mail. This explosion of large datasets coupled with the increasing profusion of computing devices has already made it impracticable for law enforcement laboratories to examine all data and devices that might contain potential evidence.

Many law enforcement agencies have responded by resorting to inefficient triage processes and case prioritization, meaning that all but those cases categorized as high priority may not be processed for months or perhaps years — hardly effective policing. Concomitant with these deficiencies are concerns expressed over practitioners with low levels of forensic skills being able to complete high-quality digital crime scene reconstructions.

To save time, practitioners sometimes use a triage process to take a snapshot of the media to determine whether it contains evidence of value prior to undertaking a more complete examination, notwithstanding efforts to reduce the size of forensic image files and case data through file compression. Storage and archiving this data is still a time-consuming task, which is not really offset by data size reduction. The number of storage devices and forensic images taken of these devices has increased significantly and raised concerns from forensic laboratories, contributing to large backlogs of work and serious processing errors. This backlog is further aggravated by the increase in the size of datasets.

Emerging problems confronting practitioners because of increasingly large and widely dispersed datasets

Despite many commercial forensic software vendors endeavoring to meet the challenges of the changing nature of digital evidence and growing volume of datasets, it has not alleviated or addressed the momentous problem of data storage. The storage problem cannot be overstated. Cataloging and saving digital evidence for future retrieval and examination is a time-consuming and costly exercise, irrespective of the lower costs and higher storage capacity of storage media. A point to consider is the availability of what become legacy or redundant forensic tools that may not be available if not backed up themselves for later use. There may also be future licensing issues to enable the use of the tools, especially problematic if the tool manufacturer/vendor is no longer in business.

Smaller-size data requires less storage and is easier to archive. The benefit of the ISeekExplorer forensic container, for example, is that it provides a permanent safe harbor for evidence and uses significantly less storage space than conventional containers (this is described in more detail later in this chapter).

Digital evidence analysis usually involves processing large datasets, and using existing forensic tools requires technical expertise and understanding seldom possessed by legal practitioners and IT managers, for example. Furthermore, the technical complexity of digital evidence sometimes leads to misunderstandings about digital evidence tendered in legal cases. Although the forensic processing of large datasets could theoretically be completed with current forensic tools, this would be hugely time-consuming and calls for urgent research to alleviate the problem of large datasets.

I contend that there is no real distinction between criminal (mostly law enforcement) and civil examinations when using digital forensics processes and tools, as each group of stakeholders is looking for the same sort of evidence, but arguably to different standards. I further contend that the approach that has been used in the past for e-discovery, which often involves large numbers of machines, now needs to be applied to digital forensics, with some refinements, as the only way to handle large data volumes, although not necessarily the same large number of different sources.

Consequently, the challenges of storing large datasets and analyzing their contents in the search for evidence is formidable, and sometimes this has a detrimental effect on legal hearings. The objectives of locating and preserving digital evidence in criminal and civil settings are similar, but the forensic processes and tools used have developed differently in each environment, which are described in the following two subsections.

Debunking the myth of forensic imaging

The courts expect that digital evidence is recovered using sound forensic processes that eliminate at best and minimize at worst any modification of the digital information. This has been misinterpreted in e-discovery and, to some extent, in criminal digital forensics to mean that in every case, the complete set of digital information on a device must be imaged.

In many jurisdictions, most notably the United States, there is no prerequisite for a forensic image to be made. What the court needs to be satisfied with is that the evidence collected is forensically sound in that it can be shown to be unmodified and uncontaminated. This should, as shown in *Chapter 4, Recovering and Preserving Digital Evidence*, include a reliable and trustworthy account and log of how the data was recovered and by what process.

Section 901(a) of the United States Federal Rules of Evidence, which holds sway in most civil and criminal court case matters, stipulates that authentication of exhibits, including digital evidence, must be supported with sufficient proof as to the authenticity of the process used to recover the evidence. In civil cases, there is a predilection by courts and parties to a case for there to be an "over-collection" of evidence, as evinced in cases where imaging has been used. There are also concerns that too much irrelevant information may be examined in breach of the privacy of other parties from whom the data is collected.

In particular, what is needed is some perceptive reasoning as to what information should be selected for recovery, rather than the bucket approach of full-drive imaging involving the complete copying of hard drives. In outdated theory, the data collected is supposed to be unmodified and must include every bit on the drive, including deleted and partially erased data from allocated space. A forensic image provides access to all data recovered during the imaging process, including deleted, erased, and corrupted data. This allows the practitioner to reconstruct crime histories but comes at a cost in terms of expertise and time and often produces no beneficial outcome to the investigation.

Forensic images are more often used as a standard process for criminal investigations but are also frequently used for corporate investigations when there is a suspicion of deliberate data deletion that requires special tools to recover evidence from an image. In fact, in cases where there is a need to recover hidden and altered data, imaging is still considered the preferred option.

The disadvantage of imaging is that the process recovers every bit of data from the device being imaged, and because of the size of the drives, images are now significantly large in size. The size is significant because the images contain mostly irrelevant data, which can make it difficult and time-consuming to locate the evidence and traditionally required a high level of expertise. Often, no more than a small percentage of the image is of evidentiary value. Moreover, the practitioner must travel to the location to access the computer device and complete the imaging process by connecting to the device or hard drive. This adds to the time taken to recover the data as well as the cost of personnel involved.

This time-consuming and resource-hungry practice of forensic imaging is fast becoming untenable because more cases involve large datasets and suggest more efficacious processes than those that exist. While forensic imaging is the norm for criminal investigations, it is estimated that in more than 90 percent of civil cases where forensic imaging was undertaken, it was an overindulgent and unjustified use of resources and money. The same trend is likely to occur in criminal investigations over the next few years. Moreover, forensic imaging tools do not effectively recover evidence from web-based e-mail accounts, Dropbox, or other accounts held in the cloud or other remote locations.

Dilemmas presently confronting digital forensics practitioners

Practitioners are now processing increasingly large, terabyte-sized datasets but are confounded by inadequate analysis tools and time-consuming and inefficient recovery processes. Forensic practitioners were struggling with processing large datasets as early as 2004, being constrained by the time-hungry hashing and indexing algorithms required to analyze data post capture. Even with moderately large datasets of, say, 500 gigabytes, processing is problematic as it is inordinately and inherently time-consuming. This is because the data extraction and analytic processes become extremely slow and inefficient.

For over a decade, researchers have argued that practitioners must address the problem of locating and recovering relevant data using what they described as inadequate forensic tools and processes. It was also predicted that the rapidly increasing size of datasets would require more sophisticated, automated analysis to help locate and identify target evidence and possibly required significantly more computing power. More astute observers recognized that enhanced automated processes were needed as part of the timely and reliable identification and classification of relevant evidence buried in large and dispersed datasets.

Overreliance on forensic imaging and a reluctance to undertake live recovery of devices such as desktop computers and network servers has stymied practitioners as well as forcing them to spend an inordinate amount of time in unnecessary recovery, storage, and analysis. The ability of conventional forensic tools to make complete images and for those images to be reconstructed so that all the data can be viewed has repeatedly foundered. Yet, imaging rules supreme—at least for the time being.

But there is some encouraging news for practitioners. Simpler processes that comply with the expectations of the legal system are needed, and these are described in the following section.

Processes and forensic tools to assist practitioners to deal more effectively with these challenges

In sharp contrast to imaging, targeted live recovery using forensically sound tools and processes is possible. Evidence is sought and not altered by the searching process in that the file data and metadata remain unaltered. Recovered data is collected in a forensically sound and password-protected evidence container. E-discovery tools have been heralding this change—a change I predict will spill over into criminal evidence recovery processes.

E-discovery evidence recovery and preservation

Recent developments in the technology available for undertaking e-discovery are now signaling a paradigm shift away from the cumbersome existing processes used to capture and identify digital evidence. For companies involved in civil litigation, there is an increase in electronic discovery involving the capture of relevant digital information for evidentiary purposes.

Existing processes involve technologies that sometimes challenge the skills and experience of digital forensic and legal practitioners, thus creating a need for specialist digital forensic practitioners. The cost of these experts is high, which is an added burden to the discovery process on top of the high cost of the mandatory teams of legal analysts processing recovered data.

Processing times for limited keyword searches of the captured e-discovery data, for example, is also time-consuming, often taking days and weeks, and the large number of search hits for review are often overwhelming to process. Evidence examinations are hampered by the limited processing capabilities of human analysts, which are further aggravated by the increase in the size of datasets and post-processing reviews. The opportunities for practitioners to complete meticulous reviews of all captured evidence and search large datasets for evidence has long since passed and clearly signals a need for better digital evidence capture and processing.

E-discovery is almost entirely a civil matter, involving disputes between different organizations, so the concept of "evidence" is slightly different. However, civil investigations sometimes result in evidence recovered being used in criminal trials, disciplinary hearings, and other tribunal proceedings, such as unfair dismissal cases. Usually, cases that center on e-discovery require the litigants to identify information relevant to the legal action, by completing searches across their networks and storage systems. Any documents that are identified as relevant to the action are extracted, processed to remove irrelevant documents, and provided to the requesting litigant. Note that no forensic imaging has taken place.

A conundrum exists between the various e-discovery processes in using automated tools to prioritize and select documents for review, typically considered cost savers but an inferior alternative to tedious, manual reviews requiring the assessment of each document in response to a production request and to determine privilege. *Grossman and Cormack* (2011) quote the *Sedona Conference Best Practices Commentary on the Use of Search and Information Retrieval Methods in E-Discovery*, which cautions that "[t]here appears to be a myth that manual review by humans of large amounts of information is as accurate and complete as possible – perhaps even perfect – and constitutes the gold standard by which all searches should be measured. Even assuming that the profession had the time and resources to continue to conduct manual review of massive sets of electronic data sets (which it does not), the relative efficacy of that approach versus utilizing newly developed automated methods of review remains very much open to debate."

The process of indexing in e-discovery is carried out by software applications that scan the readable text of numerous electronic files and incorporate them into database tables of search terms corresponding to the text files. Indexing is intended to optimize subsequent search and retrieval and is useful for managing captive repositories, centralized data archives, and business-record repositories.

Typically, in index-based and non-index-based e-discovery data collection, the software is installed on the client server or network, which permits the inspection and indexing of the selected corpus, which is held as a searchable on an agent or index server for later retrieval and processing, as shown in the following figure:

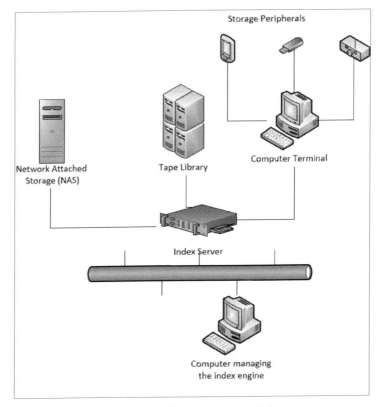

Client-server indexing of networked data

The holders of **Electronically Stored Information (ESI)**, corporations or customers, wherever they may be, certainly are not aware that in order to perform most ESI e-mail database processing, literally every intellectual property value they have, without their conscious knowledge, is being moved in bulk to the home turf of the reviewing company just to junk 90 percent of the data. It is perhaps worth noting that a huge risk of not just data breach but corporate espionage could take place at the datacenters of the reviewers as well.

I, based on case work in this field, firmly believe that it would be preferable if the processing was completed during the acquisition phase. In the end, the storage of images for the sake of it not only costs storage space, time, money, and management but also security, and it poses a potential risk of escalating data requests outside the bounds of the case at hand as well. An investigation that starts on one track might inadvertently find sufficient tangents of data of other events to expand the scope beyond the points giving rise to the matter in the first place.

Enhanced digital evidence recovery and preservation

The limitation of the indexing processes for e-discovery is that managing large archives results in slower searches and missed files. Many organizations have complained about significant difficulties managing indexes, notably, a requirement to re-index broken archives periodically, thereby negating any risk-mitigation benefit. Concerns have also been raised as to the ability of index-based e-discovery tools to locate key files subject to privilege. Checking samples of large e-mail databases that had been examined found artifacts missed during the indexing process.

Recognizing resource costs, a pressing reliance on and need for expertise in the face of the rapid increase in e-discovery, and the challenge of searching the growing size of datasets, I identified some enhancements that were required to address these challenges. A review of various tools and specialist expertise in e-discovery, my previous knowledge of e-discovery indexing servers as the predominant process to locate relevant evidence, and *Adam's* (2015) earlier experimentation prompted preliminary research into the tools available to see whether some or all of the desired enhancements were available.

In 2015, I and my co-researchers looked at the unique, patented automaton of Xtremeforensics ISeekDiscovery and noted that it made claim to a number of promising outcomes for stakeholders involved in e-discovery and potentially for law enforcement analysis. The ISeekDiscovery suite, now being marketed by eReveal Technologies Pty Ltd as eFinder, consists of a configuration utility, a search tool, and a review tool that do not require installation on the target devices or network servers. They are explained here:

- The configuration utility, ISeekDesigner, facilitates the creation of a configuration file containing the search terms, which can consist of whole paragraphs if required, to refine the search.

- The search tool, ISeekDiscovery, requires no installation and can be run by plugging in a USB device. Files containing the search term(s) are placed in an encrypted container set by ISeekDesigner.

- The review tool, ISeekExplorer, enables access to the encrypted container, allowing collected files to be reviewed and extracted as required.

The eReveal website, providing more detail about its tools and services, is located here:

`http://www.e-reveal.com/.`

The following screenshot shows the first pane of the nicely set-out wizard that assists users in using ISeekDesigner to prepare search terms for use with the ISeekDiscovery automaton:

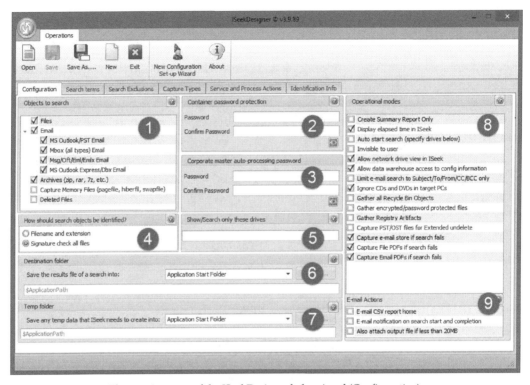

The opening pane of the ISeekDesigner help wizard (Configuration)

Some of the basic features of the tool are highlighted here:

- Select as appropriate according to what you are looking for and/or at in the **Objects to search** section
- **Container password protection**
- **Corporate master auto-processing password**
- Identify objects

- **Show/Search only these drives**
- **Operational modes** — discuss default selections
- **Destination folder**
- **Temp folder**
- **E-mail Actions**

The next screenshot shows a list of search terms and search term types, reflecting the search power of the automaton. Longer search phrases optimize the locating of specific file and e-mail content to assist the investigation. This in turn filters out many irrelevant hits and accelerates the searching process, and it reduces the data captured and facilitates more effective capture of desired datasets:

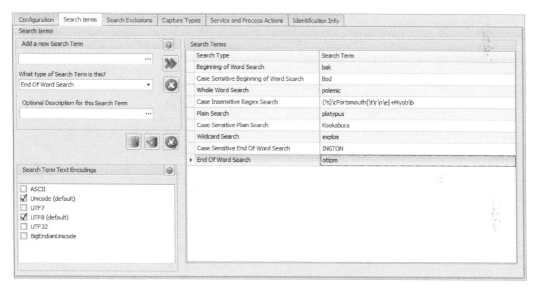

The opening pane of the ISeekDesigner help wizard (Search terms)

The purpose of ISeekDesigner is to create a configuration file containing search terms and other search process parameters. The configuration file, usually a small file of a few megabytes, is loaded with the similarly small ISeekDiscovery executable (the automaton) on a client's network server or computer terminal. No program is installed (a blessing to the network administrator), and the automaton package may be sent to a remote location by e-mail. The ISeekDiscovery executable is launched and commences a low-level sweep of the network or computer while the system is still running. No files are altered and no indexing is undertaken. This results in quicker data capture without disrupting the normal functionality of the network or attached terminals.

The following screenshot shows a view of the automaton searching one of the drives on a computer terminal and shows the drive selected being searched, the progress of the search, the amount of data read, and captured hits:

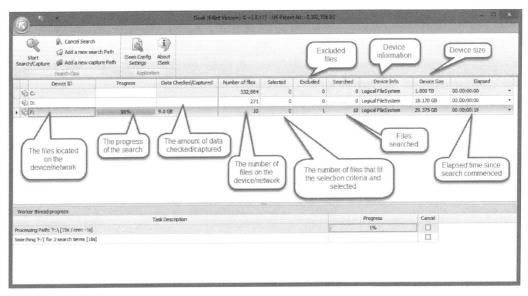

Viewing the ISeekDiscovery automaton searching a selected computer drive

Once the searching is completed, usually in only a fraction of the time it takes conventional index-based tools to complete the task, the automaton notifies the practitioner by e-mail or through the viewing panel about the number of hits recorded and the reason for the file selection. The third tool in the suite, ISeekExplorer, allows the practitioner to view the selected files and their contents and the file metadata and rationale for the search with respect to each file captured, as shown in the following screenshot. The files are stored in a password-protected .ISK encrypted forensic container for privacy as well as to facilitate legal privilege:

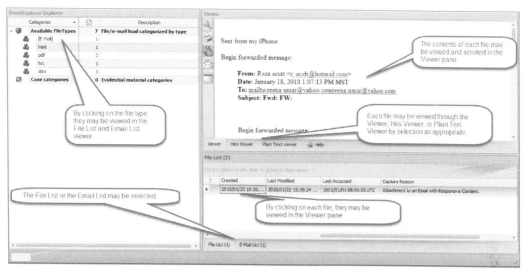

The ISeekExplorer view of the files captured and file content and metadata

The benefits of enhanced recovery tools in criminal investigations

It was noted that in contrast to traditional e-discovery or digital forensic tools, the practitioner or analyst can compile the searches and review captured data for relevance. ISeekExplorer facilitates the indexing of the processed data for quicker review after capture and not while on the target dataset, and it provides the following enhancements:

- Indexing without evidence contamination to produce sound evidence identification

- A significant reduction in the time required to complete data capture: indexing versus searching

- A significant reduction in the amount of data requiring capture

- Avoidance of site visits and associated travel

- A "safe harbor" for captured data that can be transported speedily and at lower cost

- No contamination of the evidence collated

- Simplicity of access to the target datasets without an Internet connection or software installation

- Simple executables with a minimum of technical expertise required and avoidance of the tedium of setting up complex capture processes
- Customizable search options compatible with analyst and legal team objectives
- Enhancing post-capture filtering and analysis
- A process capable of being used for crime investigations and intelligence analysis

Captured files can be indexed within the container using sophisticated software embedded in ISeekExplorer. The following screenshot shows the search results listed in the **Explorer** pane under the newly created `Search Results` folder. The name for each subfolder is based on the search terms selected, and they may be opened and viewed in the other viewer panes:

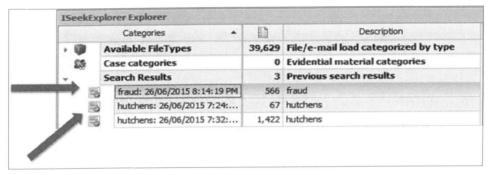

Search results cataloged in the ISeekExplorer protected forensic container

A new approach to recovering evidence is evident, and the trialing of the ISeekDiscovery suite shows that some pertinent research and design has provided a sound tool to pave the way for a more pragmatic process for evidence retrieval. The ISeek development team (incidentally incorporating experienced forensic practitioners and forensic software specialists) is presently incorporating and testing the code to enable ISeekDiscovery to recover selected Windows Registry hives and keys and deleted files from free space. This adds to the relevance of the tool being deployed by law enforcement, especially when tracking evidence on dispersed networks such as the cloud or large network servers.

Tools such as ISeekDiscovery now permit information managers and law enforcement officers with minimal training to undertake searches across a broad range of data repositories without complex forensic tools and the assistance of specialists. In theory, lawyers and auditors with a modicum of IT and forensic training can replace expensive specialists with such tools and take control of the management of their own evidence retrieval. The convenience of having only relevant data secured in a protected forensic container avoids storage issues and lengthy indexing and searching processes.

I will go further, asserting that the search and retrieval features offered by such tools can also be used in criminal investigations, where the preoccupation with forensic images can be replaced with a more pragmatic process. Such processes that are search-oriented and evidence-led offer significant enhancements to forensic analysis and significant savings in terms of resource costs. The intelligence and defense communities may also benefit as the search strategy offered through such processes could be applied to field investigations and protracted cases where computer systems and datasets are being interrogated as part of an investigation.

Chapter 10, *Empowering Practitioners and Other Stakeholders*, outlines the benefits of these new technologies, providing you with an insight into how this will shape the future of digital forensics.

Empowering non-specialist law enforcement personnel and other stakeholders to become more effective first respondents at digital crime scenes

As mentioned in *Chapter 4*, *Recovering and Preserving Digital Evidence*, well-intentioned action by a network administrator, information manager, or first respondent law enforcement officer, who are trying to determine whether a transgression has occurred and are attempting to preserve evidence, can amount to unintentional evidence tampering if they do not have some form of forensic experience and the right tools. Considering the heavy caseload of law enforcement agencies and digital forensic practitioners and the high cost of using their services, it seems long overdue that some form of basic training and tools such as ISeek be able to assist stakeholders in managing the identification and collection of potential evidence without contamination.

This section looks at this deficiency in digital evidence collection and preservation and offers some pragmatic solutions.

The challenges facing non-forensic law enforcement agents

Law enforcement field agents are often tasked to be evidence collectors. In effect, they carry out para-forensic roles because of the heavy workload of specialist crime scene personnel and forensic examiners, who may not always be readily available to help stabilize the crime scene and recover evidence in a timely manner. Law enforcement agents attending the scene of an incident are now increasingly confronted with seizing and examining computers and data held on computer networks, mobile devices, digital cameras, and video recorders.

It may often be of importance to access these devices to obtain information as a matter of operational urgency rather than primarily as evidence collection and preservation. Whether or how they do it is a judgment call for the officer at the scene. Operational requirements that, for example, may lead to the apprehension of a suspect or prevent harm to others or severe damage to property have an overriding priority over evidence collection. But that is not to say that some form of awareness and response training cannot be given to agents in the field who are not forensic specialists.

Data recovery from mobile phones, for example, has traditionally been handled by computer crime teams experienced in recovery with access to a laboratory or forensic field kits. These teams are often centrally located with heavy caseloads and regular and time-consuming court attendance as expert witnesses, and are usually focused on higher-level categories of cases. At best, they may only be able to communicate directions to field agents as to the best evidence recovery response, sometimes leaving the field agents with limited guidance, no experience, and no effective tools to preserve the evidence.

Enhancing law enforcement agents as first respondents

The use of portable mobile phone recovery units for law enforcement officers, using reasonably priced recovery software and some basic training for nominated targets in central and more widely dispersed operational locations, has provided some benefit. While it has reduced the overreliance on central forensic teams, it has been contingent on the ability of agencies to purchase sounds units in sufficiently large numbers to make a difference. Emerging mobile phone encryption and new phone models can make these field kits obsolete overnight.

The training of designated personnel who use these kits has, on occasion, proved to be ineffectual when the operator has been confronted with the quirkiness of a broad range of mobile phone types. The effectiveness of the kits and the ability of the operators observed by me on recent occasions raised doubts as to the overall benefits when evidence that could have been recovered was not. If such strategies are to be used, the soundness of the equipment must be rigorously tested. Moreover, ongoing training for the operators must be provided and monitored to guarantee the best outcomes.

Apart from mobile phones, the handling of desktop and laptop computers needs a pragmatic process to preserve evidence as well as a workable guide to evidence recovery for case prognosis. The basic requirement to achieve this consists of:

- A reasonable budget to set up and maintain the initiative
- The selection of affordable, proven, and reliable software and hardware that is relatively easy to use and update
- Reliable training personnel to ensure operators are properly trained and receive ongoing support and retraining when required
- A review made of the process to determine its success and ultimately its importance (to enhance future budgeting)
- Flexibility of review to ensure that the process keeps pace with the ongoing change in technologies

Skills required as part of the process include the ability to image devices or, preferably, search for evidence that can be stored in forensic secure digital evidence containers such as the ISeek `.ISK` evidence container. This may be achieved by using a 64-gigabyte USB thumb drive and a predesigned ISeek configuration file, with which the contents of a device, such as e-mail records or correspondence files, may be selected and recovered. This is the only tool available to boot up an Apple computer to retrieve information. The automaton can also capture the drive contents or selected folders and partitions. The critical process involved is designing the search criteria to meet the needs of the investigator. While this may appear straightforward, it does require some thought and experience in using search terms.

The recovery can take between 30 minutes to several hours depending on the size of the drive and may also be deployed on a network server with a modicum of operator training. Once the search hit results are known, the data may be selected and either accessed on site or sent to a more secure central handling center for further analysis. Recovered datasets may be migrated to processing applications such as **Relativity**; however, the ISeek suite provides an application interface, XtremeReporting, that assists legal and analysis teams to process data expeditiously.

Alternatively, the agents can use ISeekExtractor to export selected files and folders from the `.ISK` file for local or central location analysis, as shown in this screenshot:

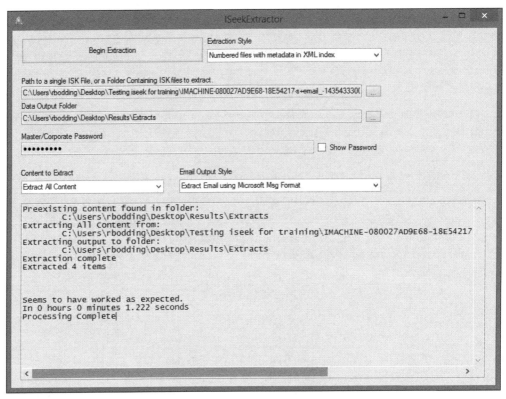

The ISeekExtractor API tool

The extracted folders may then be catalogued and conveniently searched for essential evidence, as shown here:

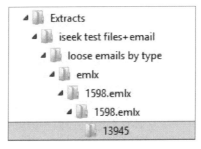

Folders of extracted e-mail messages

The following screenshot shows the contents of a typical folder, showing the e-mail header file, the body of the e-mail and the attachment—in this case, a PDF file:

Name	Date modified	Type	Size
1.header	22/01/2010 3:35 PM	Text Document	5 KB
2.body	22/01/2010 3:35 PM	Firefox HTML Doc...	4 KB
3.20080905161636738	22/01/2010 3:35 PM	Foxit Reader PDF ...	149 KB

View of the e-mail header, body, and attachment extracted into the examination folder

Use of the automaton is far simpler than imaging, even with IXImager, and only requires access to the device and appropriate design of the configuration file. There is no dismantling the device, and the tool uses the data storage virtualization technology **Redundant Array of Independent Disks (RAID)** and network servers to locate only essential data.

The sample case at the end of this chapter compares the effectiveness of old and new processes to facilitate speedy data recovery during a fraud investigation. It shows what can be done to speed up and remove the complexity of the digital forensic component of a crime investigation.

The challenges facing IT administrators, legal teams, forensic auditors, and other first respondents

The custodians of desktop and laptop machines and network administrators know the characteristics of their data holdings, user access, and running applications. They may be the first respondent to discover that some form of improper use of the system has taken place. This may include a hacker attack, insider fraud, or personnel misconduct. For organizations, personnel have access through a desktop terminal, portable laptop, or mobile device, usually linked to the organization's network server by direct cabling or remote access, Wi-Fi connection, and so forth.

Often, the investigation will require inculpatory evidence that typically is in the form of personal or business correspondence, notably e-mail messages and attachments, text files, photographs and diagrams, and logs of database access and document management systems. Also, the investigation may require a deeper level of forensic examination to look for hidden and deleted information that has been deliberately concealed.

These types of investigations may be triggered by a broad range of events, including:

- Breaches of confidentiality
- The sudden and unexplained departure of a staff member
- Evidence of fraud or misappropriation of an organization's funds or assets
- Account audit anomalies
- Misuse of Internet browsing privileges
- Complaints of misconduct made by clients and other staff members of misbehavior, sexual harassment, and other breaches of the employment code

Evidence stored on desktops and personal computing devices may well be forensically imaged or, in the case of mobile phones, data extraction can be made using a range of forensic tools. However, these tools may not be available, and no qualified users are available in-house.

For extracting data from a network server, the network administrator may use a range of data backup applications such as Safeback or ShadowProtect to make logical copies of the server and copies of available backup tapes. However, when viewing and accessing files to determine whether there has been a security breach or evidence of some transgression, there is a possibility of altering the file data, timestamps, and audit trail logs unintentionally. There is also the possibility, if the extracted information is presented in court, that the opposing team may dispute the authenticity of the data, claiming that it may have been altered during recovery or deliberately by hostile parties.

These tools take a logical copy of the server and, for example, any database files hosted on the server, such as e-mail server databases and other accounting and administrative databases. A copy of the server file at a given point and all available backup tapes (on-site or off) is an expedient measure, as it allows the organization to recommence business while the original dataset containing potential evidence remains intact. The backup will copy all system files and, to reiterate, this is time-consuming and results in more data being collected than will be required. The practitioner is also in the hands of the network administrator, who may not be on site or unavailable at critical times to make a backup of the server data.

Normally, the network administrator will save everything so that examination of relevant data may take place when desired, although, unlike a forensic imaging, it will be a logical copy of the data and not a bit-for-bit exact physical image that would facilitate locating hidden and deleted files. For a 1-terabyte network server, the copying process would take between 3 and 5 hours, but considerably more time and storage space would be required for a larger network.

It may be a matter of isolating e-mail databases relating to dubious activities based on user identities, time frames, and subject matter. In an organization of any size, it is unlikely that an investigation will examine the information holdings relating to every employee or manager, and may from the outset focus on one or more employees. On the other hand, it may be unclear as to what the identity of possible culprits is, but an event or subject matter may provide links to them.

Having an image of the server, if possible, may be useful for indexing and searching for evidence, but what if the network is dispersed and it is impractical to consider imaging the large dataset? Copying and restoring an image of a network is time-consuming and can take between a day and several days to complete. So much data is saved, yet little of it is required. If the appointed investigator is tasked to look for only certain parts of the network thought relevant to the incident, there is no guarantee that they will contain all the available evidence. Staff terminals also take time to image and then search for evidence, and this is not without its challenges, as will be demonstrated in *Chapter 6, Selecting and Analyzing Digital Evidence*.

Enhancing IT administrators, legal team members, and other personnel as first respondents

So, rather than adopting imaging as the best process, I and my co-researchers use and commend the use of the ISeek automaton to locate and recover data of potential value. This is exemplified in the case study at the end of the chapter, but consider the time benefit of being able to interrogate a server and desk terminals using the automaton to collate a manageable container of information from which an early and quick prognosis can assist the investigation.

For example, the e-mail server may contain thousands of user databases, yet the investigation is seeking the e-mails of only one or perhaps two internal users, for a specified time frame, engaging in certain activities. The automaton can be configured to look for e-mails and attachments in the context of the inquiry. It can filter by file size, type, and periods of time to avoid processing unnecessary data and speed up the process of locating evidence and leads for further inquiry.

In addition, these types of investigations require the large e-mail and document sets to be filtered and cataloged efficiently so as to reduce the time spent on and tedium experienced by the examining team personnel. The same stratagem used by law enforcement agents to search for and contain selected data applies here. Moreover, while the administrator may be able to isolate a user and e-mail accounts, the possibility remains that information of value may be overlooked in other locations on the server not evident to the examining team. The team may lack sufficient technical knowledge and experience regarding the less likely locations of evidence. The automaton does not have to rely on extracting large datasets and can work quickly and efficiently on those drives where evidence may sit.

Another benefit of administrators and auditors using the automaton is that they can be involved in configuring the search terms, which can be launched on the server or terminal without the installation of any software application and without the physical presence of a forensic practitioner. This broadens the scope of investigations that may otherwise be delayed or abandoned because of the cost of hiring an expensive practitioner and associated travel and accommodation costs. It can all be accomplished by e-mail and telephone communication.

Securing the evidence, or what appears on first inspection to be information that may assist a later investigation, is a high priority. Making sure that the evidence is kept in pristine condition has been emphasized in previous chapters, as has the likelihood of its contamination by hostile parties as well as those inspecting it and trying to save it to a safe location.

Again, the ISeekDiscovery tool has the capability of being quickly deployed with a simple configuration file to enable the capture of drives or folders where information needs to be placed in a "safe harbor". The evidence container is password protected and encrypted to restrict access to the recovered evidence to ensure confidentiality and safekeeping. This figure shows the selection of a drive folder for capture by ISeekDiscovery:

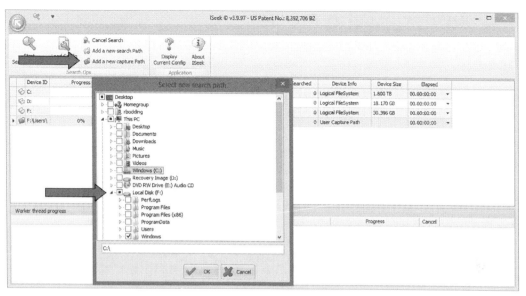

Using ISeekDiscovery to capture a drive folder for safekeeping

These are software application solutions potentially empowering first respondents. While the tools and the training necessary are not without cost, they do enable the responders to take some ownership of the problem of digital information in their care and take direct responsibility for protecting recovered evidence in civil and criminal settings. *Chapter 8, Examining Browsers, E-mails, Messaging Systems, and Mobile Phones,* will look at forensic processes to enhance the recovery and preservation of digital evidence, including data stored on remote locations, such as the cloud.

The following case study is based on what started out as a business insolvency that, as it later transpired, involved the theft of large sums of client and employee funds by the principal owner of the business. The case was prepared with a view to handing recovered evidence to a law enforcement agency for formal criminal charges to be laid as well as for civil litigation intended to recover the funds and other property.

Case study – illustrating the challenges of interrogating large datasets

Consider the case of a domestic property management firm that, over a period of some 30 years, built up a profitable business managing the sale, purchase, and rental of domestic properties in several fashionable suburbs in an Australian state capital city. The business principal bought into the business at a relatively young age and with little business management acumen, yet was full of ambition and showmanship.

The setting of the crime

The business owners, of what had always been a profitable enterprise, became aware that it was experiencing some increasingly serious financial problems. Letters of demand were received from contractors engaged in the maintenance of and repairs to rental properties managed by the firm, complaining of non-payment of their work. Clients complained that monies placed in trust funds as part of the sale and purchase of listed properties were not cleared within stipulated periods. Letters from the firm's financiers over default payments of loans and staff members not receiving salaries and commissions all added to the clamor.

The principal was questioned as to the nature of the problem and, after a month of apparent prevarication, departed the firm in possession of his work computer and mobile phone. Attempts to interview the principal failed and it was then discovered that the principal had been registered as a bankrupt. An acute shortage of funds and an inability to meet its creditors' demands forced the firm into involuntary administration.

It soon became evident that significant funds had been secreted out of the firm through a number of shelf companies and trusts controlled by the principal. These funds were the bulk of the firm's reserves, amounting to some $5 million, including trust fund holdings of clients. Even the employees' superannuation fund was devoid of funds; the firm's monthly fund contributions were 6 months in arrears.

The investigation

The forensic audit team commenced its investigation into the affairs of the firm and noted that some important business ledgers, containing recent transactions relating to funds that had been emptied just prior to the principal's unexpected departure, were missing. The principal's missing laptop and office phones denied the auditors the principal's e-mail and telephone communications. Examination of the firm's accounts through its bank confirmed that large amounts of funds had been transferred to other businesses by the authorized account holder—the principal.

The initial suspicion was that the principal had been involved in the transfer of the funds and may have used companies he owned to do so. There was some suspicion that documents relating to transfers and these companies had been forged to facilitate the transfer and avoid detection by the bank and create unwanted attention.

The practitioner's brief

While the misappropriation of the funds implicated the principal, it was necessary to demonstrate knowledge, involvement, and motivation that it was for criminal gain and not some other less onerous reason. Proof of this could be provided by the following:

- E-mail and other communications, including attachments relating to the principal and possible accomplices relating to dubious transactions

- All communications relating to the indebtedness of the firm

- Traces of electronic copies of missing business ledgers (the audit team would separately examine the financial and client business database to identify missing transactions)

- Word and Excel documents that relate to the principal and business entities relating to dubious financial transactions

- All .PDF files that appear to have been scanned and may reveal forgery relating to dubious transactions

- All applications that relate to copying and changing documents into PDF format and could facilitate the suspected forgery

- Backups of the principal's mobile phone that may provide additional proof of involvement in the fraud

- Any other information that might provide investigative leads and reconstruct relevant events

The available evidence

The data available to the practitioner consisted of:

- The network server, containing about 800 gigabytes of data, including an e-mail database, a real estate management database, and an accounting database for personnel payroll and business operations

- 17 terminals for employees

- A backup drive for the property management database

- A damaged mobile phone discarded by the principal

The data extraction process

The network server data was required to be imaged for eventual analysis by the relevant government department and as the best evidence in the event of any future legal action against the firm and the principal. As the server could not be shut down because of urgent business with irate clients and other commitments, the option of imaging the drive was not feasible. The network administrator, also an unsecured creditor of the firm, isolated the network from the principal and other personnel and made a backup of the drive. The backup took 48 hours to complete because the server refreshed itself and delayed the process. The administrator did, however, provide some 60 gigabytes of e-mail stores of the entire staff members and user terminals. This data was searched using ISeekDiscovery.

However, this data was not available for analysis for 3 days. The server backup was restored, taking a further 20 hours, and there was another delay in copying the data to a forensic container for the government department.

Examination of the personnel e-mail .PST files was completed in under 2 hours using the automaton, locating evidence in the principal's e-mail server account and minimal relevant information in one other staff member's account. This accorded with the auditing team's view that the principal had acted alone.

This e-mail data could have been recovered on day one by launching the automaton on the server. Other documentary evidence being sought, including a small number of suspected forged or fabricated PDF files and the related software application, could have been captured expeditiously using the automaton. This would have provided the audit team with an earlier insight into the principal's impropriety and identified other probative information and possible links to other perpetrators.

Six desktop computers used by other personnel were imaged for broader analysis, as it was thought possible that information relating to the fraud may be obtained. Imaging of each device using IXImager was speedy and undertaken concurrently, being completed within 3 hours. The images were mounted and ISeek was used to search for possible evidence and other leads. This was a more time-consuming process than using the automaton on the six terminals concurrently, which, as it transpired, recovered minimal probative information. However, the client was persistent in sticking to the old tried-and-tested processes that took longer, as it transpired.

Data relating to PDF files and mobile phone and e-mail messages and attachments was obtained through these combined processes and filtered using ISeekExtractor to produce a distillation of relevant data for the audit team to examine. Evidence of particular importance was extracted and included in the report provided to the forensic audit team for analysis as well as feedback to the practitioner for further searching.

The outcome of the recovery and examination

The practitioner had been provided with sufficient background of the investigation to undertake some analysis and reconstruction to assist the audit team with the digital evidence. The use of ISeekExplorer to search for and catalog possible evidence and leads from an originally large dataset was relatively uncomplicated and speedy compared to the use of conventional forensic tools.

Information of value to the audit team was distilled and consisted of:

- E-mails between the principal and the financial institution regarding the transfer of large amounts of funds out of the firm to companies controlled by the principal

- Synchronized e-mail messages recovered from the server backup of the principal's mobile phone regarding suspect financial transactions and the principal's indebtedness

- Identities of family and unit trusts and residential properties owned and controlled by the principal suspected of being involved in illegal transactions

- Documents stored on the principal's server folder relating to scanned written transactions relating to the parlous state of the firm

- Details of bank transfers of significantly large and regular amounts moved from the firm's accounts to other entities of possible relevance to the investigation

What was not found was evidence of any document forgery or software applications that may have been used to alter and forge documents. Messages between the principal and his spouse and family were innocuous and of no relevance to the investigation. No other staff members were implicated in any misdemeanor.

It was clear that any substantial digital evidence that may have existed was on the principal's missing laptop or another device used away from the workplace. The server e-mail database did provide some of the principal's e-mails but they were not of significant help to the investigation. There is a possibility that any incriminating e-mails using the firm's e-mail server may have been permanently deleted by the principal as the server did not prevent users from making permanent deletions that are unrecoverable. The backup tapes for the server did not identify any incriminating e-mails. It is more than likely that the actual acts of fraud and forgery did not take place inside the firm's premises or by using its computers.

The principal later surrendered the laptop, which was accessed using ISeekDiscovery but only produced a small, but important, amount of potential evidence in the form of a spreadsheet. The file contained what were evidently specific details of the principal's money trail involved in the theft of clients' funds.

Conclusion

The case described the examination of a small organization using a combination of old and new forensic processes and clearly demonstrated the benefits of the new technology. For a larger organization, a dump of the selected hits obtained through the automaton would be extracted using ISeekExtractor for end processing using software such as Relativity. A lot of work was done at reduced cost without an overabundance of probative evidence recovered, as it transpired, but the examination that was required and the time saved also reduced the cost to the client.

References

Adams, R. B. 2015. "Leveraging new technology that combines digital forensics and electronic discovery for intelligence purposes." Journal (25 May 2015): 1-4. Retrieved from http://www.sageinternational.com.au/product/leveraging-new-technology-that-combines-digital-forensics-and-electronic-discovery-for-intelligence-purposes/.

Grossman, M. R. and Gordon V. Cormack. 2011. "Technology-assisted review in e-discovery can be more effective and more efficient than exhaustive manual review." Richmond Journal of Law & Technology (17): 11-16.

Summary

The chapter further described the challenges posed by the rapidly increasing size of datasets that makes it difficult to seek digital evidence without considerable expenditure of time, money, and human resources. The questionability of conventional forensic image protection has also been highlighted. The continuing use of forensic imaging is predicted to become less prevalent because of the concomitant increase in the size of secure data stores to preserve the evidence and related resource costs. The use of better tools to process large datasets, identify important evidence, and preserve it in more modest storage sizes is urgently needed.

The chapter introduced the evidence-searching automaton and demonstrated its value through testing and casework, confirming its effectiveness in overcoming challenges posed to practitioners, with some encouraging results being observed. Such processes offered in the suite of tools should attract the attention of practitioners, not just in the e-discovery field, but also in law enforcement and the intelligence community—communities facing escalating costs, reduced manpower, and limited time to process information in a timely manner. Information managers and the legal fraternity also seek some autonomy from costly specialists and vendors to better manage, capture, and preserve information that may later be required in legal cases.

I hope that you will benefit from the knowledge gained from this chapter by providing a glimpse into the newly emerging environment of digital evidence handling. These new technologies address the challenges posed by increasingly large and disparate datasets that can no longer be copied through conventional imaging processes for much longer. Not only do these new technologies help address these challenges, the relative simplicity of using them removes much of the mystery surrounding e-discovery experts and vendor hype. IT administrators can now take the opportunity to become involved in the sound capture and management of information likely to be used in court and can become empowered by the new technologies.

Chapter 6, *Selecting and Analyzing Digital Evidence*, introduces the use of structured processes to navigate acquired forensic images and containers, notably the ISeekExplorer .ISK container file, to locate and select evidence based on sound forensic practice. The case study provided in this chapter shows how the complexity of a case can become challenging, and so, it is important to have some structured approach to assist the practitioner. Each case is different and can vary quite remarkably, but all share some common characteristics. While there is no substitute for experience, some flexible, pragmatic schema is required to ensure that the examination proceeds in an organized manner.

The very size of the data recovered means that the best forensic tools are used to complete examinations. *Chapter 6*, *Selecting and Analyzing Digital Evidence*, provides an insight into the forensic tools used to extract and select evidence. It will further describe the emergence of forensic tools that reduce the tedium of and time spent on analysis and retrieving more evidence. The exciting part of forensic examinations is knowing where to look for potential evidence, what you are looking for, and why it may be important and relevant to the investigation, and then finding it. All this comes with experience, for there are many blind canyons to explore, and while the brain is the best forensic tool, it can become tired, confused, and frustrated in trying to locate and understand the evidence. For the seasoned and novice practitioner, these new tools do make a significant difference in reducing fatigue and impatience, resulting in more complete and satisfactory examinations.

6
Selecting and Analyzing Digital Evidence

This chapter will introduce the procedure of undertaking a digital forensic examination of acquired digital information through the iterative and interactive stages of selecting and analyzing digital evidence. It will outline the key stages of digital evidence selection and analysis in line with accepted forensic standards. The chapter will look at:

- The use of structured processes to navigate acquired forensic images to locate and select evidence based on sound forensic practices
- The emergence of forensic tools that reduce the tedium and time spent on analysis and that retrieve more evidence

Structured processes to locate and select digital evidence

Various digital forensic examination models are in use, each emphasizing slightly different stages in the investigation process, with no universally agreed-upon model used by practitioners. I have examined the structure of each model and propose that a typical digital forensic examination may be divided into the evidence-recovery and preservation stage and then locating, sorting, selecting, and analyzing the evidence recovered that may support (or refute) a legal argument. The next stage is validating the evidence, ensuring that it is what it purports to be. The final stage is presenting the selected evidence in a formal report. This may be to the legal team or the investigator or may be made by the practitioner testifying during a legal hearing.

The examination is often an iterative process, in that the various stages may be revisited before the examination is finally concluded. For example, another device that may be recovered later will require data recovery and preservation of the data, as was described in detail in *Chapter 4, Recovering and Preserving Digital Evidence.*

Recovery and preservation has traditionally involved the imaging of devices and storing the data in bulk in a forensic file or, more securely, in a forensic image container, notably the ILookIX `.ASB` container. *Chapter 5, The Need for Enhanced Forensic Tools*, described the recovery of smaller, more manageable datasets from larger datasets from a device or network system using the ISeekDiscovery automaton. Whether the practitioner examines an image container or an extraction of information in the ISeekDiscovery `.ISK` container, it should be possible to overview the recovered information and develop a clearer perception of the type of evidence that should be located. Using a structured process to locate the evidence makes the certainty of locating it more likely and the process less arduous than using an unstructured approach.

Once acquired, the image or device may be searched to find evidence. Locating evidence requires a degree of analysis combined with practitioner knowledge and experience. As outlined in *Chapter 2, Hardware and Software Environments*, evidence may be located in a broad range of devices and in various locations on those devices. Information of interest may be located in the e-mail folder, containing messages and attachments of interest to an investigator. The process of selection involves analysis, and as new leads open up, the search for more evidence intensifies until ultimately a thorough search process is completed.

The searching process involves the analysis of possible evidence, from which evidence may be discarded, collected, or tagged for later re-examination, thereby instigating the selection process. It must be stressed that the selection of candidate evidence by the practitioner does not mean that it is proof of guilt or innocence—it simply means that the evidence selected appears to be relevant to and supportive of the matter at hand. This means that the evidence supports or adds to a legal argument or hypothesis—the ultimate *probandum* of a case, such as the defendant using the computer to strike the deceased's head, resulting in his demise! Some theorists and practitioners have a clearly defined stage in their models they call analysis, but that may be somewhat confusing as analysis is part of all stages and not really a separate process.

The following diagram is a simple model proposed by me, which highlights the examination of digital evidence in the investigative and legal domains. The penultimate stage of the investigative process is the validation of the evidence, aimed at determining its reliability, relevance, authenticity, accuracy, and completeness. The final stage is the presentation of the evidence to interested parties, such as the investigators, the legal team, and, ultimately, the legal adjudicating body. Evidence validation is covered in more detail in *Chapter 9, Validating the Evidence*. Once the legal process is completed, the digital evidence containers and digital devices may require safe storage pending the outcome of any review or legal appeal:

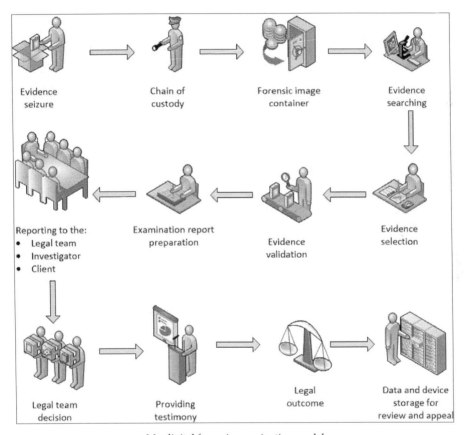

My digital forensic examination model

The following subsections describe the evidence searching and selection processes.

Locating digital evidence

Locating evidence from the all-too-common large dataset requires some filtration of extraneous material, which has until recently been a mainly manual task of sorting the wheat from the chaff. But it is important to clear the clutter and noise of busy operating systems and applications, from which only a small amount of evidence really needs to be gleaned. This section describes the processes involved that practitioners follow in their endeavors to locate relevant material to assist an investigation.

Search processes

Search processes involve searching in a filesystem and inside files; common searches for files are based on:

- Their names or patterns in their names
- Keywords in their content
- Temporal data (metadata), such as the last-accessed or last-written time

A pragmatic approach to the examination is necessary, where the onus is on the practitioner to create a list of keywords or search terms to cull specific, probative, and case-related information from very large groups of files. The advanced search terms in ISeekDesigner provide practitioners with a high level of flexibility to locate evidence, notably the following:

- Plain search
- Case-sensitive plain search
- Whole-word search
- Case-sensitive whole-word search
- Regex search
- Case-insensitive regex search
- Wildcard search
- Hex sequence search
- Beginning-of-word search
- Case-sensitive beginning-of-word search
- End-of-word search
- Case-sensitive end-of-word search
- Disabled

Hashing is used to compare the signature of files against a range of databases that include malware and child exploitation material. It can also assist in locating files on a suspect computer against previously known signatures. For example, locating a forged text document held on one computer and suspected to be on another was made possible by using the hash of the file contents, despite the file extension and name being changed to conceal the forgery.

Searching desktops and laptops

The next figure shows a computer terminal linked to the Internet via a modem. Various peripheral devices are attached: a scanner, printer, external hard drive, thumb drive, storage device, digital camera, and mobile phone. In an office network, this would be a more complicated system. A typical household may include local area networks and a range of users and their digital devices. The linked connections between the devices and the Internet through the terminal leave a range of traces and logging records in the terminal and on some of the devices and the Internet. E-mail messages will be recorded externally on the e-mail server; the printer may keep a record of print jobs; the external storage devices and the communication media also leave logs and data linked to the terminal. All of this data may assist in the reconstruction of key events and provide evidence related to the investigation:

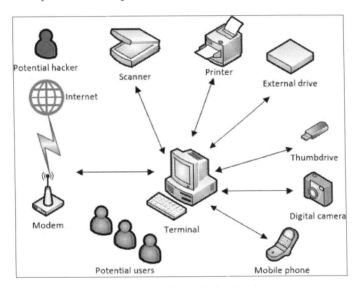

A typical single-terminal network

If we look at the data stored on the terminal, which may be a desktop, laptop, or netbook, traces of relevant data may be located there. In the following diagram, we have recovered a deleted MS Word document from **Recycle Bin**, containing a death threat to another person.

The intended victim has reported receiving an e-mail message with a Word document attachment from the suspect, whose computer was later seized for examination. In this hypothetical scenario (based on an actual case), the practitioner's task is to locate evidence of the e-mail message and attachment. This simple task may reveal the e-mail file and attachment, but it may only locate traces of the message:

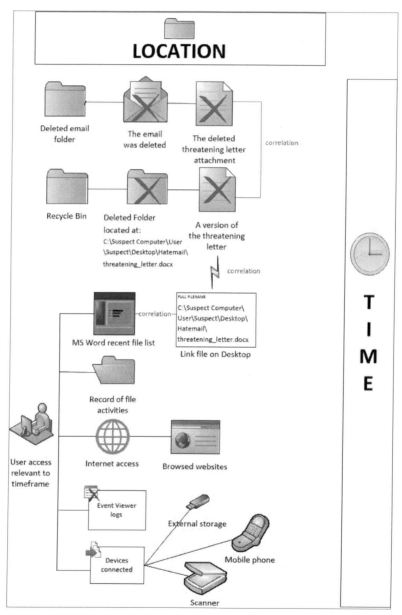

A relationship between a recovered evidence artifact and its correlation with other artifacts

Anomalies in timestamp metadata may also complicate the reconstruction of key events.

In this scenario, we have an e-mail message that may have a number of relationships with other files that record events that seem to link to the e-mail message and are within the relevant time frame. From this recovered file, it is possible to reconstruct a timeline based on relevant timestamps and the locations of the additional files. This will assist in the more complete selection of useful information to assist in the analysis of the threads of evidence. This will be looked at in more detail in the following subsection on evidence selection, but first, it is important for the practitioner to know where to look for helpful leads.

From this simple yet common scenario, note that the file does not exist in isolation. There is related information that should be located—and within a period corresponding to the creation and transmission of the e-mail message. Firstly, it is expedient to look for other information that correlates with the e-mail message; information that may clarify:

- When the message was created and posted
- Whether it was created and dispatched on the suspect's computer
- Where the attachment was created
- When the attachment was created
- The identity of the user who created the Word document

The previous diagram highlights that there are what appear to be related events based on deleted files and applications that created or modified these files, which are as follows:

- The Deleted e-mail folder held the deleted e-mail and attachment
- Recycle Bin held a deleted folder and a deleted version of the threatening Word document that was previously located on the computer desktop
- The Word document file contained metadata relating to the previous location of the file and its recorded author
- A link file (or Jump List log) refers to the location of the file of the same name in this folder that was previously located on the desktop
- Microsoft Word is installed and shows a record of the creation and modification of a file with the same name in a recent document log

Files created, modified, transferred, or stored on a computer will often leave a trail of links that record its presence on the device. They often contain metadata, including authorship, file location, and timestamps, which may help in event reconstruction, and they certainly assist in locating such links. The following screenshot shows the **Quick access** feature in the **File Explorer** pane. In this example, it shows frequent folders accessed by users of the computer. The screenshot displays folders and an individual file, which is a typical default setting. By booting up the forensic image of the device, this may be readily observed, and it cannot contaminate evidence on the original device:

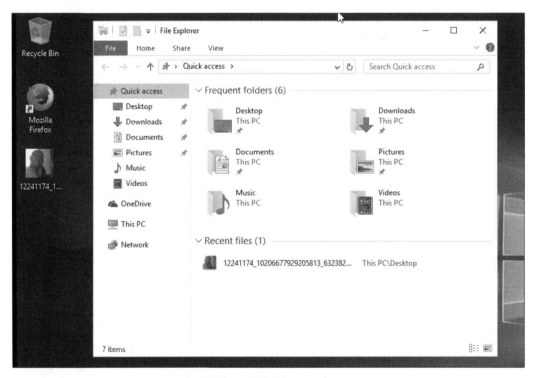

The Windows 10 Quick access feature

However, this data is stored in Jump List files since the launch of Windows 7 and intended to assist users with quick and convenient access to files and applications at various locations in the computer. During the physical examination of a device, Jump List details may be accessed in Windows Registry at `HKCU\Software\Microsoft\Windows\CurrentVersion\Explorer\Advanced\Start_JumpListItems`.

These Windows proprietary files, known as **Object Linking and Embedding,** embed and link documents and applications for quick retrieval and may be located in Windows 10 folders such as `C:\Users\LCDI\AppData\Roaming\Microsoftg\Windows\Recent\`.

Jump Lists are compartmentalized into two directories:

- **AutomaticDestinations**: These are created by the operating system and other default applications that contain the `DestList` stream recording the most recently or frequently used files
- **CustomDestinations**: These files are created when a user pins an application to the taskbar or **Start** menu, for example, in Windows 10

Careful analysis of these files may assist in determining the number of times the file was accessed and the dates when that occurred. The following screenshot shows a Jump List on the taskbar for Microsoft Word listing any pinned files and recently accessed files:

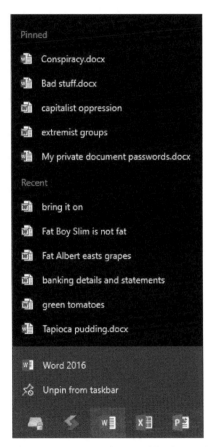

Word document Jump List showing recent files used by the application on the taskbar

The next screenshot is a view of a Word document file that provides some antecedents of the document, its creation and last-modified dates, and its authors and file location—again, all useful potential evidence to assist event reconstruction, if you know where to look for it:

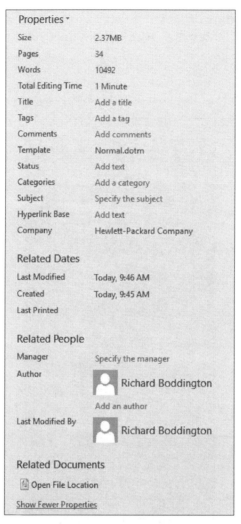

File metadata stored in a Word document

The following screenshot shows a small menu tab from the same page that allows inspection of the document to search for hidden properties or personal information. The tool looks for embedded documents that may include information that is not visible on the file or has been formatted to appear invisible:

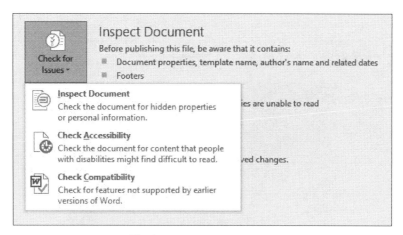

The document inspection menu

The file, the Word document in this instance, may be located by opening the **Related Documents** tab, as shown here:

The Related Documents tab–seeking the folder location of a Word document

It is important to determine whether other activities on the computer may identify a specific user during the creation and dispatch of the e-mail message and attachment. The previous screenshot, for example, indicates a correlation between a recovered artifact and corroborating artifacts. It is critical to show that such additional events occurred or could have occurred during the relevant time frame. Windows 10 has an abundance of links to frequently and recently used files, as shown in the Smart Screen feature in the following screenshot, which shows a link to a Yahoo! Mail account and a number of recently visited websites:

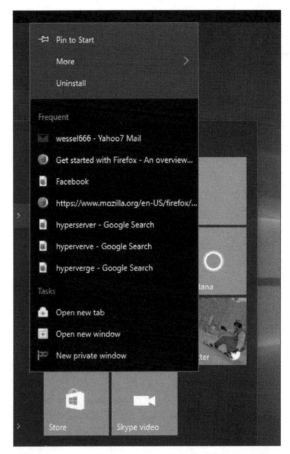

The Start Up form showing a list of frequently visited sites

Using the logical examination process (booting up the image), we can see, in the example shown in the following screenshot, a deleted file in **Recycle Bin** that was previously on the computer **Desktop**. Right-clicking on the file shows the creation and deletion dates:

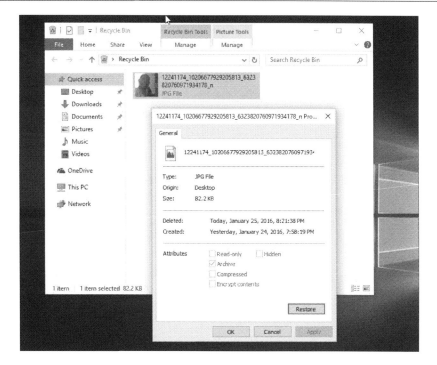

The Mozilla Firefox browser history shown in the following screenshot lists a number of visited websites. This feature is switched on in most browsers as a default setting but will be deactivated if the user has chosen to browse in private mode to avoid leaving history logs:

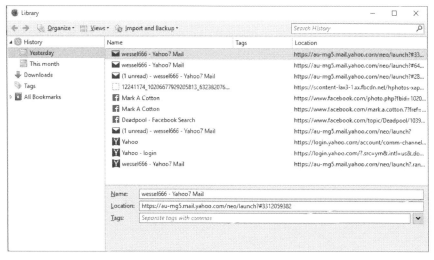

Mozilla Firefox browsing history

This screenshot shows a similar history list recovered from IE browser history:

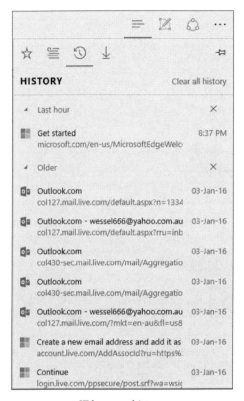

IE browser history

It may not always be possible to boot up a forensic image and view it in its logical format, which is easier and more familiar to users. However, viewing the data inside a forensic image provides, in its physical form, unaltered metadata and files that provide accurate information about applications and files. To elaborate, as shown in the following screenshot, it is possible to view the containers that hold these histories and search records that have been recovered and stored in a forensic file container:

Structure	Tag			Parent Archive Path
Archive St...		45,378	3,001	
addon...		5	1	iseek crime simula...
Archiv...		5	1	iseek crime simula...
Archiv...		5	1	iseek crime simula...
bistat...		4	1	iseek crime simula...
blist.s...		6	1	iseek crime simula...
chrom...		146	8	iseek crime simula...
chrom...		1	1	iseek crime simula...
conte...		3	1	iseek crime simula...
Cookies		2	1	iseek crime simula...
Cookies		2	1	iseek crime simula...
cooki...		1	1	iseek crime simula...
Datab...		2	1	iseek crime simula...
dc.db		5	1	iseek crime simula...
dc.db		254	1	iseek crime simula...
downl...		1	1	iseek crime simula...
eas.db		6	1	iseek crime simula...
exten...		6	1	iseek crime simula...
Favico...		5	1	iseek crime simula...
Favico...		56	1	iseek crime simula...
FirstU...		91	1	iseek crime simula...
FirstU...		91	1	iseek crime simula...
glas-b...		12	1	iseek crime simula...
glas-g...		12	1	iseek crime simula...
glas-r...		12	1	iseek crime simula...
global...		185	1	iseek crime simula...
History		9	1	iseek crime simula...
History		9	1	iseek crime simula...
hp600...		57	1	iseek crime simula...
hp600...		57	1	iseek crime simula...
hp600...		57	1	iseek crime simula...
hp600...		57	1	iseek crime simula...

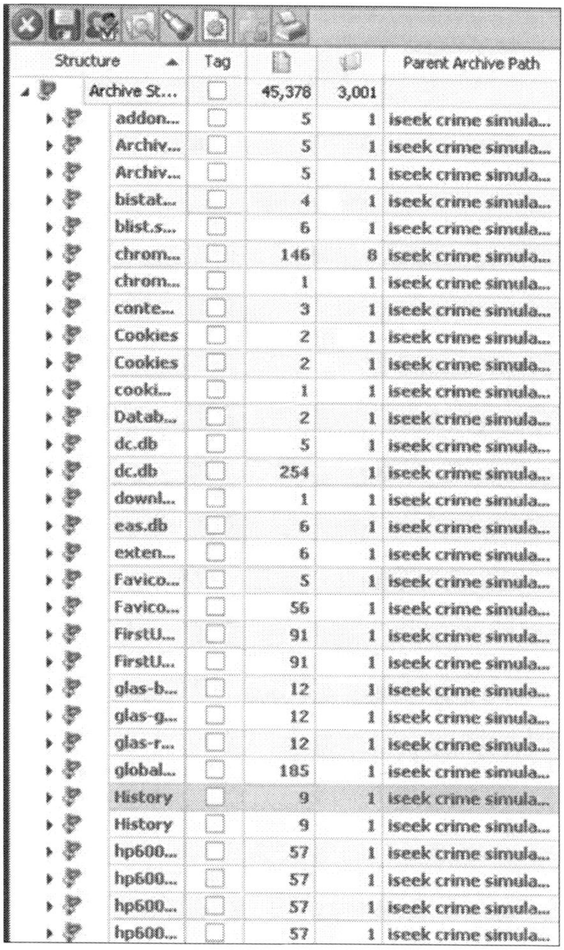

A list of containers recovered, including the browser history database

ILookIX has recovered and deconstructed the containers to reveal their contents, as shown in the following screenshot. The contents in this case are spreadsheets (`.csv` files) that may be viewed with ILookIX or exported for further analysis and presentation as evidence during trial. The file and folder locations are stated along with the timestamps they had at the time of imaging. The disadvantage of viewing files in the logical environment is that the process of booting and using various applications alters the metadata.

Even though the image is write-protected and any such alterations are non-persistent, the view presented also shows the current alterations to the metadata and removes the original timestamp. For example, the last-accessed dates will be altered to the current time of the viewing of the file once the file has been opened by the practitioner:

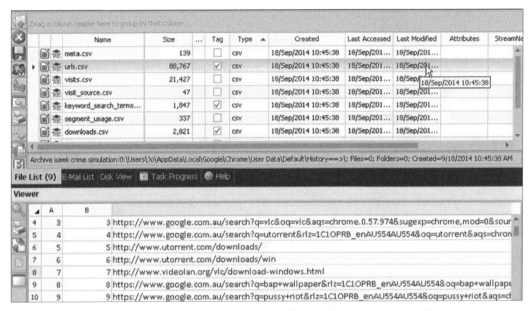

Spreadsheets and a list of contents extracted from the browser history database

The practitioner should have some understanding of the nature of the transgression and some of the key "players". The case may center on e-mail or chat messaging, or it may relate to browsing activities of the suspect and so forth. If examining Skype communications, for example, it is helpful to locate the database file that records chat logs, which are usually `.csv` spreadsheet files. The file is `main.db` and is usually located in the specific user's directory folder.

The short extract shown here provides details of the names of the Skype accounts used, timestamps of each message, and the content:

Messages	chatname [text]	author [text]	from_dispname [text]	timestamp [integer]	body_xml [text]
1	charliefarlie	bettygrunt	bondie pool	4/03/2015 9:32	WAIT WHAT
2	kroek911	bettygrunt	bondie pool	4/03/2015 9:32	U OK?!
3	charliefarlie	bettygrunt	bondie pool	4/03/2015 9:32	No not really
4	lincolo888	bettygrunt	bondie pool	4/03/2015 9:32	But I com 2 work
5	jhojkj	bettygrunt	bondie pool	4/03/2015 9:32	U STILL IN HOSPITAL?!
6	davirah44	bettygrunt	bondie pool	4/03/2015 9:32	OHH yes
7	ali35012	bettygrunt	bondie pool	4/03/2015 9:32	I was on a drip for 1 hour
8	alaar.44	bettygrunt	bondie pool	4/03/2015 9:32	OMG U OK?!
9	glover	bettygrunt	bondie pool	4/03/2015 9:32	It was for my leg
10	yliu666	bettygrunt	bondie pool	4/03/2015 9:32	sulphuer
11	dansper	bettygrunt	bondie pool	4/03/2015 9:32	U ok!!???
12	gpe66	bettygrunt	bondie pool	4/03/2015 9:32	<null>
13	hugfnercku	bettygrunt	bondie pool	4/03/2015 9:32	<null>

A spreadsheet of message conversations extracted from the Skype database — heavily culled

It is prudent to assume that the users of the accounts may not necessarily be the account owners. To establish the identity of the person using the application at the time may require some compelling corroboration. For example, the identity of the user could be established by some form of triangulation of the device with other digital devices. This could be using tracking data of the user's mobile phone that has shown it to be in the same location as the computer used to communicate with others.

Other cases have involved recovering personal information disclosed during communications that has been recorded in the conversation logs, known only to the communicator or a small number of close friends or relatives. The identity of the user may be established by other persons present who witnessed the user at the keyboard and observed the Skype communication on the computer monitor at a time relevant to the transgression. Skype and other messaging systems such as Kik and Whatsapp are a rich source of information that is potentially stored on computers and mobile phones. Video clips, pictures, audio, text, and voice calls may all be linked to these widely used applications.

The next screenshot shows spreadsheets recovered from a MacBook Air, which provides details of messages exchanged and the names of the user accounts involved. The **MediaDocuments** file provided details of illegal pictures sent between two parties to the conversation that were later recovered from the Recycle Bin:

Name	Date modified	Type	Size
Accounts	28/01/2016 5:35 PM	Microsoft Excel Comma Separated Values File	4 KB
Alerts	28/01/2016 5:35 PM	Microsoft Excel Comma Separated Values File	1 KB
AppSchemaVersion	28/01/2016 5:35 PM	Microsoft Excel Comma Separated Values File	1 KB
CallMembers	28/01/2016 5:35 PM	Microsoft Excel Comma Separated Values File	1,535 KB
Calls	28/01/2016 5:35 PM	Microsoft Excel Comma Separated Values File	294 KB
ChatMembers	28/01/2016 5:35 PM	Microsoft Excel Comma Separated Values File	203 KB
Chats	28/01/2016 5:35 PM	Microsoft Excel Comma Separated Values File	475 KB
ContactGroups	28/01/2016 5:35 PM	Microsoft Excel Comma Separated Values File	3 KB
Contacts	28/01/2016 5:35 PM	Microsoft Excel Comma Separated Values File	479 KB
Conversations	28/01/2016 5:35 PM	Microsoft Excel Comma Separated Values File	266 KB
DbMeta	28/01/2016 5:35 PM	Microsoft Excel Comma Separated Values File	8 KB
LegacyMessages	28/01/2016 5:35 PM	Microsoft Excel Comma Separated Values File	1 KB
MediaDocuments	28/01/2016 5:35 PM	Microsoft Excel Comma Separated Values File	861 KB
MessageAnnotations	28/01/2016 5:35 PM	Microsoft Excel Comma Separated Values File	1 KB
Messages	28/01/2016 5:35 PM	Microsoft Excel Comma Separated Values File	42,773 KB
Participants	28/01/2016 5:35 PM	Microsoft Excel Comma Separated Values File	711 KB
SMSes	28/01/2016 5:35 PM	Microsoft Excel Comma Separated Values File	3 KB
tracker_journal	28/01/2016 5:35 PM	Microsoft Excel Comma Separated Values File	1 KB
Transfers	28/01/2016 5:35 PM	Microsoft Excel Comma Separated Values File	28 KB
Translators	28/01/2016 5:35 PM	Microsoft Excel Comma Separated Values File	1 KB
VideoMessages	28/01/2016 5:35 PM	Microsoft Excel Comma Separated Values File	1 KB
Videos	28/01/2016 5:35 PM	Microsoft Excel Comma Separated Values File	853 KB
Voicemails	28/01/2016 5:35 PM	Microsoft Excel Comma Separated Values File	2 KB

Spreadsheets extracted from the Skype database contained in a MacBook Air

Selecting digital evidence

The next stage in the examination process is to select and analyze the evidence that will form part of a legal case. For those unfamiliar with investigations, it is quite common to misread readily available evidence and draw incorrect conclusions. Business managers attempting to analyze what they consider are the facts of a case would be wise to seek legal assistance in selecting and evaluating evidence on which they may wish to base a case.

Selecting the evidence, sometimes referred to as the analysis stage or event reconstruction stage, involves analysis of the located evidence to determine what events occurred in the system and their significance and probative value to the case. The selection analysis stage requires practitioners to carefully examine the available digital evidence, ensuring that they do not misinterpret the evidence and make imprudent presumptions without carefully cross-checking the information. It is a fact-finding process, where attempts are made to develop a plausible reconstruction of the facts. It may be expedient to liaise with the investigation and legal teams to ensure that relevant and probative information is selected.

As in conventional crime investigations, practitioners should look for evidence that suggests or indicates the *motive* (why?), *means* (how?), and *opportunity* (when?) of suspected offenders. In cases dependent on digital evidence, it can be a vexatious process to determine this. However, it is important for the practitioner to be aware of seeking clarification of the three fundamental components of crimes while at the same time remaining neutral and dispassionate as to the likelihood of a suspect's guilt.

Seeking the truth

The primary role of the practitioner when seeking the truth of a matter under investigation includes locating evidence that supports the preliminary hypothesis, but just as important is locating evidence that refutes the hypothesis. This is also known as **exculpatory evidence**. It is important to stress that in the interest of justice, even the most hard-pressed practitioner must always keep this requirement in mind and comply with it under all circumstances.

Law enforcement agents seek a conviction and are often preoccupied with selecting the lowest-hanging fruit. This is referred to as cherry-picking and is selective, biased, and can sometimes lead to important evidence being located that may challenge other evidence. Any prosecutor worthy of presenting a case in court always looks for the weaknesses in the prosecution case, primarily as a strategy to deflect a counterattack. In the interest of justice, all evidence procured by the prosecution that has a bearing on a case must be shared with the other party. For the defense team, the requirement to reciprocate varies in different jurisdictions and is based on the adversarial court process of the prosecution having to prove that the defendant is guilty, not for the defendant to prove innocence.

Trials increasingly rely on digital evidence, and there are documented cases where the innocent are convicted, hence the need for a high level of certainty that the evidence is valid. This is described in more detail in *Chapter 9, Validating the Evidence*.

Some order is required during the process rather than taking a haphazard approach. It is important to define the general characteristics of the evidence being searched for and then look for the object in a collection of data. For example, if searching for an image file, say a JPEG file, the practitioner would look for all images with the `.jpeg` extension. In the case previously mentioned that involved the recovery of incriminating Skype chat messages that had illegal pictures posted by the two parties, the attachments had been saved and later deleted, most likely to prevent detection. A sample of the deleted pictures in PNG format, shown in the next screenshot, was recovered from the user's protected and hidden folders. They were readily identified, as the name of the file incorporated the date and time when each file was saved to the MacBook Air. These timestamps correlated with the chat message logs and were used to reconstruct these communications more fully. This was a circumstantial but compelling relationship that contributed to a just outcome in this case:

Name	Date	Type	Size	Tags
Screen Shot 2015-05-16 at 5.40.46 pm	16/05/2015 5:40 PM	IrfanView PNG File	426 KB	
Screen Shot 2015-07-04 at 8.29.08 pm	4/07/2015 8:29 PM	IrfanView PNG File	12 KB	
Screen Shot 2015-07-16 at 7.16.44 pm	16/07/2015 7:16 PM	IrfanView PNG File	82 KB	
Screen Shot 2015-07-16 at 7.22.36 pm	16/07/2015 7:22 PM	IrfanView PNG File	147 KB	
Screen Shot 2015-07-16 at 7.22.43 pm	16/07/2015 7:22 PM	IrfanView PNG File	181 KB	
Screen Shot 2015-07-16 at 7.22.50 pm	16/07/2015 7:22 PM	IrfanView PNG File	157 KB	
Screen Shot 2015-07-16 at 7.23.30 pm	16/07/2015 7:23 PM	IrfanView PNG File	124 KB	
Screen Shot 2015-07-16 at 7.23.39 pm	16/07/2015 7:23 PM	IrfanView PNG File	133 KB	
Screen Shot 2015-07-16 at 7.23.45 pm	16/07/2015 7:23 PM	IrfanView PNG File	129 KB	
Screen Shot 2015-07-16 at 7.23.55 pm	16/07/2015 7:23 PM	IrfanView PNG File	106 KB	
Screen Shot 2015-07-16 at 7.24.08 pm	16/07/2015 7:24 PM	IrfanView PNG File	140 KB	
Screen Shot 2015-07-16 at 7.24.20 pm	16/07/2015 7:24 PM	irfanView PNG File	168 KB	
Screen Shot 2015-07-16 at 7.25.35 pm	16/07/2015 7:25 PM	IrfanView PNG File	81 KB	
Screen Shot 2015-07-16 at 7.25.40 pm	16/07/2015 7:25 PM	IrfanView PNG File	89 KB	
Screen Shot 2015-07-16 at 7.26.16 pm	16/07/2015 7:26 PM	IrfanView PNG File	142 KB	
Screen Shot 2015-07-16 at 7.26.20 pm	16/07/2015 7:26 PM	IrfanView PNG File	144 KB	
Screen Shot 2015-07-16 at 7.26.28 pm	16/07/2015 7:26 PM	IrfanView PNG File	145 KB	
Screen Shot 2015-07-16 at 7.26.34 pm	16/07/2015 7:26 PM	IrfanView PNG File	141 KB	
Screen Shot 2015-07-16 at 7.26.42 pm	16/07/2015 7:26 PM	IrfanView PNG File	130 KB	
Screen Shot 2015-07-16 at 7.26.47 pm	16/07/2015 7:26 PM	IrfanView PNG File	138 KB	

Screenshot of pictures recovered from a suspect's hidden folder

As the investigation proceeds, the practitioner will develop various hypotheses as to the nature of the transgression and possible suspects. The practitioner looks for data that supports or refutes hypotheses about the incident. Timestamps, for example, may be changed in most systems; therefore, it is helpful to locate log entries, network traffic, and other events internal and external to the suspect computer. This information may then be used to triangulate the accuracy and reliability of the data of relevance to the overall investigation.

Examination of the evidence involves the use of a potentially large number of techniques to find and interpret significant data. It may require the repair or salvage of damaged data in ways that preserve its integrity and potential usefulness. What the practitioner must always be aware of is that evidence distinguishes a hypothesis from a groundless assertion—it may confirm or disprove a hypothesis. Therefore, reliability and integrity are key to its admissibility and weight in a court of law, and this must be heeded during the selection process.

There are often too many potential suspects, and linking a suspect to the incriminating events is not always as straightforward as it may seem at first glance. The following diagram shows a typical family network setup using Wi-Fi connections to the home modem that facilitates connection to the Internet. In this example, based on a real case, the parents provided the broadband service for themselves and for three other family members. One of the children's friends completed a university assignment on the child's computer and synchronized their iPad to the child's device:

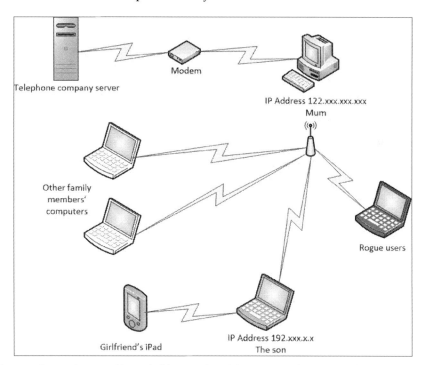

The complexity of a typical household network and determining the identity of the transgressor

This scenario lends itself to exploitation as other family members and friends visiting the residence have unrestricted access to the children's computers and, through them, contact with the Internet. The Wi-Fi connection is also vulnerable to being hijacked, and external rogue attackers are capable of gaining access to and control of the small local network. Assuming one of the devices contains incriminating data, the questions that must be asked are how it got there, who put it there, and, possibly, why it was done.

With traditional offenses, the offending act or event is usually manifested — there is a corpse, a theft, or at least a complaint to work with and, usually, a list of potential suspects, based on these criteria:

- Who knew the victim?
- Who had physical access to the scene?
- Who had a motive?

The Internet, for example, may offer over 700 million suspects according to connectivity. It should not be assumed that the owner of the computer that holds incriminating data or other family members in this scenario are the only suspects. Clearly, this is a natural, intuitive assumption, but a dangerous one if in fact it can be shown that others had access to the terminal at the relevant time.

It is sometimes problematic to identify the crime during the selection process. Here are some examples:

- In cybercrime, the nature of the event is often less obvious and immediate
- If a hacker steals confidential information, victims may not find out what has been stolen
- Victims usually rely on being informed by system administrators
- The administrators may not notice until long after the event — as evinced in the case study at the end of the chapter
- Identity theft fraud, the fastest-growing financial crime, may take years to be exposed

The practitioner should also consider the quality of the evidence during selection and take heed that digital evidence is circumstantial and often involves the examination of a large amount of data that may prove to be irrelevant to the investigation. It rarely provides sufficient weight by itself to prove guilt or innocence unless soundly corroborated.

The next section looks at emerging tools that help in the evidence-selection process.

More effective forensic tools

Various forensic tools are available to assist the practitioner to select and collate data for examination analysis and investigation. Sorting order from the chaos of even a small personal computer can be a time-consuming and complex process. As the digital forensic discipline develops, better and more reliable forensic tools are being developed to assist practitioners locate, select, and collate evidence from larger, complex datasets. It should be pointed out that in many cases, more than one device is involved, and they require examination as well. This of course adds to the challenge of the overall forensic examination.

The following subsections show how the data can be organized through a range of managed processes.

Categorizing files

To varying degrees, most digital forensic tools used to view and analyze forensic images or attached devices provide helpful user interfaces to locate and categorize information relevant to the examination.

The most advanced application that provides access and convenient viewing of files is the **Category Explorer** feature in ILookIX, as shown in this screenshot; it divides files by **Type**, **Signature**, and **Properties**:

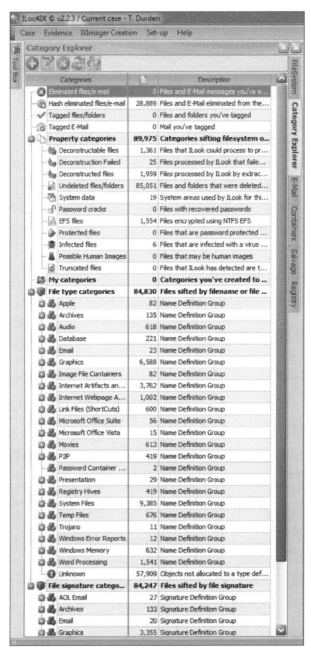

ILookIX Category Explorer

Category Explorer also allows the practitioner to create custom categories called **My Categories** to group files by relevance. For example, in a criminal investigation involving a conspiracy, the practitioner could create a category for the first individual and one for the second individual. As files are reviewed, they would then be added to either or both categories. Unlike tags, files can be added to multiple categories, and the categories can be given descriptive names.

To add a file or group of files to a category, the practitioner may select as desired one or more files in the **File List**. Selecting the **Save Selected File(s) to a Category** button brings up the **My Categories** window. The following screenshot shows all currently existing categories (including those created during the initial case creation); the examiner is given the option to add new or delete redundant categories. In this screenshot, the files selected for inclusion in the category are Skype messaging files. The **My Categories** folder can be viewed and accessed conveniently in the **Category Explorer** window, allowing the practitioner to select, edit, deselect, and later export the files as part of the case preparation:

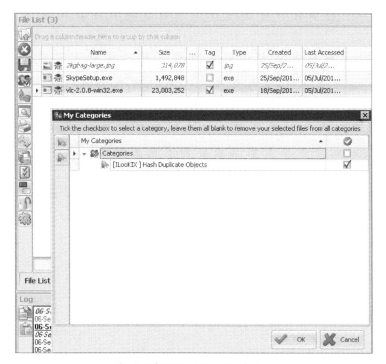

The ILookIX My Categories feature

It is common during evidence selection to find some tantalizing information and later forget where it was located, consequently wasting much time trying to relocate it and follow up any essential leads it may offer. Adding files of possible relevance to various containers within this application minimizes unnecessary repetition of the process. It also offers the practitioner the opportunity of pigeonholing interesting snippets of information for future analysis. This avoids the problem of being waylaid too early in the selection process by looking at interesting leads that may detract from a more formal search for the key evidence.

Eliminating superfluous files

The prospect of trawling for evidence through large numbers of files located on computers could be compared with being unable to see the trees for the forest, let alone seeing any wood (evidence). Computers store many of the same files in duplicate, triplicate, or more versions, which are often scattered in various obscure parts of the system. Files with no content or zero-length files also add to the clutter; eliminating these files by hiding them from view can significantly reduce the ones that need to be searched manually or by automated applications.

The ILookIX **Data Reduction** feature, shown in the following screenshot, allows the elimination of files from view, but these files have not been destroyed and can be returned to the case at any time. When they are in an eliminated category, they will not appear in any lists, and processes such as indexing, hashing, and searching will not be run against them. ILookIX allows files to be eliminated through a number of processes. These include running a hash elimination or hash deduplication process or manually eliminating files based on type or path. File elimination is usually used to remove files from an image before processing to speed it up, and it is also used to suppress duplicate files. Hash deduplication can be used prior to review to ensure that the reviewer is given only one copy of each file of interest, instead of multiple identical copies under different names:

The ILookIX Data Reduction feature

ILookIX's **Hash Set Manager** allows the examiner to review loaded hash sets and determine for each whether it is active for file elimination, hash search, or both. Its **Hash Elimination** function takes all of the files in the case that have been hashed, compares them against all of the hash values for the hash sets selected for elimination, and transfers the matching files to the **Hash Eliminated Files/E-mail** category. The **Hash De-duplication** function takes all of the files in the case that have been hashed, compares their hash values, and sends all but one copy of each file to the **Hash Eliminated Files/E-mail** category.

Once the files are in this category, they will no longer appear in any list of files or e-mail unless the examiner selects the **Hash Elimination** category to view the files, or selects a file within the category and restores the file.

Deconstructing files

Deconstructable files are compound files that can be further broken down into smaller parts, such as e-mail, archives, thumb stores, and files. Once deconstruction is complete, the files will either be classified as deconstructed files or deconstruction failed files. ILookIX's built-in file deconstruction allows the practitioner to deconstruct a range of complex files during the processing of an image or attached device, as shown here:

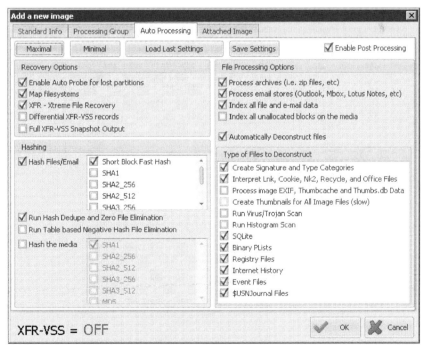

ILookIX Data Deconstruction feature

The deconstruction of files involves processing compound files such as archive, e-mail store, registry store, or other files to extract useful and usable data from a complex file format and generate reports. Manual deconstruction adds significantly to the time required to complete an examination.

Searching for files

Depending on the type of image being mapped and the options selected, it can take a considerable amount of time to make data available to the examiner. Options that take the most time upfront are hashing, indexing, and salvaging. Depending on the purpose of the examination, the time consumed by these activities should be weighed against the future time savings. Hashing, for example, can significantly reduce the number of superfluous files to be reviewed by the examiner. Indexing saves time in almost any examination in which multiple keyword searches are needed.

 Indexing is the process whereby chunks of data are catalogued. It is the process of generating a table of text strings that can then be searched almost instantly any number of times.

The two main uses of indexing are to create a dictionary to use when cracking passwords and to index words for almost-instant searching. Indexing is also valuable when creating a dictionary or when using any of the analysis functions built in to ILookIX. ILookIX facilitates indexing of the entire media at the time of initial processing, all at once. It can also be done after processing. Indexing facilitates searching through files and archives, Windows Registry, e-mail lists, and unallocated space. This function is highly customizable via the setup option and can be optimized for searching or for creating a custom dictionary for password cracking.

Sound indexing ensures speedy and accurate searching. Searching is the process of looking through the evidence for a specific item, such as a string of text or an expression. An expression, in terms of searching, is a pattern used to structure data in a search, such as a credit card number or e-mail address. ILookIX offers a comprehensive range of searches, including keyword searches, which simply look for certain characters on disk.

This type of search will miss files within compound files if they are not deconstructed into their constituent parts first, that is, mails within PSTs or `.docx` and `.xlsx` files within zipped archives. The indexed search is fast and reliable, as the prior indexing process has eliminated the need for repeated and time-consuming searches over the entire drive or image.

ILookIX's **Search History** view displays historical records of all searches undertaken in the case and allows the investigator to send the results of any historical search back to the ILookIX **List Pane** at a later date, as shown in the next screenshot. Examples of search results and files located are illustrated later in this section:

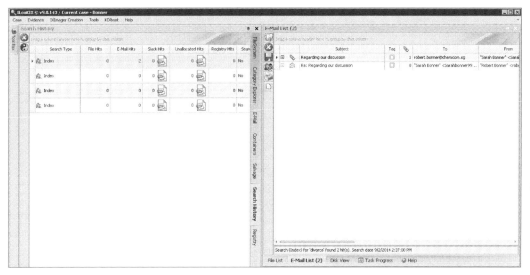

The ILookIX List Pane showing the results of various searches

The Event Analysis tool

ILookIX's **Event Analysis** tool provides the practitioner with a graphical representation of events on the subject system, such as the following:

- File creation, access, or modification times
- E-mails sent or received
- Other events, such as the modification of the Master File Table on an NTFS system

The graph itself shows the following:

- Time (in months) along the x axis
- The number of items along the y axis

The events are color-coded by event type, with the total of each type of event displayed above the bar for that month's events, as shown here:

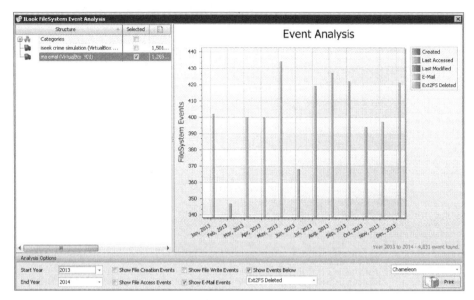

ILookIX Event Viewer showing events between selected dates

The application allows the practitioner to zoom in on any point on the graph to view more specific details, as shown here:

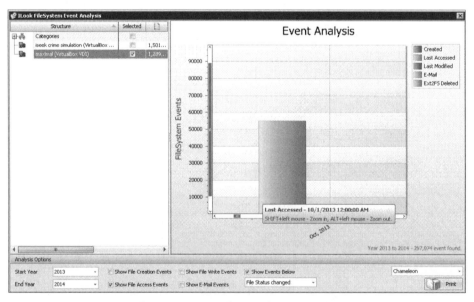

ILookIX Event Viewer showing last-accessed times

Left-clicking on any bar on the graph will return the view to the main ILookIX window and display the items from the date bar selected in the **List Pane**. A sample of such results is shown in the following screenshot. This can be most helpful when analyzing events during specific periods:

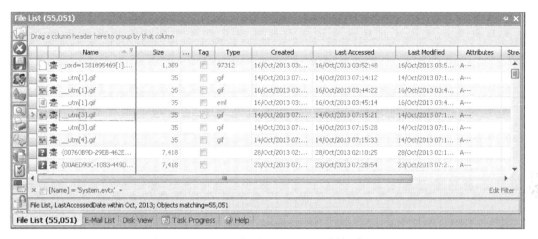

ILookIX Event Viewer displaying extracted files for review

The Cloud Analysis tool

The **Cloud Analysis** tool embedded in ILookIX is a visual representation of the frequency with which individual words appear in a case. The analysis is based on the current index database, so the practitioner must index the case data prior to initiating an analysis. The analysis is presented in data cloud form, removing the complexity of the underlying analysis and presenting the practitioner with an easy-to-understand picture of the analysis.

In the top-right section of the **Cloud Analysis** viewer, shown in the following screenshot, there is a **Highlight List** to help organize groups of case words under easy-to-remember headings. This is so the analysis brings these words immediately to the practitioner's attention with no special effort required to find them:

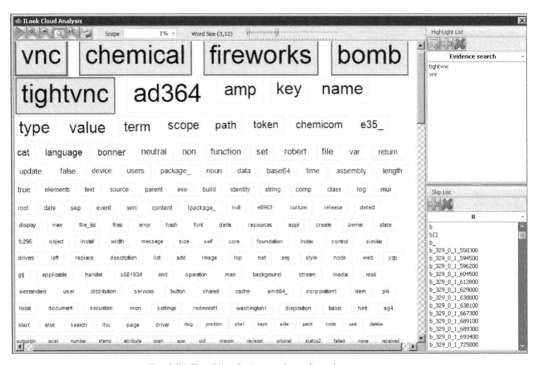

ILookIX Cloud Analysis searching for relevant terms

Cloud Analysis has a number of features designed to make it easy to refine analysis and bring case-relevant data to the fore. Since it is based on index data and takes only a simple click to initiate, functionality issues are the only ones that must be described. Since the display generated is an interactive pictorial, the user can interact with selections by left-clicking on the words one at a time. It is then possible to initiate a search of that word selection by a simple double-click on the word.

In the following example shown, the search word selected was **fireworks**:

A Cloud Analysis search result for the word "fireworks"

Selecting that search history entry will in turn reveal a file-list response of all objects containing that term, as shown in the following screenshot:

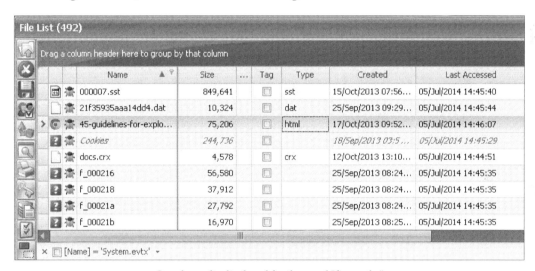

Search results displayed for the word "fireworks"

The Lead Analysis tool

The **Lead Analysis** tool is an interactive evidence model embedded in ILookIX that allows the practitioner to assimilate known facts into a graphic representation that directly links unseen objects. It provides the answers as the practitioner increases the detail of the design surface and brings into view specific relationships that could otherwise go unseen.

The primary aim of **Lead Analysis** is to help discover links within the case data that may not be evident or intuitive and which the practitioner may not be aware of directly or has little background knowledge of to help form relationships manually. Instead of finding and making notes of various pieces of information, the analysis is presented as an easy-to-use link model. The complexity of the modeling is removed; we get the clearest possible method of discovery. The analysis is based on the current index database and, again, it is essential to index case data prior to initiating an analysis.

The application interface will initially be blank, as shown in the following screenshot. In the center of the analysis dialogue is the canvas: this is the main modeling area for evidential links. To the left is the **Lead Objects** section: these objects may be dragged onto the **Canvas** to set up start points for the analysis or to manually model linkage. In the top right is the **Potential Links** list. In the bottom right is the **Skip List**. This is a same global **Skip List** that is also used by the application:

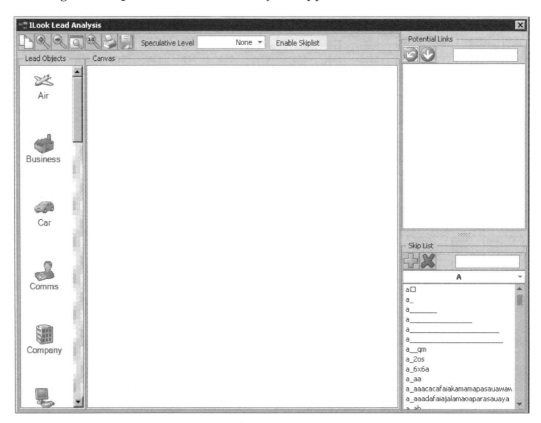

ILookIX Lead Analysis

The first task is to state some facts about the case and to use these as the starting point of the analysis. These facts may be stated by establishing start points on the canvas, by dragging lead objects from the **Lead Objects** section onto the canvas. Then, the user may pick a lead object that represents the piece of information of relevance or concept and drag it onto the canvas. Then, by clicking on the object's text tag, it will shift into edit mode and replace the default text with something specific to the lead, such as a person's surname. Right-clicking on the avatar and then on **Find Links** collates a list of words that appear to be associated with the name of the avatar, as shown here:

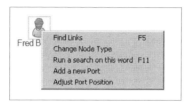

ILookIX Lead Analysis creating the avatar node

Once a list of potential links has been generated, it is important to review them to see whether any are potentially relevant. By highlighting any that are and then clicking on the green **Link Transfer** button on the Mini Toolbar of the **Potential Links**, it is possible to look for words in the catalogs if they have been included. In the example scenario shown in the following screenshot, the word **divorce** was located as it was known that **Sarah** was divorced from the owner of the computer (the initial suspect). By selecting any word by left-clicking on it once and clicking on the green arrow to link it to **Sarah**, as shown in the screenshot, relationships can be uncovered that are not always clear during the first inspection of the data:

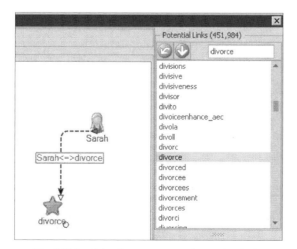

ILookIX Lead Analysis creating relationship links

Once **Lead Objects** has commenced, it is possible to begin discovery by right-clicking on a **Lead Object** and using the `Find Links` function. If there are any links, they will be displayed in the **Potential Links** list. If no links are located, then it might be necessary to refine the lead object's text or increase the **Speculative Level** from the drop-down box on the Mini Toolbar, as shown in the following screen snippet. In normal use, it is preferable to leave **Speculative Level** set to the **None** setting:

ILookIX Lead Analysis setting the Speculative Level for searching for leads

Each of the stated facts becomes one starting lead on the canvas. If the nodes are related, it is easy to model that relationship by manually linking them together by selecting the first **Lead Project** to link, right-clicking, and selecting **Add a New Port** from the menu. This is then repeated for the second **Lead Object** the practitioner wants to link. By simply clicking on the new port of the selected object that needs to be linked from and dragging it to the port of the **Lead Object** that it should be linked to, a line will appear linking the two together. It is then possible to iterate this process using each start node or discovered node until it is possible to make sense of the total case data. A simple relationship between suspects, locations, and even concepts is illustrated in this sample:

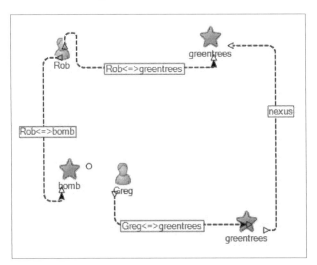

ILookIX Lead Analysis discovering relationships between various entities

In more complex cases, this allows the practitioner to locate and analyze relationships more efficaciously than a manual search. It is then possible to review the documents supporting the model to glean further information, as shown by the number of file hits evident in the following screenshot:

ILookIX Lead Analysis hits on the relationship were found in the **File Hits** (448) and **E-Mail Hits** (20)

The following screenshot shows some of the relationship hits obtained as a result of using **Lead Analysis**:

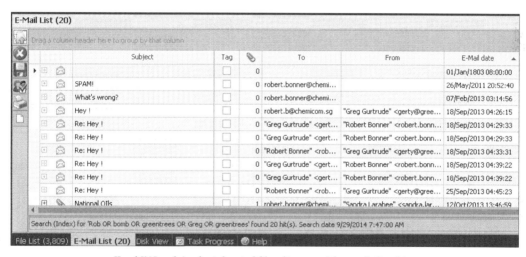

ILookIX Lead Analysis located files discovered from relationships

Analyzing e-mail datasets

Analyzing and selecting evidence from large e-mail datasets is a common task for the practitioner. ILookIX's embedded application, **E-mail Linkage Analysis**, is an interactive evidence model to help practitioners discover links between the correspondents within e-mail data. The analysis is presented as an easy-to-use link model; the complexity of the modeling is removed to provide the clearest possible method of discovery. The results of analysis are saved at the end of the modeling session for future editing.

An important concept that must be understood is the homogenous nature of all e-mail types supported in ILookIX. All e-mail client deconstructions become part of the same basic explorer e-mail concept. This removes the differences between clients so that functions such as **E-mail Linkage Analysis** can be used to analyze and explore in a new, much easier-to-use interface. This more easily deciphers complex e-mail relationships. It allows the deconstruction of e-mail during the wizard case load process, or it provides the option of deconstructing the pieces one at a time or in groups. Either way, the Interface provides an object model that encompasses all of the characteristics of an internet e-mail item using the RFC standards that apply to all Internet e-mail send/receive clients.

If there is a large amount of e-mail to process, this analysis generation may take a few minutes. To make the analysis more readable, it is necessary to only select one or a few e-mail stores to analyze at a time when first using the tool. Once the analysis is displayed, the user will see the e-mail linkage itself. It is then possible to see a line between correspondents, indicating that they have a relationship of some type. Here, in particular, line thickness indicates the frequency of traffic between two correspondents; therefore, thicker flow lines indicate more traffic.

The application allows the selection of an e-mail store by clicking on the checkbox next to its name. On the canvas, once the analysis is generated, the user may select any e-mail addressee node by left-clicking on it once. Creating the analysis is really simple, and one of the most immediately valuable resources this provides is group identification, as shown in the following screenshot. ILookIX will initiate a search for that addressee and list all e-mails where the selected addressee was a correspondent. Users may make their own connection lines by clicking on an addressee node point and dragging to another node point. Nodes can be deleted to allow linkage between smaller groups of individuals:

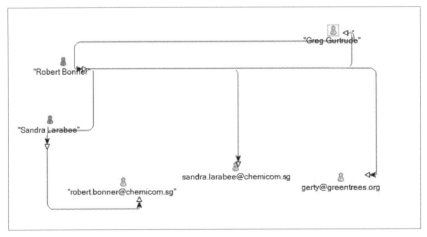

The E-mail Linkage tool showing relationships of possible relevance to a case

Detecting scanned images

Searching for scanned images is a process that may assist in document authentication or detecting forged documents. It may be completed using the **ILookIX Detect Scanned Images** application. The results may be viewed in the **Category Explorer**, as shown in the following screenshot. The case studies in *Chapter 3*, *The Nature and Special Properties of Digital Evidence*, and *Chapter 5*, *The Need for Enhanced Forensic Tools*, included searches for evidence of scanned documents:

▲ 🔊 My categories	51,967	Categories you've created to ...
[ILooKIX] Hash Duplicate Objects	51,902	
[ILooKIX] Probable Scanned Images	6	
Dat file web history	58	
Skype	1	

A list of probable scanned images in ILookIX Category Explorer

Scanned documents are also displayed in the **File List** viewer, as shown in the following screenshot:

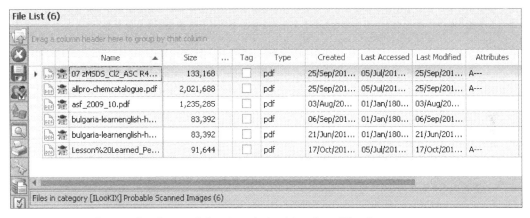

	Name	Size	...	Tag	Type	Created	Last Accessed	Last Modified	Attributes
	07 zMSDS_Cl2_ASC R4...	133,168		☐	pdf	25/Sep/201...	05/Jul/201...	25/Sep/201...	A---
	allpro-chemcatalogue.pdf	2,021,688		☐	pdf	25/Sep/201...	05/Jul/201...	25/Sep/201...	A---
	asf_2009_10.pdf	1,235,285		☐	pdf	03/Aug/20...	01/Jan/180...	03/Aug/20...	
	bulgaria-learnenglish-h...	83,392		☐	pdf	06/Sep/201...	01/Jan/180...	06/Sep/201...	
	bulgaria-learnenglish-h...	83,392		☐	pdf	21/Jun/201...	01/Jan/180...	21/Jun/201...	
	Lesson%20Learned_Pe...	91,644		☐	pdf	17/Oct/201...	05/Jul/201...	17/Oct/201...	A---

Files in category [ILooKIX] Probable Scanned Images (6)

The E-mail Linkage tool showing relationships of possible relevance to a case

Volume Shadow Copy analysis tools

A shadow volume, also known as the **Volume Snapshot Service** (**VSS**), is a service that creates point-in-time copies of files. The service is built in to versions of Windows Vista, 7, 8, and 10 and is turned on by default. ILookIX can recover true copies of overwritten files from shadow volumes, as long as they resided on the volume at the time the snapshot was created. VSS recovery is a method of recovering extant and deleted files from the volume snapshots available on the system. It is a valuable resource for locating previously unavailable data to assist an investigation, as illustrated in the case study at the end of this chapter.

ILookIX, unlike any other forensic tool, is capable of reconstructing VSS copies in a readable structure in differential or full recovery modes, including VSS and deleted files and folders. Either option is available in the image-loading window of the tool, as shown in the following screenshot:

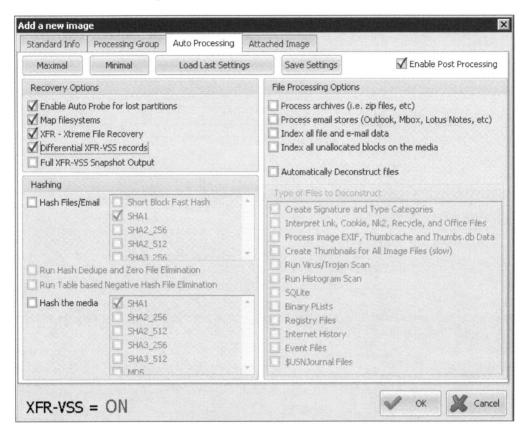

The ILookIX Volume Shadow Snapshot tool with differential records selected

In the test scenario, shown in the following screenshot, the tool recovered a total of 87,000 files, equaling conventional tool recovery rates. Using ILookIX's **Xtreme File Recovery**, some 337,000 files were recovered. The **Maximal Full Volume Shadow Snapshot** application recovered a total of 778,000 files. Using the differential process, 354,000 files were recovered, which filtered out 17,000 additional files for further analysis, as shown in the following screenshot. This enabled the detection of e-mail messages and attachments and Windows Registry changes that would normally remain hidden or difficult to find:

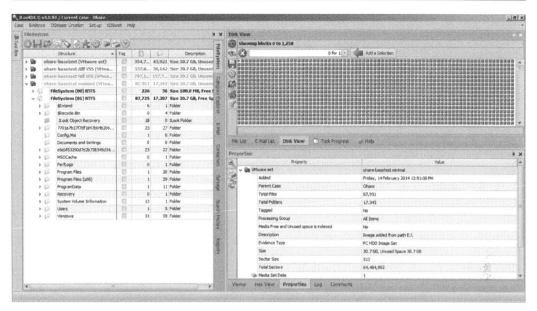

The ILookIX Volume Shadow Snapshot tool showing different search results

Differential XFR-VSS records reports on only those VSS where there is a difference (of even one file) between each record to speed up identification of evidential material. Deleted snapshots were recovered and further deconstructed, resulting in more than a terabyte of compressed data being recovered from the original 30-GB drive—believe it or not!

Timelines and other analysis tools

Timelines are often used to reconstruct a chronology of events of given periods. However, they can become too densely populated and extended over lengthy periods, so some thought should be given to producing more reader-friendly charts. For example, the overall reconstruction could be provided as a simple, uncluttered chart showing the key events and so on. Each of the major event nodes could be shown as a separate chart with some linkage to contiguous events.

The following diagram shows a fairly simple reconstruction of an actual bank fraud that involved two suspects and some electronic transactions and e-mail messages:

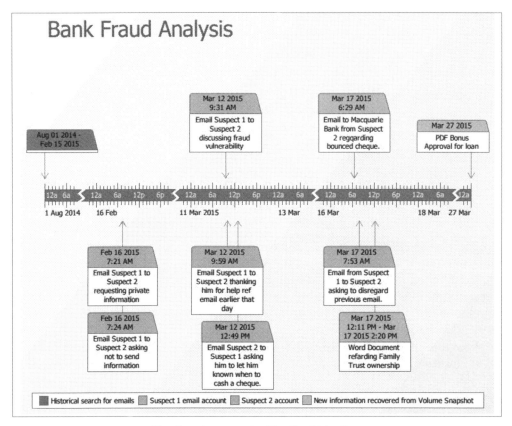

Timeline of events using Timeline Maker Pro

Time event charts aim to correct these shortcomings, as do flow diagrams that assist in interpreting complicated processes. When confronted with a complicated scheme or a process that is unfamiliar, flow diagrams facilitate the visualizing of the event.

These models are beyond the scope of this book but are worth incorporating as part of any practitioner's analysis toolkit.

Case study – illustrating the recovery of deleted evidence held in volume shadows

The case study involves an emerging business providing specialist technical services to a range of mining exploration companies. The business had lost a number of its technical experts to a rival business and noticed a drop in in its market share. There was a suspicion that departing staff members may have stolen some proprietary knowledge and expertise, which they later shared with the competing business. A forensic examination of the business' server and the computer terminals used by the departed staff members was initiated to determine whether some form of industrial espionage or sabotage had occurred.

With little to go on other than the CEO's hunch that there was mischief afoot, the former employees' computer terminals and external storage devices were searched for evidence of possible misconduct. Logically, the employees' e-mails were considered to be a sound starting point, but examination only recovered details of their dissatisfaction and contempt for the business and plans to move to the competitor. The e-mails did, however, provide details of the former employees' contacts at the competing business, from which further leads could be developed.

What was noticed was the presence of a Dropbox account that had been installed and used on one of the former employees' computers. The application had been used and contained a number of folders synchronized and evidently uploaded to the employee's online account. Most of the files appeared to be of a personal and social nature and not relevant to the investigation. However, there was one large deleted archive (compressed) file some 4 GB in size named `Calibration.rar` that appeared to be of a technical nature. This file could not be opened during the preliminary examination and may have required some specialist recovery, provided the file was not too seriously corrupted.

The CEO was advised of the location of the file and questioned about its significance and the presence of the Dropbox account on the employee's terminal, which seemed appalling security practice. The file appeared to be an essential record of technical calibrations critical to the operation of the business, and it transpired that:

- The folder containing the data was insecurely stored on the business server but had been removed at about the same time as it appeared in the employee's terminal

- Poor security on the server allowed all users to access and potentially sabotage and steal any data without hindrance and without recording the event

- Unless the data could be recovered, the business faced serious operational problems that could lead to its closure

It seems likely that the archive folder was removed as a deliberate act of sabotage but also exported to the employee's Dropbox folder for some other purpose. A "deep rinse" of the employee's computer was then completed and ILookIX recovered 12 VSS folders, one relating to an earlier period provided a readable copy of the archive file. The file was not password protected, and examination by the CEO established that it contained the missing data so important to the company's operations intact. The file is highlighted in the following screenshot, where it was recovered from the Dropbox synchronization account:

Recovered data from a Dropbox folder held in a volume shadow snapshot

While the company was relieved to have its precious data returned to it in a short period of time, the following points were noted regarding the business' inability to protect its vital electronic assets:

- The business was not aware that the archive was missing and would not have learned of its disappearance for several weeks if it had not been recovered during the examination
- The server and terminals had no password protection and no sound backup to protect and preserve critical data
- No security auditing of data access management was in place
- The inadequate physical protection of the premises added to the general vulnerability of the business
- The network administrator was a friend of the CEO and an amateur with poor network security abilities

Evidence of theft and malicious destruction of electronic information and serious personnel misconduct was evident as well as evidence being identified for civil action against the former employee. With little information to base a meaningful search on hampered by the absence of any sound information security management system, it was mostly intuition that led to the discovery of the security breach and recovery of the evidence. Such favorable outcomes involving the recovery of stolen data and evidence implicating a specific suspect are not always the usual outcome. It is saddening to write that the information security at the business remains inadequate and the business obviously did not learn from its mistakes.

Summary

This chapter described in more detail the process of locating and selecting evidence in terms of a general process. It also further explained the nature of digital evidence and provided examples of its value in supporting a legal case. Various advanced analysis and recovery tools were demonstrated that show you how technology can speed up and make more efficient the evidence location and selection processes. Some of these tools are not new but have been enhanced, while others are innovative, and seek out evidence normally unavailable to the practitioner.

The majority of laptop, desktop, and network-based computers use Windows operating systems, which have been covered in varying details in this and previous chapters. *Chapter 7, Windows and Other Operating Systems as Sources of Evidence*, will outline Windows Registry and system files and logs, and some additional benefits of VSS recovery will be introduced as a resource for digital evidence recovery and analysis. It will describe in some detail other operating systems that are commonly examined, including Apple and Linux. The chapter will also touch on remote access and malware attacks and the prevalence and challenges of anti-forensics that hamper the recovery and identification of evidence.

7
Windows and Other Operating Systems as Sources of Evidence

The majority of laptop, desktop, and network-based computers use Windows operating systems, and this chapter will describe this in some detail and provide a brief description of other operating systems that are commonly examined. The chapter will provide you with an understanding of the complexity and nature of information processed on computers that assists forensic examinations and facilitates the recreation of key events relating to the presence of digital evidence stored in a range of operating systems.

The chapter will look at:

- The Windows Registry and system files and logs as a resource of digital evidence
- Apple and other operating system structures
- Remote-access and malware attacks and the prevalence and challenge posed by anti-forensics to the recovery of digital evidence
- A case study relating to Windows Registry analysis

The Windows Registry and system files and logs as resources of digital evidence

Windows-based systems have a central repository of settings called the **Windows Registry**. The registry is often a valuable source of information that can be used to clarify and corroborate other information of relevance to an investigation recovered from the filesystem. The Windows Registry is a vital part of the Windows operating system and maintains the configuration of the system and supported application programs as well as the users accessing the system and attached devices and networks.

The registry consists of a directory structure containing folders or "hives" that contain files or keys that contain values and, sometimes, sub-keys. Each key contains specific values that are used by the operating system or an application that relies on the value, for instance, the time zone used by the computer, the status of remote access settings, or details of a storage device attached.

The **Registry Explorer** allows the practitioner to explore the content of registry hives that must be processed before they can be viewed. Depending on the purpose of the examination taking place, the registry can hold valuable information. The Registry keys have an associated value called the **Last Write** time, which records the last modification time of the key. The last modification time may disclose what was changed in the key. Some Registry keys contain several values, which also makes it difficult to determine which of the values was changed.

The following screenshot shows samples of **Registry Hives** viewed using ILookIX Registry Explorer, which contains all of the processed registry hives, along with a viewer to review selected keys and values:

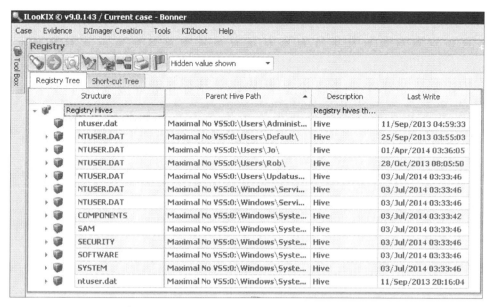

Looking at Registry Hives using ILookIX Registry Explorer

It is important that the practitioner have some knowledge of the workings and layout of the Registry and what corroboration it may provide. Knowing where to look and the sort of information required is covered in the following sub-sections.

Seeking useful leads within the Registry

Registry Explorer has two sections:

- The upper section displays the hives, keys, and sub-keys
- The lower section shows the names and properties of registry values

The structure of the hives is displayed in the top panel, shown in the following screenshot. Clicking on any key in a hive displays the values for that key in the lower panel. Clicking on a value in the lower panel reveals the data for that value, which is displayed in the viewer panel.

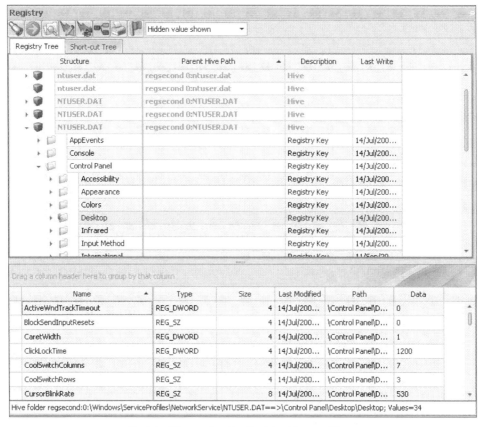

Registry Viewer showing Registry hives and keys

Registry Explorer has functions not present or poorly implemented in other forensic tools, such as these:

- **Search**: It searches the loaded hives' value data
- **List**: This is used to list all of the values under the key you have currently selected in the top panel
- **Key structure report**: This function creates a report of the structure as it is currently viewable in the upper panel

- **Hive value report**: This function creates a report of the values currently shown in the lower panel
- **Value name find**: This function allows you to search for value names
- **Hidden value list**: This is used to list all of the hidden values (if any) under the key you have currently selected in the top panel

Registry Explorer flags some hives, keys, and values that may be hidden from normal view in the Registry. Hidden keys and values, often used to store virus and Trojan data, may have additional data. ILookIX will allow the practitioner to view this extra data if it is present. Programs in Windows, including viruses and Trojans, have the ability to read and write values to the Registry by writing directly to the Registry, which programs using the standard **Win32 Application Programming Interface (Win32 API)** cannot detect. These values are referred to as hidden values.

There are also programs available that do not rely on the Win32 API and are capable of writing hidden values to the Registry. This could be used to conceal data. Hidden values should not automatically be interpreted as malicious, as Windows XP, for example, came with about 27 hidden values.

By selecting a key or sub-key or using either of the **Generate List** buttons, a list of values will be transferred to the **Value List** box in the lower portion of Registry Explorer. The list in the lower window will display relevant information about the value, as shown in the following screenshot:

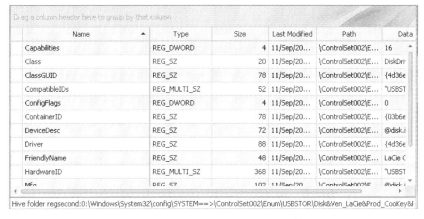

Registry Viewer showing some values of keys

The following screenshot shows the hex editor view of the value:

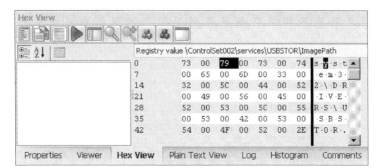

Hex view of key values

The search function shown in the following screenshot uses an index search to identify useful data such as a word search in the appropriate field:

- **Registry Key**
- **Registry Value**
- **Registry Data**

Searching for information in the Registry

Mapping devices through the Registry

By mapping a device to determine partitions and mounted and attached storage devices, the practitioner will gain a deeper insight into the usage of the device. For example, consider an instance where an internal hard drive detached from a computer was recovered and contained some probative evidence.

The following should be considered:

- Can it be linked to the device?
- If so, does it increase the likelihood that a relationship exists between users of the device and the drive?
- If not, does this affect the strength of the link between the suspect and the evidence contained on the device?

ILookIX will identify device partitions and extract data from them. However, the examination of other artifacts may provide more specific details about the antecedents of the device.

Windows makes a record of various internal and external drives attached to the device as well as details of other peripherals, such as printers, optical drives, and thumb drives. The previous connection of an external device that is no longer connected may be shown through this device logging. In Registry, the SYSTEM\ MountedDevices key records previously mounted devices. It can provide the actual serial number of many attached USB devices—a most useful attribute for the practitioner to use in reconstructing key events. The following screenshot shows a collection of devices attached to a desktop computer:

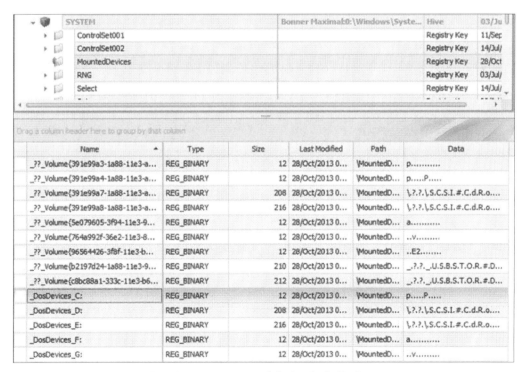

Viewing system-mounted devices in the Registry

Detecting USB removable storage

To reiterate, details of external devices, most notably, USB devices, mobile phones, and digital cameras, that have been connected to the computer are stored in the Registry. The Registry records some basic information about attached peripheral devices, such as the internal hard drive, monitor, keyboard, and mouse, but it also keeps information about other devices that may have been temporarily attached to the computer, such as external drives, thumb drives, cell phones, and digital cameras.

The following screenshot shows a record of an attached USB thumb drive stored in the registry, showing the manufacturer's name. Often, the unique serial number of the device can be recovered.

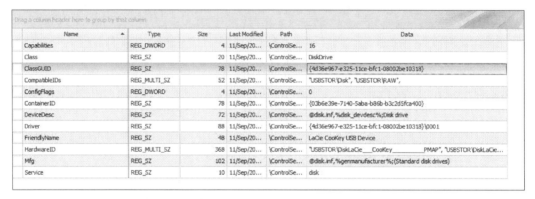

Name	Type	Size	Last Modified	Path	Data
Capabilities	REG_DWORD	4	11/Sep/20...	\ControlSe...	16
Class	REG_SZ	20	11/Sep/20...	\ControlSe...	DiskDrive
ClassGUID	REG_SZ	78	11/Sep/20...	\ControlSe...	{4d36e967-e325-11ce-bfc1-08002be10318}
CompatibleIDs	REG_MULTI_SZ	52	11/Sep/20...	\ControlSe...	"USBSTOR\Disk", "USBSTOR\RAW",
ConfigFlags	REG_DWORD	4	11/Sep/20...	\ControlSe...	0
ContainerID	REG_SZ	78	11/Sep/20...	\ControlSe...	{03b6e39e-7140-5aba-b86b-b3c2d5fca400}
DeviceDesc	REG_SZ	72	11/Sep/20...	\ControlSe...	@disk.inf,%disk_devdesc%;Disk drive
Driver	REG_SZ	88	11/Sep/20...	\ControlSe...	{4d36e967-e325-11ce-bfc1-08002be10318}\0001
FriendlyName	REG_SZ	48	11/Sep/20...	\ControlSe...	LaCie CooKey USB Device
HardwareID	REG_MULTI_SZ	368	11/Sep/20...	\ControlSe...	"USBSTOR\DiskLaCie___CooKey_____PMAP", "USBSTOR\DiskLaCie...
Mfg	REG_SZ	102	11/Sep/20...	\ControlSe...	@disk.inf,%genmanufacturer%;(Standard disk drives)
Service	REG_SZ	10	11/Sep/20...	\ControlSe...	disk

The Registry showing a record of an attached USB device

Not all USB thumb drives have serial numbers. This may be determined by the second character of the device ID being & and not a number. When examining each attached device, it can be seen that various values are displayed, including `ParentIdPrefix`, but there is very little else to assist the practitioner in determining the origin of the value or its use by the system. However, the Registry does hold other information that may assist, such as the `HKEY_LOCAL_MACHINE\System\MountedDevices` key, which is, in effect, a database of mounted volumes. The database records persistent volume names associated with unique identifiers for these volumes. By examining this additional data, it can often be shown that names assigned to the volumes, such as the drive letter `F`, will be associated with the `ParentIdPrefix` value for an attached thumb drive. If the thumb drive has been given a specific name by the user, this may also be recorded in the Registry.

User activity

The Registry holds various files, such as the NTUSER.DAT file, for each user granted permission to use the device, and stores the settings specific to that user. The contents of these files are mapped to the HKEY_USERS\SID hive so that it records users logging in. The process creates and updates the HKEY_CURRENT_USER hive, which can provide useful information regarding the actions taken by users after logging in to the device.

Reviewing Most Recently Used and Jump List activity

The registry maintains **Most Recently Used (MRU)** lists and **Jump Lists**, which were introduced in *Chapter 6, Selecting and Analyzing Digital Evidence*. This facility is intended to assist users to keep track of recent activities, such as providing quick access to word processing documents or pictures and videos that were viewed. However, from a forensic perspective, they act as a burglar's "footprints in the flowerbed," which are useful for recreating some history of entries made due to specific actions taken by the user. They are stored to keep track of items the user may return to in the future.

The Registry maintains a list of commands that the user types into the **Start** | **Run** box in this key:

```
HKEY_CURRENT_USER\Software\Microsoft\Windows\CurrentVersion\Explorer\
RunMRU
```

When an entry is made in the **Run** box, this action is recorded to this key and a list of the most recently used value is maintained, although this data may correlate with file and application metadata. It would be prudent to check this data as a matter of course to ensure there are no unexplained anomalies that might bring the fidelity of the evidence into doubt.

Detecting wireless connectivity

Network connections on Windows machines provide **Service Set Identifiers (SSID)** data confirming the existing and previous wireless network or networks connected to the desktop or laptop computer. This often useful data is stored in the Registry in the HKEY_LOCAL_MACHINE\ Software\Microsoft\WZCSVC\ Parameters\Interfaces hive. This repository can provide details of the network settings, including the IP address, from the KEY_LOCAL_MACHINE\System\ CurrentControlSet\Services\TCPIP\Interfaces\GUID key. The value of linking an IP address to recovered evidence from the computer may be assisted by this data.

Observing Windows Event Viewer logs

The Event Viewer logs maintained in Windows 7 onward record additional information to that contained in the Registry. It can, for example, corroborate the connection of a USB device, which may or may not be retained in Registry logs. It can record the frequency of usage of some programs, such as virtual networks, that may have been operating and can corroborate logging recorded by the application.

A portion of the text formatting, shown in the following screenshot, contains some of the same information about a USB device that can be found in the `System` hive. The registry should also show the date the device driver was installed, and this is typically recorded in Event Viewer logs.

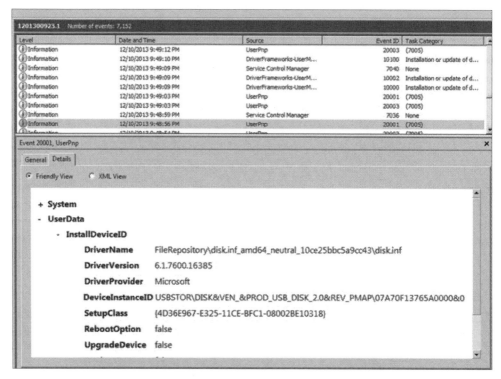

Windows Event Viewer showing a record of an attached USB device

Disconnected USB devices generate logs that can justify a more detailed examination of the circumstances surrounding the disconnection of an external device and may provide a timestamp of the time of the disconnection. This information may be located in the `System` hive `CurrentControlSet\Enum\DeviceType\DeviceID\ InstanceID\ \Properties\xxxx`.

Recovery of hidden data from a VSS

Recall from *Chapter 5*, *The Need for Enhanced Forensic Tools*, that the recovery of additional data can be achieved from Windows systems that have the VSS feature enabled. In the case study in the previous chapter, files important to the victim organization were recovered from Dropbox accounts in one of the VSS folders. In the instance shown in the following screenshot, ILookIX's **Differential XFR-VSS records** feature was used to recover only those VSS folders that contain differences in the file content:

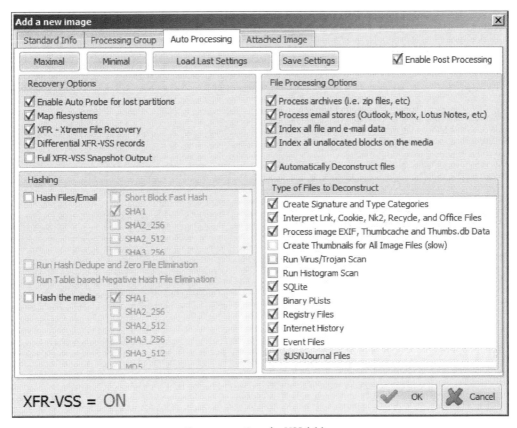

Recovery options for VSS folders

In this laboratory simulation, seven VSS folders were recovered, as can be seen in the following screenshot:

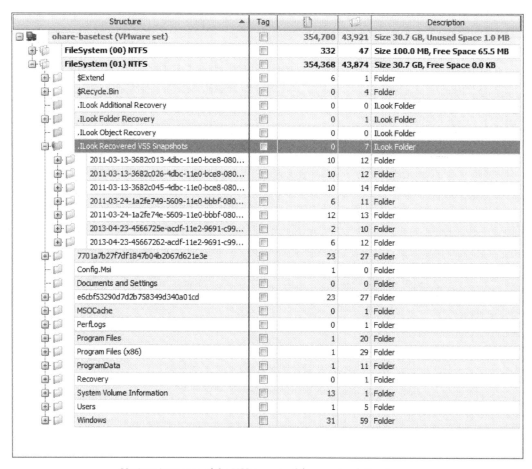

Structure	Tag	📄	📄	Description
ohare-basetest (VMware set)	☐	354,700	43,921	Size 30.7 GB, Unused Space 1.0 MB
FileSystem (00) NTFS	☐	332	47	Size 100.0 MB, Free Space 65.5 MB
FileSystem (01) NTFS	☐	354,368	43,874	Size 30.7 GB, Free Space 0.0 KB
$Extend	☐	6	1	Folder
$Recycle.Bin	☐	0	4	Folder
.ILook Additional Recovery	☐	0	0	ILook Folder
.ILook Folder Recovery	☐	0	1	ILook Folder
.ILook Object Recovery	☐	0	0	ILook Folder
.ILook Recovered VSS Snapshots	☑	0	7	ILook Folder
2011-03-13-3682c013-4dbc-11e0-bce8-080...	☐	10	12	Folder
2011-03-13-3682c026-4dbc-11e0-bce8-080...	☐	10	12	Folder
2011-03-13-3682c045-4dbc-11e0-bce8-080...	☐	10	14	Folder
2011-03-24-1a2fe749-5609-11e0-bbbf-080...	☐	6	11	Folder
2011-03-24-1a2fe74e-5609-11e0-bbbf-080...	☐	12	13	Folder
2013-04-23-4566725e-acdf-11e2-9691-c99...	☐	2	10	Folder
2013-04-23-45667262-acdf-11e2-9691-c99...	☐	6	12	Folder
7701a7b27f7df1847b04b2067d621e3e	☐	23	27	Folder
Config.Msi	☐	1	0	Folder
Documents and Settings	☐	0	0	Folder
e6cbf53290d7d2b758349d340a01cd	☐	23	27	Folder
MSOCache	☐	0	1	Folder
PerfLogs	☐	0	1	Folder
Program Files	☐	1	20	Folder
Program Files (x86)	☐	1	29	Folder
ProgramData	☐	1	11	Folder
Recovery	☐	0	1	Folder
System Volume Information	☐	13	1	Folder
Users	☐	1	5	Folder
Windows	☐	31	59	Folder

Various instances of the VSS recovered from a simulation image

Not only may deleted files be recovered that otherwise may have remained obscured, but system information and logs that assist in the reconstruction of a transgression may also be recovered. The previous iterations of Registry keys and hives and Event Viewer logging records are shown in the following screenshot. These records may reveal various activities of potential relevance, including remote access, changes to clock and desktop settings, and malicious intrusion exploits of the Registry.

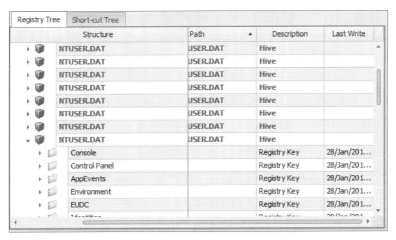

Various instances of Registry hives and keys recovered from VSS folders

The recovery of additional information such as archive stores, including zipped files, is also possible. The following screenshot highlights some additional ZIP files extant in various VSS folders, shown with different dates:

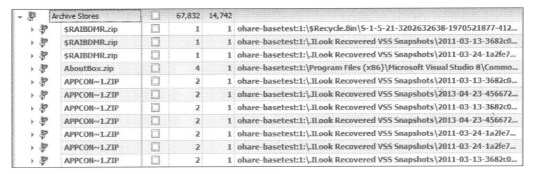

Archive stores recovered from VSS in the ILookIX Container Category

The additional recovery of e-mail stores from VSS folders, shown in the following screenshot, reflects e-mail messages during different periods. In the simulation, one of the vss folders surrendered a deleted e-mail that was not located in the current view of the drive:

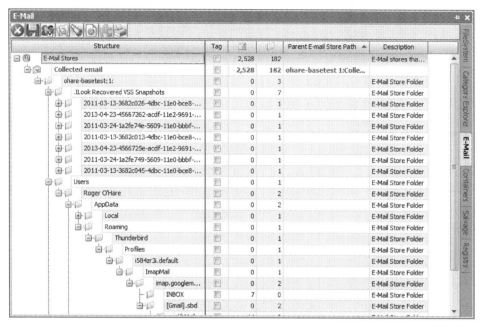

E-mail recovered from a VSS folder

Examining prefetch files

The process of booting a Windows system results in a range of files being read to RAM, which can be a lengthy process, so Windows creates prefetch files whenever a program is first run. This information may provide the practitioner with information about the history of various programs of relevance to an investigation running on the system.

Application execution may indicate that an anti-forensic program, for example, was used to obfuscate a transgression. In the event that a program has been deleted, it may be possible to locate a prefetch file that confirms the use of the program prior to its deletion—much more helpful than a bland statement that the program was installed, but whether it had been executed was unknown.

Malware activity can sometimes be established by examining a prefetch file that can provide some history of its download and execution. The `prefetch` folder and `ReadyBoot` folder are shown in the following screenshot:

View of the Prefetch folder and subfolder

Application prefetching uses a similar process, but it is localized to a single application's startup and typically stores its trace files in `C:\Windows\Prefetch`. Prefetch data is reflected in a file called `Layout.ini` that keeps a catalogue in sequential order. It holds the details of files and folders active in the boot process as part of system housekeeping:

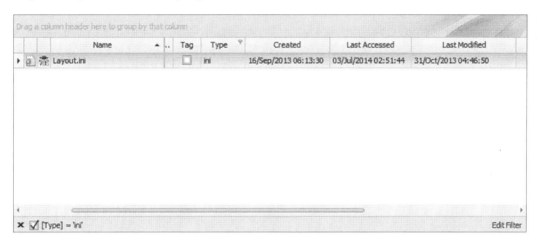

View of the Layout.ini file

Prefetch file analysis is uncomplicated, and it is really not difficult to confirm that the files contain details about the frequency of application runs, volume details, and timestamps of applications' first and last runs. Windows 10 records up to eight timestamps for each occasion an application was run and stores them in the `ROOT/Windows/Prefetch` folder.

Pagefiles

Windows uses `pagefile.sys` to store frames of memory that do not currently fit into physical memory. Windows supports 16 pagefiles, but typically, only one hidden file is used and is stored in `%SystemDrive%\pagefile.sys`. Acting in effect as virtual memory files, the hidden `pagefile.sys` file runs when RAM is pushed to its limit, and it becomes a virtual memory file. When the system is running out of RAM, it places memory dumps on the hard drive as a pagefile to supplement scarce memory. This can result in the system slowing down, which often occurs when too many applications are running.

This operation is not dissimilar to the functioning of `hiberfil.sys`, as it stores processes running at a specific time. However, it should be noted that `pagefile.sys` does not record all RAM activity.

The `pagefile.sys` file is essential for the sound performance of the system and undergoes constant changes as the device is being used. The following screenshot shows duplicate copies of a large-sized `pagefile.sys` file:

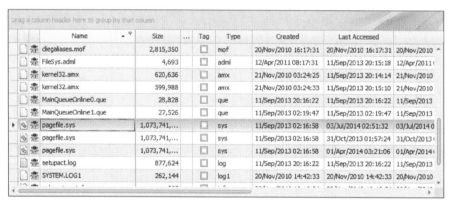

Locating pagefile.sys files

Hibernation and sleep files

The `hiberfil.sys` file is the default file used by Windows to save the machine's state as part of the hibernation process. As the operating system keeps the file open, it is not possible to read the file while the system is running. Internet artifacts are commonly found in memory and typically remain in the form of the pagefile or hibernation file. Recovering the deleted hibernation data can assist in determining what was in memory prior to hibernation.

Sleep mode does not provide much useful information as RAM is still working in the background and dissipates once the device restarts. Hibernation mode may provide more useful data from laptop computers because during hibernation, a snapshot of all the data in RAM is captured, and this is written to the hard drive.

The following screenshot shows a search for hibernation files to search for information that may assist the practitioner:

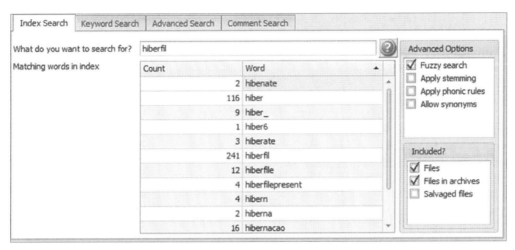

Searching for hiberfile.sys instances

Detecting steganography

Steganography is the process of concealing data in a communication so that only the sender and receiver know of its existence and are able to access the concealed information. It is common to encrypt data hidden in digital files or images whenever possible. The detection of steganographically encoded files is referred to as **steganalysis**. Steganalysis is limited to the detection of an embedded message, which may identify the embedding process. When the application or method of concealment has been identified, it might be possible to extract the message.

Unusual patterns in the steganographic image are obvious and create suspicion but can be hard to detect initially. A number of disk analysis utilities, such as ILookIX, are available, which can report on and filter hidden information in unused clusters or partitions in storage devices. By identifying repetitive patterns, it may be possible to detect hidden information in what appear to be innocuous files. Such repetition might reveal the presence of a steganography tool as well as hidden information. Comparing an authentic original file with one suspected of containing hidden information is a viable process, but that is contingent on having two samples for comparison.

Watermarking is often used to legitimately identify and protect copyrighted material. Although watermarks are often concealed, they are sometimes identified by forgers and subject to illicit removal to thwart the investigator.

To assist in the detection of hidden information with various tools, practitioners must identify and match the hash value of each suspected file. Doing so involves the importing or building of a library of hash sets, notably steganography software, as part of a comparison library.

Apple and other operating system structures

While Microsoft dominates the household market and many network systems, other popular operation systems such as Apple and Linux are also very much in use and likely to have to be examined by the forensic practitioner. The following subsections provide a brief introduction to these systems.

Examining Apple operating systems

Apple Macintosh devices use a different operating system (currently called OS X), which, unlike Microsoft's systems, enables applications to run independently of users, who do not have direct access to the filesystem. Simplicity and convenience is the general convention, which is based on the Unix filesystem.

Applications installed on an Apple machine have limited interaction with the filesystem, being restricted from doing so from within directories inside the application's sandbox. The sandbox protects systems and users from malware attacks. In effect, it limits the access privileges of each application to tighten the security of the device.

When applications are installed, a number of containers are created with specific roles. Typically, the application's operating files are held in a bundle container and the data files are held in data containers and subdirectories. Users access files through the **Finder** facility. The filesystem consists of four main domains, separating resources from files for ease of access and use and sound security protection. These consist of the following:

- **The user domain**: This has user-specific resources restricting each user's access and control to only their own home directory.
- **The local domain**: This is concerned with applications installed on the current computer and shared among all users, consisting of several directories on the local boot volume, which is managed by the system. Users with administrative privileges may add, remove, or modify this domain.

- **The network domain**: This contains applications and documents shared among all users of a local area network.

- **The system domain**: This contains Apple system software installed by Apple, which prevents users from adding, removing, or modifying items.

As part of its attempt to simplify the use of applications, the Finder function and several other functions, such as the **Open** and **Save** panels, conceal files and directories that do not require user access or intervention. A typical directory structure viewed through a forensic tool is shown in the following screenshot:

Apple file hierarchy

The various categories of files held on Apple desktops and laptops are available to the practitioner and shown cataloged in the following screenshot of ILookIX **Category Explorer**:

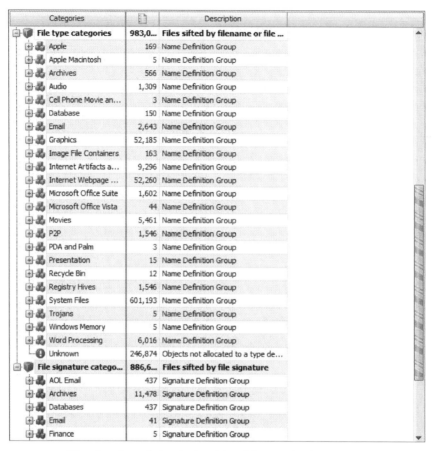

File categories and signatures cataloged from an Apple computer

File metadata, including timestamps, EXIF data for picture images, and file locations, may also be recovered from iOS, as shown in the following screenshot:

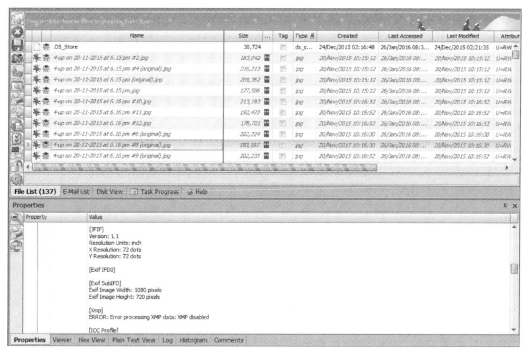

File metadata collated from an Apple computer

The Linux operating system

The Linux operating system, a variant of Unix, relays instructions from an application to the computer's central processing unit and processor. The processor performs the instructed task and then sends the results back to the application via the operating system. Although Linux has many features common to Windows and OS X, it is an open source operating system, developed in collaboration with users, companies, and partners. This has resulted in economic research and development endeavors to produce an innovative and, many say, superior operating system. Linux has become an important desktop system as well as the foundational operating system for networks and many devices, such as mobile phones.

Because Linux is on the system BIOS of laptop and notebook computers and cellphones, it dramatically increases the speed of booting up these devices. Linux increasingly runs a significant number of web servers, including Amazon's cloud service. Twitter, LinkedIn, YouTube, and Google use Linux as their operating systems.

Operating systems' architectures have kernels that contain a set of coded instructions that make the computer hardware respond to the operating system and, by default, application-level programs. Unlike the Microsoft Windows kernel, which many regard as cumbersome and inaccessible to all but a few of its own programmers, the flexibility and modular structure of the Linux kernel offers a number of advantages to developers. In particular, the size of the kernel can be increased or decreased to meet the requirements of developers wishing to redesign the system for different operating environments and devices. This is especially helpful in system miniaturization for smaller-sized handheld devices.

A collective set of tools embedded in the Linux kernel is, in effect, its operating system, which also has the advantage of being modular in form. Linux provides users with a range of choices in the way they may wish to make use of its system, including the windows-and-desktop functionality that most users are familiar with in Windows and OS X.

A system of users, groups, and privileges is embedded in Linux to keep the security of the operating system as secure as possible. It does provide self-contained user accounts in much the same way as other operating systems. For example, personal files are held within the user's `home` directory and are readily available for use. However, a typical Linux filesystem can contain a confusing array of local and remote files and running processes and, unlike Windows, there is no `Program Files` directory. The following screenshot shows a menu view of a Linux system:

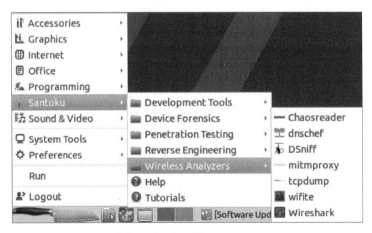

Menu view in a Linux system

The archive view of a sample Linux operating system is shown in the following screenshot:

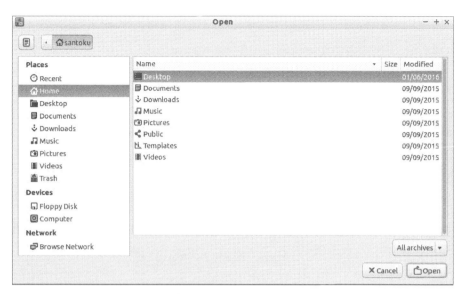

Archive view of a Linux system

Remote access and malware threats

The prevalence of malware and other exploits through hacker attacks, often through remote-access exploits, remains a significant threat to computers and network systems that are vulnerable because of poor security management. These issues are discussed in the following subsections.

Remote access

The "Trojan defense" has been used by guilty as well as innocent computer users to support claims of their innocence by blaming the presence of illegal activities on their computers on remote attackers. While this is plausible, there seems to be a reversal of the onus of proving innocence, with the defendant instead of the prosecutor taking on the role. The big bugbear in all digital forensic examinations is linking the suspect to incriminating events. It would be fairer, but obviously too time-consuming on occasion, for the practitioner to clarify the possibility or likelihood of a remote-access exploit.

Windows operating systems permit remote access for legitimate purposes, but it is quite common for Windows updates needed to resolve vulnerability in the feature in including its Remote Desktop Protocol service, which is inherently unsecure and vulnerable to exploitation.

Remote access can also be gained through a malware attack that assists hackers in gaining access to the target device or network. This is especially problematic if there is an absence or only a low level of security protection.

Wi-Fi connections, while convenient, often allow the snooping of sensitive network traffic to take place, potentially providing easy access to accounts held on computers and handheld devices. A lack of sound encryption of these communications will enable a cyberattack to be mounted against online banking and other accounts that involve financial transactions, for example.

Detecting malware attacks and other exploits

The registry stores autostart keys at various locations, which launch applications without direct user intervention. One of the keys that hackers most commonly exploit is the run key that allows many of these exploits to remain on the system: `HKEY_LOCAL_MACHINE\Software\Microsoft\Windows\CurrentVersion\Run`. The startup key will launch programs when the system starts up, when a user logs in to the system, or the user undertakes some other specified action.

The `HKEY_LOCAL_MACHINE \SOFTWARE\Microsoft\Windows NT\CurrentVersion\ Image File` Registry entry is intended for the administrator to debug various executive options, but it is vulnerable to outside attackers who can use it to redirect an application to a hijacked copy of the application. The addition of an autostart key for Word can direct the process to a copy of Word containing malicious code that allows access to the computer whenever the program is launched. These autostart keys often leave some electronic fingerprint of such intrusions that may clarify whether the computer user or an intruder is responsible for events of interest.

In *Chapter 4, Recovering and Preserving Digital Evidence*, mention was made of reading and recovering the contents of RAM for analyzing malware that antivirus programs do not detect. IXImager can reboot fast enough to enable capture of the system's RAM so that running programs, passwords, and so on can be captures. This is achieved by inserting the USB, CD, or SD card into the computer port, rebooting the computer and commencing the imaging process, and recovering and storing the captured RAM data for analysis.

The ISeekDiscovery automaton provides a novel and highly effective means of searching for bogus files. If, for example, the practitioner wants to find all Word and Excel files on a machine that are misnamed or spelled wrong or have no extensions by type, all that is needed is to use the **auto capture** feature by signature for Excel and Word, but to also use the **Search Exclusions** tab, shown in the following screenshot, and add in the following file extensions:

- `*.xls`
- `*.xlsx`
- `*.doc`
- `*.docx`

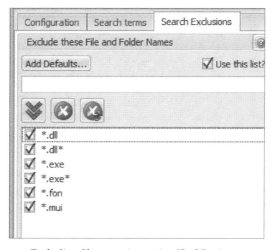

Excluding file extensions using ISeekDesigner

When this routine is run, it will remove the files with legitimate names, leaving only the ones that have bogus names. This should be helpful for intrusion detection because of the large number of security breaches caused by hidden hacker-executable code.

The prevalence of anti-forensics processes and tools

Obscuring and destroying evidence is not a new phenomenon and has emerged alongside digital forensics to challenge and frustrate evidence recovery. It consists of a broad range of software tools that obfuscate events linked to transgressions as well as deleting or modifying data. Anti-forensics may also be intended to delay the time it takes to complete an examination. Sometimes, it may cast doubt on the validity of the evidence later relied on in court. These tools often hide their existence and may persist on a device after it has been seized.

Specific uses of this illicit practice include:

- Overwriting or altering data and metadata, including timestamps
- Hiding and encrypting data and steganography (mentioned previously)
- Encrypting folders, partitions, and network traffic
- Using external devices that enable computers to be booted up but leave no trace of activities on the host machine

Detecting anti-forensics activity is not necessarily an intuitive process, but the fact that it may have been done on a device being examined should always be considered. Tools that detect and even prevent anti-forensics activity seem in short supply, and there is certainly a case for further research into the problem.

This book will not promote or provide any information about these toolkits that are freely available on the Internet, but I acknowledge that they are already bringing into disrepute digital forensic tools that continue to be heavily relied upon. Of concern is the use of these tools to protect the guilty and possibly implicate the innocent. *Chapter 8, Examining Browsers, E-mails, Messaging Systems, and Mobile Phones,* describes the Dark Web and the use of such anti-forensic tools to encrypt and hide information, such as Tor and 12P.

Case study – corroborating evidence using Windows Registry

This case study exemplifies how digital evidence should always be corroborated and verified whenever possible.

The case is related to downloading illegal child exploitation pictures and movie files. One of the potentially damaging files recovered was a pornographic picture of an underage child. The prosecution contended that this file had previously been displayed as the computer's desktop wallpaper, clearly visible on startup of the computer. It contended, not unreasonably, that it could hardly not have been noticed by the users of the computer, thus implicating the user's complicity in handling illegal, obscene material.

When seized, the computer desktop displayed an innocuous blank picture that raised no immediate interest. However, later examination of the computer located a `.jpg` file depicting an obscene image of an underage child. This disturbing image was located at `C:\Documents and Settings\xyz\Application Data\Opera\Opera\xxx.jpg`. The prosecution's practitioner demonstrated that on a confirmed date and time, `xxx.jpg` was converted to be used as the desktop wallpaper. A picture file of that name was located at `C:\Documents and Settings\xyz`, which was confirmed to be the default directory containing files and folders associated with the user account `xyz`.

Testing by the practitioner suggested that this entry is not created until a non-Windows-standard picture is applied as the desktop wallpaper. If the desktop is changed to another nonstandard picture, the Registry key is altered to reflect the new picture without maintaining a list of the old files. When a standard Windows picture is selected for the desktop, this key will remain to show the last used nonstandard picture.

Analysis of Registry entries relating to the `xyz` user account revealed that non-human intervention to create the desktop wallpaper and place the illegal image file in the user account was not evident but could not be entirely discounted, as traces of such events are not easily identifiable for further examination. In this instance, the system stored the usual background wallpaper bitmap in the wallpaper registry hotkey located at the `HKEY_CURRENT_USER\Control Panel\Desktop\Wallpaper` Registry key. Windows Registry does not record a history of the use of previous standard Windows files.

The metadata for `xxx.jpg` revealed creation, modified, and last-accessed dates, which correlated with Internet usage identified during the reconstruction of the offense timeline. Examination indicated that the file existed in another location on the computer, but no record of whether it was downloaded from the Internet or copied from an external device could be confirmed.

It is unlikely that the user would make the image the desktop wallpaper by manually installing it through a directory search through `C:\Documents and Settings\xyz \Application Data\Opera\Opera\`. What is more usual, and therefore more likely, is that the image was viewed through Opera and then set as the wallpaper by a user using the right mouse button. The file was also saved to the `xyz` folder, which suggests two manual processes that imply deliberate actions on the part of a user or users. These actions could be effected by the presence of malware such as a Trojan horse, but that seemed highly unlikely considering other testimony in the case.

Unfortunately, no data was available to show when the image was removed as wallpaper when some user reverted to a blank (black) screen choosing the default setting, **None**, or no image in the desktop frame. This information would have provided a more precise time of the manipulation of at least one illegal file. VSS was not present on the Windows XP operating system, which, had it been, may have provided some clarification of such Registry changes.

While Registry can be helpful in many cases, in this instance, it left some uncertainty. This was most unhelpful when it was presumed that the users of the computer, tenants in the defendant's home as distinct from the actual owner who was charged with possession of child exploitation material, became aware of the law enforcement interest in the computer 14 hours before its seizure. It is suspected they removed the incriminating wallpaper in haste along with some other incriminating files, when it was later proven that the owner (defendant) had no access to the computer.

The owner had a cast-iron alibi showing he was in a different suburb at the time these deletions to the computer files were made. Had this been heeded at the time charges against the defendant were being prepared, it is unlikely that the case would have progressed to trial. On reflection, it seems that the investigating detectives and forensic practitioner did not see this glaring conflict in user access and did not attempt to determine the involvement of others with access to the computer. This is again a prime example of suspect-led investigation.

As the forensic examination of the device proceeded, it became clear that more than one local user had access to it. It was thought sound practice to determine whether a remote attack may have occurred and an outsider may have been responsible for the presence of the illegal files. The computer settings showed that the facility for an external user to access the computer was disabled at the time of seizure but not necessarily at the time of the relevant events.

The practitioner claimed that the computer was searched for malicious applications with no results. However, the defense practitioner located the `ZLOB.JN` Trojan horse downloader at `C:\Documents and Settings\xyz\My Documents\setup.exe`. The file was removed and quarantined by the defense practitioner pending further examination.

Unsubstantiated information about this malware ranges from describing it as a serious threat to a nuisance that slows down the computer and launches pop-up commands. Some observers claim that it can be used as a means of gaining access to a computer, allowing hackers to gain remote access. Some versions of Zlob automatically load on bootup and hide their presence by hijacking the Windows Explorer program. The Trojan has been claimed to have the ability to take complete control of the computer, but that claim was never substantiated.

Some commentary suggests that a Zlob infection will begin to take over the computer browser, causing constant popups, the redirection of a URL to other sites, the erasing of documents and images, and even invasion into personal information that can be erased or distributed to other websites. Manual Zlob removal requires some knowledge of the technical aspects of the target computer. It is difficult to remove because it is known for replicating itself under different names. Even if removed, it may have replicated and reinstalled itself on the computer.

Examination of the suspect Zlob file, `setup.exe`, showed it was created prior to the illegal activity recorded on the computer and it had not been identified or removed by the antivirus program. The Trojan horse reportedly creates a number of files in the system, including `stdole3.tlb`, and registry entries are created in an attempt to run `Troj/Zlob-JN` on startup, including `HKLM\SOFTWARE\Microsoft\Windows\CurrentVersion\policies\explorer\run wininet.dll` and `HKLM\SOFTWARE\Microsoft\Windows\CurrentVersion\policies\explorer\run regperf.exe`.

However, examination of the computer failed to locate these three files inside Windows Registry or on the computer. It seemed unlikely that an external attack had occurred, leaving the possibility that one or more of the local users were responsible for the illegal activity. Although this extra work by the defense practitioner to examine the possibility of an external attack proved fruitless, it had to be done, but why not by those laying the charges? The defendant was acquitted by the jury of the charge, but no further charges were laid against those others users implicated in using the computer.

To reiterate, ad nauseam, this case highlights the benefits of a counterargument forming an essential part of an examination, which then lends itself to search for exculpatory evidence, which, if it exists, may modify or refute an argument, for, to recall the simple yet powerful catchphrase of practitioner and academic *Dardick* (2010): "There is nothing more deceptive than an obvious fact."

References

Dardick, G. S. 2010. "*Cyber Forensics Assurance*." 8th Australian Digital Forensics Conference, Perth, Western Australia. SECAU: 57–64.

Summary

This chapter described the Windows operating system in some detail as well as other operating systems that are commonly examined, including Apple and Linux. Windows Registry, system files and logs, and some additional benefits of VSS recovery were introduced as a valuable resource for digital evidence recovery and analysis. The chapter also touched on remote access and malware attacks and the prevalence and challenges of anti-forensics that hamper the recovery and identification of evidence.

Chapter 8, Examining Browsers, E-mails, Messaging Systems, and Mobile Phones, will describe the processes of locating and recovering digital evidence relating to records of personal communications, including e-mails and browsing records stored in computer devices and telephonic communications retained on mobile phones. It will look specifically at the recovery of Internet browsing and search records and other messaging systems, including Skype and virtual private networks as well as e-mail analysis.

Mobile phone forensics will be introduced and its importance in forensic examinations will be discussed, along with the growing challenge of evidence acquisition from personal computing and GPS devices. The chapter will provide you with an appreciation of the value of locating, extracting, and examining records of communications between persons of interest stored on computers and mobile phones.

8

Examining Browsers, E-mails, Messaging Systems, and Mobile Phones

This chapter looks at Internet browsers, e-mail and messaging systems, and mobile phones and other handheld devices—often considered to be rich sources of digital evidence. The processes of locating and recovering digital evidence relating to records of personal communications, including e-mails and browsing records stored in computer devices and telephonic communications stored on mobile phones, are described. You will appreciate the value of locating, extracting, and examining records of communications between persons of interest stored on computer and mobile phones that are often a rich source of evidence.

The chapter will provide you with a basic understanding of the following concepts:

- The recovery of Internet browsing and search records and other messaging systems including Skype and virtual private networks
- E-mail analysis and the processing of large e-mail databases
- Mobile phone forensics and the growing challenge of evidence acquisition from personal computing devices, including tablet and GPS devices

A range of Internet browsers are available for desktop and laptop devices as well as for tablets and other handheld devices, including Mozilla Firefox, Google Chrome, Microsoft Internet Explorer and, more recently, Microsoft Edge, Safari, and a range of others. The value of data stored as a result of using browsers is outlined in the next section and in the *The growing challenge of evidence recovery from mobile phones and handheld devices* section.

Locating evidence from Internet browsing

Information relating to the web-browsing activities of a user are often found stored as cookies, cache files, URL history, search terms, histories, and other files on the computer. This forms an important part of many forensic examinations, as it can help reconstruct a suspect's online browsing behavior in relation to cases such as infringements of intellectual property, cybercrime and child pornography, and other serious crimes. The following subsections describe some of the basic features of web-browsing events that assist in crime reconstruction. They also outline the recovery of evidence from browser data, which may be done from unallocated space as well, providing the practitioner with an insight into private browsing activities.

Typical web-browsing behavior

Typical browsing activities involve searches for specific topics stored on websites, such as a person, event, organization, or e-mail or messaging account—virtually anything that the searcher is looking for. During the process of visiting or linking to a remote site, there is, as per *Locard's exchange principle*, some exchange of data: traces are left behind and some are transferred to another device. The remote website may record some details of user visits to a varying extent. Web-based e-mail servers such as Hotmail and Yahoo! would log account holders and often record their IP addresses at the point of accessing their accounts. This information is useful in reconstructing transgressions, even more so if they correlate with the device used by the account holder to sign in to an account.

Gmail, for example, stores e-mail messages on its cloud server and not on local machines, so it is unlikely that much e-mail evidence will be recovered from these accounts, other than what may be in the transient RAM state. However, such e-mail accounts can now be synchronized and backed up into a **Post Office Protocol** (**POP**) client, a standard protocol to retrieve and manage messages from remote servers over an Internet connection. This results in messages being downloaded and stored on the local machine. Windows 10 e-mail messaging similarly caches these messages on the local drive, thereby potentially assisting forensic recovery.

Browsing records are often cached on the user's local machine. For example, the default browser setting will record browsing activities in a number of different forms, most notably:

* Cached folders storing HTML and multimedia files of webpages visited
* History databases of webpages visited and, to some extent, the date and time of a range of times in which an individual webpage was visited

- A database record of searches made using applications such as Google and Bing
- Cookie stores that record websites visited and the timestamps of each visit
- Records of online accounts visited by users
- E-commerce activities, including e-banking records and accounts

Forensic tools process common file types that could contain useful evidential material. Many of these small database files require deconstruction, including history databases and image thumbnail database `.db` files, `index.dat` and other such files that record Internet history, and so forth. The following table shows a collection of image and Shockwave files recovered from the Firefox default cache and a default temporary folder located in a suspect's laptop. This information formed part of the evidence to bring charges against the suspect and helped establish browsing activities during a relevant period relating to the main charge. The table shows recovered image and media files from the browser cache and the default `temp` folder.

Name	Type	Path	Created	Modified	Accessed
E3A65A2Ed01	.jpg	\Documents and Settings\User\Local Settings\Application Data\Mozilla\Firefox\Profiles\7yyxpig9. default\Cache	17/07/2015 5:54	17/07/2015 5:54	14/09/2015
25C1B625d01	.jpg	\Documents and Settings\User\Local Settings\Application Data\Mozilla\Firefox\Profiles\7yyxpig9. default\Cache	17/07/2015 5:49	17/07/2015 5:49	14/09/2015
PV.SWF	.swf	\Documents and Settings\User\Local Settings\Temp\TMP27340-11320	5/03/2015 0:04	5/03/2015 0:04	14/09/2015
PE.SWF	.swf	\Documents and Settings\User\Local Settings\Temp\TMP27340-11320	5/03/2015 0:04	5/03/2015 0:04	14/09/2015
PR.SWF	.swf	\Documents and Settings\User\Local Settings\Temp\TMP27340-11320	5/03/2015 0:04	5/03/2015 0:04	14/09/2015

In the following table, the first image file, which had been deleted, has been recovered from a cache folder. Its previous location is unknown, but the file does provide some potentially useful timestamps. The remaining deleted files have no location or timestamps but they do have a hashed filename and signature that may be used for comparison with other files recovered on the device. The file-carving process recovered these files from sectors, which could be examined in more detail to attempt to discover more about their antecedents. Without some form of corroboration, the evidentiary weight of this evidence is weakened. The table shows the deleted files recovered from unallocated space, recording the filename and, on one occasion, timestamps:

Name	Type	Path	Created	Modified	Accessed
12DffGbbvt	jpg	\Path unknown\ Cache	23/08/2014 01:58	23/08/2014 01:58	23/08/2014 01:58
00049.jpg	jpg	\Path unknown\ Carved files			
00476.jpg	jpg	\Path unknown\ Carved files			
00352.jpg	jpg	\Path unknown\ Carved files			
00573.jpg	jpg	\Path unknown\ Carved files			
00700.jpg	jpg	\Path unknown\ Carved files			
00865.jpg	jpg	\Path unknown\ Carved files			
00869.jpg	jpg	\Path unknown\ Carved files			
00886.jpg	jpg	\Path unknown\ Carved files			
01492.jpg	jpg	\Path unknown\ Carved files			
01931.jpg	jpg	\Path unknown\ Carved files			

The following table shows some .db database files holding traces of images that existed in a folder at an unknown location on the device. There are no timestamps, although the naming convention of the files suggests two dates in August 2015 when they may have been created or accessed. The reliability of this data obtained by the X-Ways Forensics tool is probably insufficient for this evidence to be considered admissible without some other sound corroboration.

Name	Type	Path	Created	Modified	Accessed
Thumbnail.jpg	jpg	\Path unknown\ Carved files\ C120,D380 2015-08-13 03:15:03.jpg			
Thumbnail.jpg	jpg	\Path unknown\ Carved files\ C120,D380 2015-08-22 05:22:04.jpg			

The following screenshot shows URLs and keyword search history files recovered from a laptop computer. This information was used to reconstruct the suspect's browsing activities and the nature of the search terms used as part of online crime activity. The spreadsheets extracted from the database provided timestamps, details of websites visited, and search terms used as part of the commissioning of the offense:

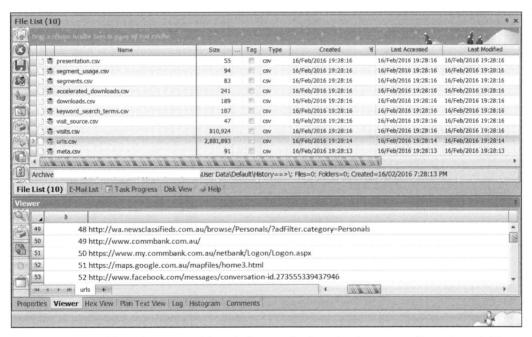

Recovered spreadsheets deconstructed from the browser database showing a range of browsing activities

Recovering browsing artifacts from slack and unallocated space

Using ILookIX's indexing of unallocated sectors will index the raw sector contents of each sector not assigned to a file or folder. The following screenshot shows the result of a search for the term **tightvnc** in an attempt to explore the possibility that this remote-access program may have been used to compromise the desktop computer. **116** hits in the file slack were recovered, with a further **423** file hits being recorded, thereby shedding much more light on a remote attack against the device:

	Search Type	Search Terms	Run Date	What was searched?	File ...	E-Mail...	Slack Hits	Unallocated Hits	Registry Hits	Search Summary
	Keyword	tightvnc, chemicals ...	23/Sep/201...	maximal (0); iseek crime si...	6	0	0	0	0	No
	Keyword	tightvnc	23/Sep/201...	maximal (0); iseek crime si...	423	0	116	0	0	No

Search hits recovered in files and file slack sectors

A sample of recovered sectors containing traces of the search terms or hits is shown in the following screenshot. Note that there are no timestamps for this data, and what is shown is the date the practitioner extracted the traces after free and unallocated space on the forensic image was indexed. In many instances, not all of the data is readable, even using the inbuilt hex editor—there is often an absence of timestamps and the original file location.

In this instance, BitTorrent activity was recovered, providing details suggesting the suspect using the BitTorrent peer-to-peer protocol to download media from other torrent users. In this example, the timestamps of some of the activity are clearly visible as well as the nature of the media being downloaded:

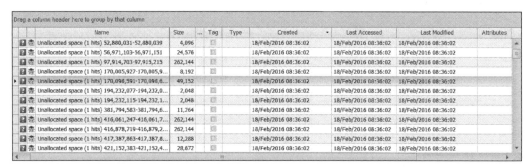

Name	Size	...	Tag	Type	Created	Last Accessed	Last Modified	Attributes
Unallocated space (1 hits) 52,880,031-52,880,039	4,096				18/Feb/2016 08:36:02	18/Feb/2016 08:36:02	18/Feb/2016 08:36:02	
Unallocated space (1 hits) 56,971,103-56,971,151	24,576				18/Feb/2016 08:36:02	18/Feb/2016 08:36:02	18/Feb/2016 08:36:02	
Unallocated space (1 hits) 97,914,703-97,915,215	262,144				18/Feb/2016 08:36:02	18/Feb/2016 08:36:02	18/Feb/2016 08:36:02	
Unallocated space (1 hits) 170,005,927-170,005,9...	8,192				18/Feb/2016 08:36:02	18/Feb/2016 08:36:02	18/Feb/2016 08:36:02	
Unallocated space (1 hits) 170,098,591-170,098,6...	49,152				18/Feb/2016 08:36:02	18/Feb/2016 08:36:02	18/Feb/2016 08:36:02	
Unallocated space (1 hits) 194,232,077-194,232,0...	2,048				18/Feb/2016 08:36:02	18/Feb/2016 08:36:02	18/Feb/2016 08:36:02	
Unallocated space (1 hits) 194,232,115-194,232,1...	2,048				18/Feb/2016 08:36:02	18/Feb/2016 08:36:02	18/Feb/2016 08:36:02	
Unallocated space (1 hits) 381,794,583-381,794,6...	11,264				18/Feb/2016 08:36:02	18/Feb/2016 08:36:02	18/Feb/2016 08:36:02	
Unallocated space (1 hits) 416,061,247-416,061,7...	262,144				18/Feb/2016 08:36:02	18/Feb/2016 08:36:02	18/Feb/2016 08:36:02	
Unallocated space (1 hits) 416,878,719-416,879,2...	262,144				18/Feb/2016 08:36:02	18/Feb/2016 08:36:02	18/Feb/2016 08:36:02	
Unallocated space (1 hits) 417,387,863-417,387,8...	12,288				18/Feb/2016 08:36:02	18/Feb/2016 08:36:02	18/Feb/2016 08:36:02	
Unallocated space (1 hits) 421,152,383-421,152,4...	28,672				18/Feb/2016 08:36:02	18/Feb/2016 08:36:02	18/Feb/2016 08:36:02	

Search hits recovered in files and file slack sectors

In this example, data was recovered from slack file sectors using the term `search terms`. One of the hits shown in the following screenshot provided details of the drive sector and contiguous sectors where the record was held. Data carving of the sectors may provide a partial reconstruction of the data, but unless there were some timestamp included in the body of the information, analysis of temporal data would be guesswork at best:

Properties of recovered Internet browsing from slack space

By opening this data, it was possible to glean some important information. The following screenshot highlights a website visited to delete a Skype account. This information was commensurate with the suspect's presumed attempt to delete the account to prevent future investigation of illegal activities involving communication with organized crime personalities:

A view of some of the readable data from Internet browsing records recovered from slack space

The data held some temporal material that correlated with deleted HTML data to assist in determining the likelihood of the month and year when the search was made. The following diagram suggests the likelihood that Skype was installed on the computer, but there is no evidence of the program and deleted data files in the Recycle Bin or in slack space. Windows Event Viewer did provide evidence of its earlier installation and use during specific periods. This was reinforced by the remnants of Skype activity recovered from slack space, including message text and the search for an uninstallation process. A partially recovered webpage located in slack space provided an approximate period when the webpage was created on the website. Such corroboration of these scattered remnants is useful in reconstructing key events.

In this case, it was an attempt to remove Skype and data associated with it and could be considered potentially incriminating:

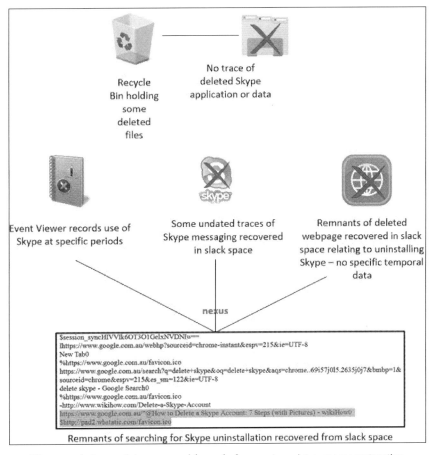

Remnants of searching for Skype uninstallation recovered from slack space

The nexus between data recovered from slack space to assist event reconstruction and an attempt to obfuscate the use of Skype

ILookIX includes a shortcut feature that takes commonly used values, such as the most recently typed web addresses in Internet Explorer and Internet Explorer settings, and regenerates those hives, keys, and values into a shortcut tree for easy review, as shown in the following screenshot:

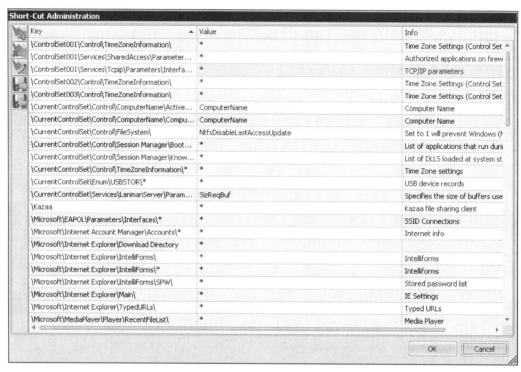

Activity antecedents recovered from the Registry

Private browsing

Private browsing is a facility provided by some web browsers, including Google Chrome, Mozilla Firefox, and Internet Explorer, for the purpose of avoiding all traces of the user's activity during a browsing session for privacy and, possibly, security reasons. It is also typical of users wishing to hide browsing activities that involve a degree of illegality. This makes the analysis and location of evidence relating to web browsing activity potentially difficult, as the private browsing may have removed all evidence of browsing activities that may be relevant to an examination.

Research was undertaken by me to gain a clearer understanding of the nature of the private browsing function and its implications for forensic examination. Previous research had looked at recovering browsing data from computer hard drives, while other research stressed the wisdom of recording browsing activities from RAM data stored on the computer. A range of forensic programs used for the analysis of web browsers, including EnCase, AccessData's Forensic Toolkit, Nirsoft Internet Tools, and Internet Evidence Finder, had been used in earlier experiments.

My experiments were intended to identify those areas of the computer system that are modified or accessed during normal and private browsing sessions. This showed that during private browsing, IE stored everything normally but deleted it once the browser was exited. Chrome modified the safe browsing databases, cookies, and history, and Firefox modified the Firefox profiles and safe browsing database. These results could potentially help researchers focus their search when analyzing web browsers.

Some variances were noted in whether `pagefile.sys` files contained information relevant to private browsing, but that may have been due to the size of RAM available, as memory swap files are created when the memory is fully used, storing data on the hard drive. This seems more of a matter of chance than something that can be relied upon during a dead analysis of the hard drive, with the chance of finding them decreasing as time and computer use after the session increases.

The results of experiments using ILookIX and IXImager to image and examine each browser under identical conditions on Windows 7 Ultimate showed that both Chrome and Firefox had more secure private browsing modes than Internet Explorer, with no information relating to the private browsing session other than the date changes on related files found for Firefox or Chrome. The following general observations could be made:

- **Google Chrome**: Examination of the slack space, `pagefile.sys` files, unallocated spaces, and string searches for Google Chrome did not recover any artifacts. Earlier researchers had found only timestamp changes in SysVolume information, and in files such as `Safebrowsingcookies.db`.

- **Mozilla Firefox**: Analysis found only timestamp changes in **Firefox | Profiles** files.

- **Internet Explorer**: Commensurate with previous research, more recoverable data was retained after private browsing sessions, with browsing artifacts recovered from all the websites visited. Most information recovered was located in cache, history, and temporary Internet files as well as in unallocated space. The study found browsing information in both the usual folders and unallocated space. These differences in locations where browsing artifacts were found may be due to system, web browser version, or forensic analysis software differences. This study also found that there were differences between the number of artifacts that could be recovered after a private browsing session in Internet Explorer. This appeared to depend on the different process used to access files in private browsing, with fewer artifacts recovered when Internet Explorer was opened directly in InPrivate Browsing mode.

These results show that while there are timestamp changes to relevant browser files that indicate a browsing event has occurred, if someone has used Firefox or Chrome for a private browsing session, the recovery of any browsing artifacts would be very difficult—impossible or unlikely at best—from a dead analysis of the hard drive, as nothing was found during this research. However, information relating to the web browser session from private browsing using Internet Explorer was recoverable. However, there was less information available when Internet Explorer had been opened directly in private browsing mode than when it had been opened in normal mode and then switched to private mode.

Microsoft Edge, a variant of Internet Explorer, also incorporates a private browsing feature, as shown in the following screenshot. Preliminary research shows that like Internet Explorer, traces of this feature do remain on the device and are recoverable:

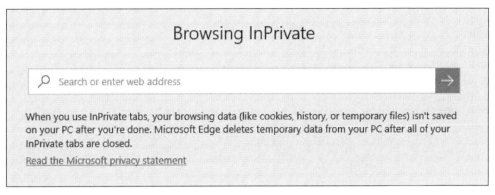

Activity antecedents recovered from the Registry

Messaging systems

There are a range of messaging applications that are installed on computers that often provide useful digital evidence about the activities, contacts, and intentions of wrongdoers. Mobile phones are increasingly used for such communications, and this is described in more detail later in the chapter.

MSN Messenger, Skype, Yahoo! Messenger, and other web-based e-mail applications are a common feature on many computers. Chat rooms that appeared destined for the scrap heap have undergone a renaissance on computers, tablets, and mobile phones because of their ease of use and general convenience. Banter, for example, enables casual chatting with others who are nearby.

Social networking sites such as Facebook, Twitter, LinkedIn, Google+, Flickr, and Meetup are just a few of the sites available for users to meet friends, contacts, and others with similar interests. Other sites host chat rooms catering to every form of human interest and endeavor—and not all legal or in good taste.

Examining Skype and chat room artifacts

The following screenshot shows the file property sheet of recovered chat messages between a suspect and young persons through the social networking site **TeenChat** (`http://www.teenchat.com/`). The site is intended for use by adolescents, but its users are sometimes exploited by cyberstalkers and pedophiles:

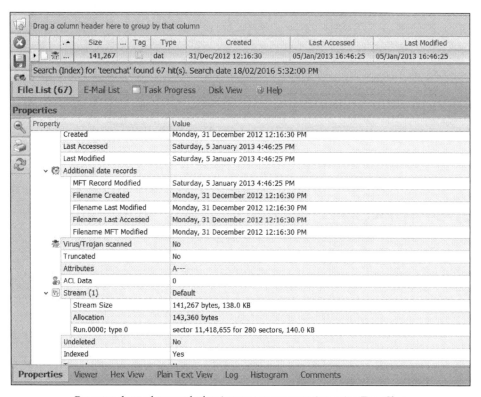

Property sheet of a record of an innocuous conversation using TeenChat

Data relating to chat rooms is often logged and conversations and an exchange of multimedia files may also remain on the device, despite attempts by wrongdoers to delete and remove incriminating evidence. Skype, by default, leaves a collection of spreadsheets that are helpful to the investigator. In the following screenshot, there are samples of files that contain records of conversations between various parties:

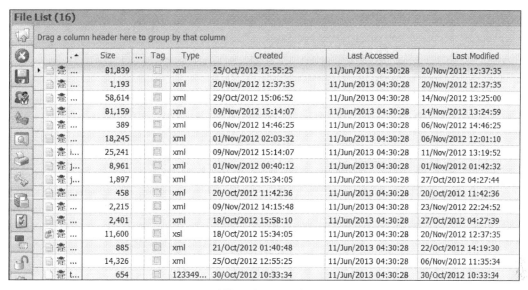

Recovered files relating to Skype activity

Often, attempts are made to delete or obfuscate these communications, and in doing so, the offender may assume that the records of conversations have been permanently destroyed. However, other parties to the conversations and responsible website-hosting services may retain some of the traffic data and will be obliged by law to share this with investigation teams.

To confound law enforcement investigations, offenders will adopt anti-forensics processes that were introduced in *Chapter 7, Windows and Other Operating Systems as Sources of Evidence*, including the use of the invisible Internet.

The invisible Internet

It is estimated that the World Wide Web is a small representation of networked sites, with the bulk, which some observers estimate to be well in excess of 90 percent, comprising what is termed the invisible Internet or the Deep Web. Search engines such as Google are incapable of recognizing and indexing its sites. Locating them requires some insider knowledge, a modicum of skill, and a web browser such as Tor.

The Dark Web, on the other hand, is not invisible, but the sites that host them in the background are, as they have been encrypted and hidden using special tools provided by Tor and I2P. The infamous Silk Road online drug-trafficking site used these tools to undertake its covert activities. Others use it for legitimate purposes but are keen to maintain their anonymity while browsing the web.

Obviously, locating remnants of these covert communications on devices is another challenge for practitioners, but remnants do in fact often get left behind. In the following screenshot, subject to rendition, ILookIX was able to recover some traces of Tor activity on a laptop. This information supported the likelihood that the suspect was covertly accessing illegal sex sites, among others, and was anxious for this to remain secret from other computer users. Regrettably, pedophile rings use the network to exchange illegal and obscene material and communicate with others in this disgusting traffic in the hope it will avoid detection and prosecution:

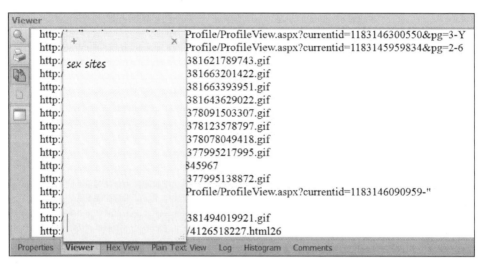

Browsing Dark Web websites for pornography

The following screenshot shows a sample of .TOR files recovered from another device. While many files were deleted and non-recoverable, some were extant and provided useful information confirming breaches of intellectual property relevant to the case.

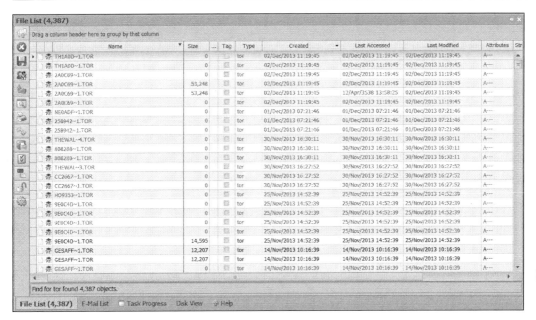

Recovered .TOR files revealing the use of Tor to download multimedia.

In many instances, not all of the data is readable, even using the inbuilt hex editor, and there is an absence of timestamps and the original file location. In this instance, BitTorrent activity has been recovered, providing details of the suspect using the BitTorrent peer-to-peer protocol to download media from other BitTorrent users. In this example, the timestamps of some of the activity are clearly visible as well as the nature of the media being downloaded:

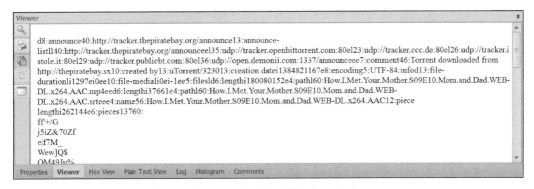

Recovered torrent download data from slack space

E-mail analysis and the processing of large e-mail databases

E-mail recovered from a desktop or laptop computer can hold substantial amounts of data, but e-mail stores held on network servers, even modest-sized stores, can hold numerous messages and attachments, requiring special programs to select and manage them properly. The following subsections further describe how these datasets are managed and how the practitioner may undertake a more efficacious approach to e-mail analysis and identification.

Recovering e-mails from desktop and laptop computers

In the following figure, ILookIX has deconstructed e-mail messages from a single account holding more than 28,000 e-mail messages and attachments. The files appear in a structure, reflecting the e-mail directory structure, files, and attachments as shown on the original device. This makes it easy for the practitioner to become oriented with the e-mail layout and gain a quick perspective of the mail system:

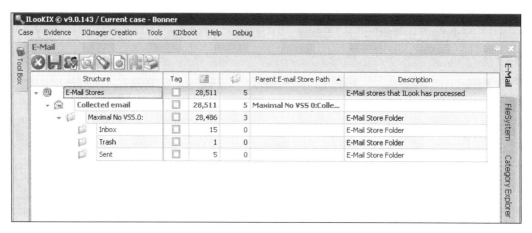

E-mail directory structure viewed in the ILookIX e-mail viewer

An **E-mail Stores** file is any file that contains e-mail messages or similar data, such as the calendar and contact information in a Microsoft Outlook .OST or .PST file. This includes .EML, .MSG, .NSF, .MBOX, .MBS, or even .HTML-based e-mails. Some e-mail stores, such as .EML or .MSG files, contain a single message per file, but even these files need to be deconstructed by ILookIX for them to appear in the e-mail explorer. Each e-mail store is listed as an entry in the e-mail explorer, whether the store contains a single message, such as a .EML or .MSG file, or a complete structure of messages in folders and subfolders. such as a .PST file.

An important concept that must be understood is the homogenous nature of all e-mail types supported in ILookIX. All e-mail client deconstructions become part of the same basic explorer e-mail concept. This removes the differences between clients so that functions such as e-mail links can be analyzed and explored in a new, much-easier-to-decipher interface. The interface provides an object model that encompasses all of the characteristics of an Internet e-mail item using the RFC standards that apply to all Internet e-mail send/receive clients. Within this process, items such as Lotus Notes are fitted into the same model as Outlook .OST files—this interface comprises the explorer bar for e-mail.

The e-mail explorer takes all of the e-mail stores, such as Microsoft Outlook's .PST files, and shows the folder structure for each. Inside the folder structure, the practitioner may view messages, contacts, attachments, and other items, depending on the type of mailbox processed. When working with files, e-mail messages are displayed in the **List Pane** by selecting an e-mail store or a subfolder in the store, as shown in the following screenshot:

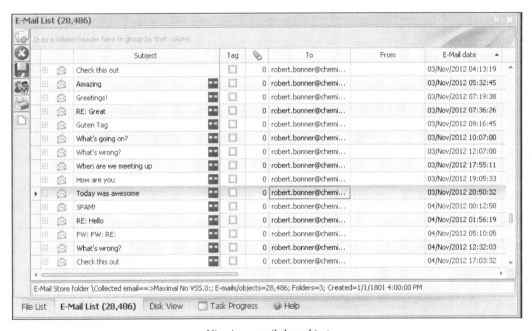

Viewing e-mails by subject

Messages may be viewed using **Viewer**, **Hex View**, or **Plain Text View**. In the following screenshot, the message and attachment is viewed in the **Viewer** pane:

Reading e-mails and attachments

E-mail file property sheets provide important file and metadata information about messages and are invaluable exports for case preparation:

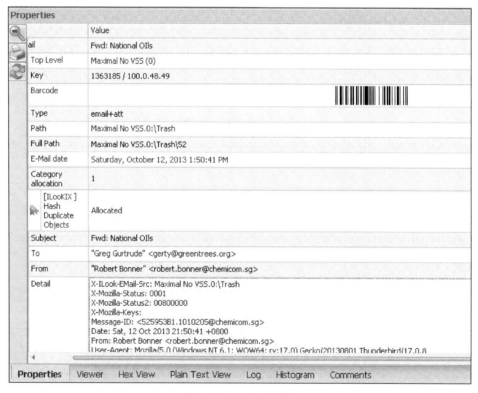

E-mail property sheet

Attachments to e-mail messages can be viewed by displaying the messages in the **E-Mail List** and then selecting the **File List**. Each message will have an icon associated with it in the leftmost column by default. This icon is either an envelope to denote an e-mail message with no attachment or a paper clip to denote a message with a file attachment, as shown here:

Checking e-mail attachment status

This will show all the files attached to the messages and allow the practitioner to work with them as a group, but it does not show the specific source of each attachment. By selecting the **E-Mail List**, the practitioner has more options for viewing attachments in the context of the messages to which they were originally attached:

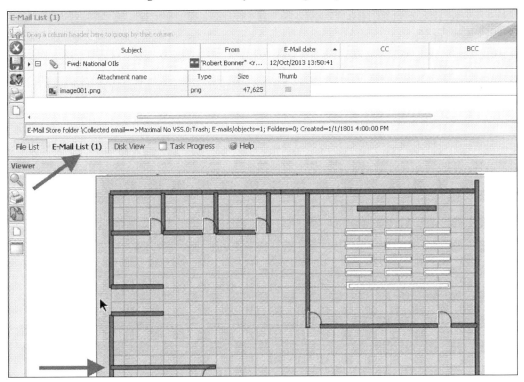

Viewing e-mail attachments

In addition, the attachment column shows the number of attachments for each individual message:

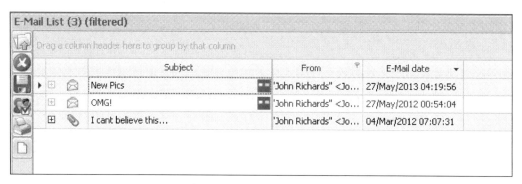

Headers, attachments, and e-mail body

ILookIX can also group and filter messages in the **E-Mail List**. Grouping allows the practitioner to take all messages displayed and group them by a single column. This can save time and enhance the cataloging of relevant evidence as the practitioner works through evidence selection:

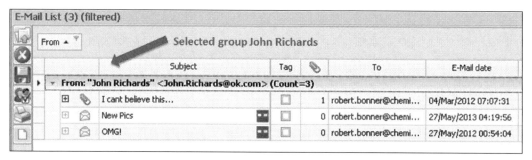

Cataloging e-mail evidence of potential relevance

E-mail messages can be included in the same categories as files or in separate categories specifically created for correspondence, as determined by the practitioner. Whole e-mail stores or subfolders therein can be added to categories by selecting the store or folder in the e-mail explorer and selecting **Save Messages to My Categories**:

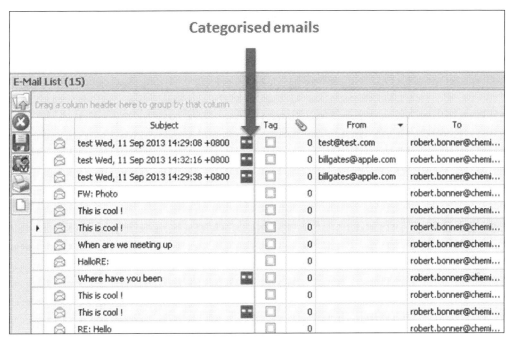

Categorizing e-mails of potential relevance

The categorized file(s) may be viewed in the **Category Explorer**, where they are collated for convenient access:

My categories	51,903	Categories you've created to allocate useful evidential material to
[ILooKIX] Hash Duplicate Objects	51,902	
Email of probative Value	1	

Good housekeeping seen by cataloging evidence of value during the selection process

Recovering and analyzing e-mails from larger datasets

As outlined in *Chapter 5, The Need for Enhanced Forensic Tools*, the ISeekDiscovery automaton is a distributed collection tool that captures **electronically stored information** (**ESI**) from unlimited populations of computers and digital storage. Unlike other tools, it harnesses its patented technology to use each targeted machine for processing with minimum impact on the user of that computer. ISeekDiscovery greatly improves ESI collection and has been enhanced for use by forensic examiners to enable live acquisition of data that traditional digital forensic tools would be unable to capture remotely in large-scale networks (including RAM and Windows Registry data).

To reiterate, the automaton only requires access to the device and appropriate designing of the configuration file; it collects only the evidence needed, thereby making endpoint analysis less daunting because of the smaller size of the dataset, which enhances filtering and searching for evidence. However, the extracted data may still be large and require substantial post-recovery processing.

The 32-bit and 64-bit APIs provided by XtremeForensics allow users to make use of companies' servers to extract large datasets from a .ISK evidence container. This is a relatively simple process of opening the application and logging on to our server, which then allows ISeekExtractor to commence the operation.

The extraction process provides a number of extraction style options:

- Original folders and filenames, discarding metadata
- Original folders and filenames, adding .XML metadata
- Numbered files with metadata in a .XML index

The API can be initialized in minutes using **Dynamic Link Library** (DLL) files and guided to facilitate the expeditious and secure transport of all captured data in an ISeekExplorer container into:

- Any database or review system intended for a basic review platform in current use
- Another file format suitable for import to any other system

This is especially time-saving when large sets of data have been captured from extensive network servers.

Searching for scanned files

Searching for scanned images may be done using the **Portable Scanned Images** tool provided by ILookIX, shown in the following screenshot. Locating scanned objects can be helpful in identifying those documents that cannot be indexed and searched because, during the scanning process, they were not converted using **optical character recognition** (OCR) to allow them to be indexed as text documents. These files may contain relevant information and so they may require manual viewing, or conversion through OCR processes if the number is too large.

The process is also useful for determining the provenance and authenticity of documents relating to forgeries and deception:

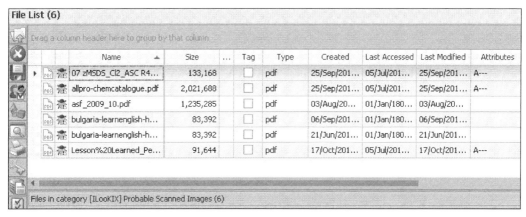

File List (6)										
Drag a column header here to group by that column										
	Name ▲	Size	...	Tag	Type	Created	Last Accessed	Last Modified	Attributes	
▶	07 zMSDS_Cl2_ASC R4...	133,168		☐	pdf	25/Sep/201...	05/Jul/201...	25/Sep/201...	A---	
	allpro-chemcatalogue.pdf	2,021,688		☐	pdf	25/Sep/201...	05/Jul/201...	25/Sep/201...	A---	
	asf_2009_10.pdf	1,235,285		☐	pdf	03/Aug/20...	01/Jan/180...	03/Aug/20...		
	bulgaria-learnenglish-h...	83,392		☐	pdf	06/Sep/201...	01/Jan/180...	06/Sep/201...		
	bulgaria-learnenglish-h...	83,392		☐	pdf	21/Jun/201...	01/Jan/180...	21/Jun/201...		
	Lesson%20Learned_Pe...	91,644		☐	pdf	17/Oct/201...	05/Jul/201...	17/Oct/201...	A---	

Files in category [ILooKIX] Probable Scanned Images (6)

Recovered scanned files ready for manual inspection

The growing challenge of evidence recovery from mobile phones and handheld devices

Digital evidence may come from a range of devices, including mobile phones, GPS navigation devices, printers, digital cameras and video recorders, voice recorders, Kindles, home security devices, motor vehicle computers, Xbox and Wii players, black-box flight recorders, and digital watches.

Mobile phones and other handheld devices store users' personal information, including call history, Internet browsing records, file downloads and uploads, geographical locations, text messages, e-mails, multimedia files, contact lists, calendar events, and private information. They also record the position of users if they have the positioning setting activated—all in all, a considerable amount of data that may assist an investigation. For example, stored information may reveal details of the user's contacts and details of their communications relating to some transgression as well as an insight into their motivation and mindset.

The following screenshot shows a report of items and deleted items regarding the activity of the phone user, including messages, calls, locations, and browsing activities:

View Statistics		
View	Items	Deleted Items
Device / Network Information	87	
Device / Event Log	598	340
Device / App Usage	4	
Device / Installed Apps	75	
Device / Keyboard Cache	8840	
Device / Accounts	95	
Contacts	1509	200
Calls	304	133
Calendar / Calendar Events	2	
Calendar / Tasks	1	
Calendar / Notes	28	18
Messages / SMS	9502	141
Messages / MMS	36	
Messages / Chat	12125	108
Messages / Status Updates	10	
Locations / History	630	
Locations / Searches	2	
Web / History	3189	4
Web / Bookmarks	117	4
Web / Searches	9	
Web / Cookies	2123	

Page : 2

Saturday, 1 August 2015   Summary

Web / Forms History	20	
Files / Pictures	43417	
Files / Audio	689	
Files / Videos	38	
Files / Documents	7641	
Files / Archives	31	
Files / Databases	499	
Files / Unrecognized	6996	2

A general forensic report of mobile phone accounts and files

However, mobile phones pose challenges to the forensic practitioner, especially with the rapid development of new phone types and operating systems with increased reliance on protection and encryption that effectively challenges evidence recovery. The rapid growth of mobile phones using different hardware and operating systems has made it difficult to develop a single process or tool to address all eventualities. In addition to a growing variety of smartphones and platforms, including Android, Blackberry, Apple iPhone, and Windows Mobile, there is a staggering range of inexpensive phones using legacy systems. The following section provides an outline of evidence recovery from mobile phones.

Extracting data from mobile devices

Evidence of different types of files is stored in mobile phones and may be found in several locations, including device memory, detachable memory such as SD cards, and removable SIM cards.

Each mobile phone is provided with a usually unique identifier known as the **International Mobile Station Equipment Identity (IMEI)** to uniquely identify a broad range of mobile phones. The unique number is normally printed inside the battery compartment or on the outside casing of the phone. It is also stored inside the embedded memory of the phone and, from there, may be displayed on the screen and recovered using forensic tools. The IMEI identifies and validates the phone hardware to a GSM network to prevent stolen phones from accessing that network. The IMEI is an important record of a phone's use and identity.

In the following screenshot, the XRY Micro Systemation forensic tool has extracted general information about an iPhone 4, including its IMEI number. The SIM identification number is recorded at the bottom of the report:

Forensic report of an iPhone 4 showing the basic device settings

[Subscribers are identified by another unique identifier: the IMEI number stored on the SIM card, which identifies and authenticates subscribers. This facilitates a practitioner liaising with the telephone network to obtain billing information, locations of calls, and contacts—all potential evidence.]

Among practitioners, it is considered best practice to document manual and technical processes used to access and recover evidence from mobile phones and to minimize any loss or changes to data. Android and Apple phones and a host of others store a significant amount of user information in SQLite databases—information which sometimes remains on the device after other information has been deleted. This can be a useful source of information, and forensic tools often recover a broad range of file types, including databases.

In the following screenshot, the mobile forensic tool NowSecure Mobile Forensics was used to recover information from an Android mobile phone. These new-generation tools organize the examination into a project so that all the recovered data is cataloged and may be analyzed with simple-to-use graphic interfaces:

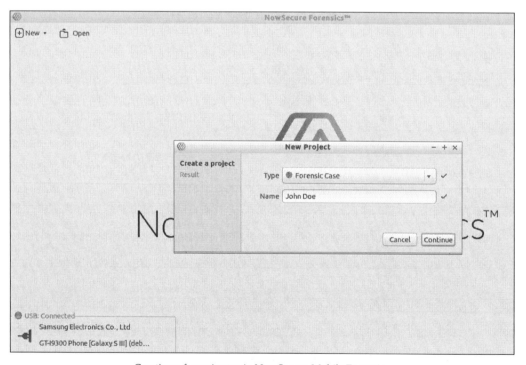

Creating a forensic case in NowSecure Mobile Forensics

The device under examination is a late-model Android and cannot be rooted to extract a physical dump, as shown in the following screenshot:

Options available to recover data from an Android phone

A logical extraction or backup of the device is available for analysis, and in this instance, a backup of the device was selected:

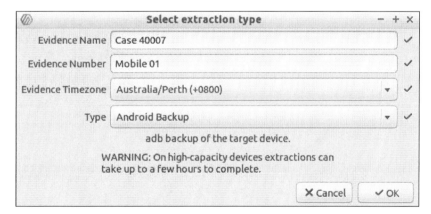

Preparing the forensic examination and inserting case details

Once the extraction is complete, the practitioner may select from a range of recovered categories of items, as shown here:

Directory in NowSecure Mobile Forensics of recovered data from an Android phone

In the following instance, an array of Internet browsing activity showing the title of the webpage, URLs, and timestamps is available to the practitioner:

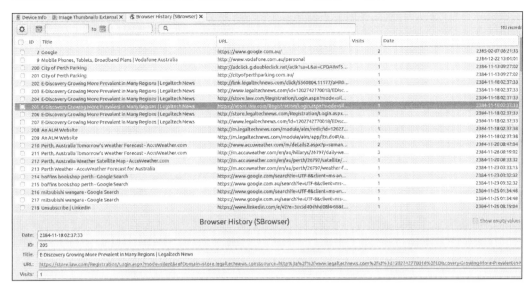

Recovered webpages, including titles, URLs, and timestamps

In the following screenshot, a list of downloaded files and the originating websites is shown with the associated timestamps:

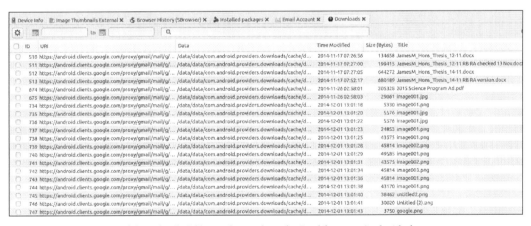

List of downloaded files and metadata obtained from an Android phone

In the next screenshot, the tool has recovered video and music files located on the external SD card housed in the phone:

View of data recovered from an attached SD card

A range of different applications were installed on the phone, and some of those can be seen in the following screenshot:

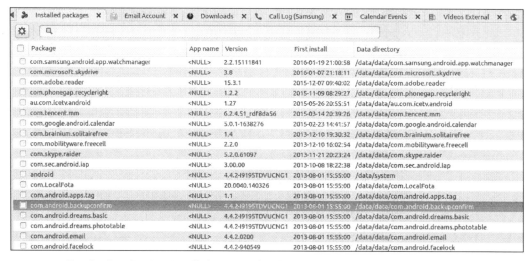

Details of applications installed on an Android phone and the dates of their installation

In the following crime simulation, XRY Micro Systemation has recovered some chat messages of an incriminating nature:

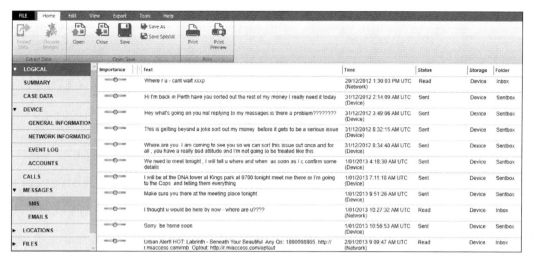

Record of SMS conversations, which can be traced back to caller and sender phones

E-mail may also be recovered from mobile phones, and the following simulation shows some communications between the suspect and his wife:

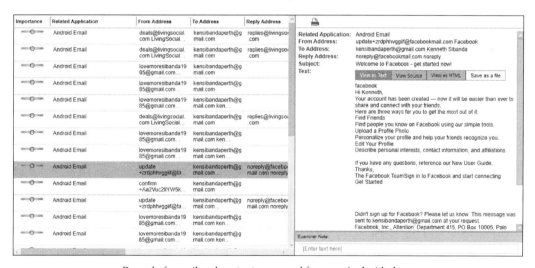

Record of e-mail and content recovered from an Android phone

General information about the suspect's iPhone 5 was recovered and reveals the IMEI and **International Mobile Subscriber Identity (IMSI)** numbers and general information about the phone:

General information obtained from an iPhone 5

In the following screenshot is a Google Map extraction, showing the specific location of the mobile phone on **23/12/2012**. In this simulation, it was possible to track the phone at its location in western Australia and then to another destination in Victoria on the eastern Australian seaboard. These records can be triangulated, with Telco information being recorded of the location of the device as it passes each cell tower while it is active. Records of its location when making and receiving calls can also be obtained:

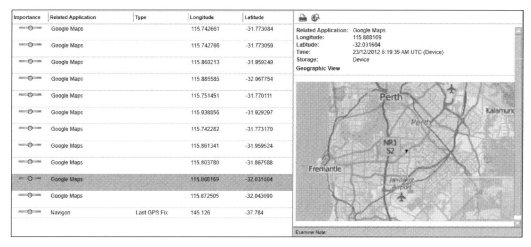

Recovered map showing the location of the phone

In the following screenshot, a new location has been recorded, showing the position of the phone approaching a major road intersection:

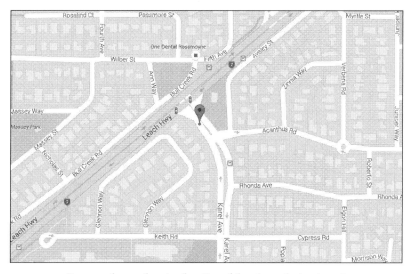

Recovered map showing location of the phone during transit

The following table is an extract of chat messages recorded on an iPhone that was used to rebut an allegation of rape by the spouse. It served as a record of conversation between the two parties showing a greater degree of friendliness and empathy than the victim had previously disclosed. The case was dismissed in a lower court:

Message	Time	Status	Folder	Deleted
Always	2011-01-15 07:52:40 (UTC)	Read	Inbox	Yes
U up for a phone call	2011-01-15 07:50:46 (UTC)	Sent	Sentbox	Yes
I home now.I doing ok	2011-01-15 07:45:10 (UTC)	Read	Inbox	Yes
How far away r u now?	2011-01-15 07:12:40 (UTC)	Sent	Sentbox	Yes
Yes but I will be coming straight back	2011-01-15 06:13:16 (UTC)	Sent	Sentbox	Yes
Well do u have 2 go bac 2moro?	2011-01-15 06:12:07 (UTC)	Read	Inbox	Yes
Don't know probably could do with a couple days rest	2011-01-15 06:10:50 (UTC)	Sent	Sentbox	Yes

Chat messages between spouses used as alibi evidence

In the following extract from a civil case over a disputed will, one chat message between the deceased and her spouse and a number of voicemail notifications recorded on the Nokia mobile phone were recovered. Regrettably, the phone did not provide any further information to assist either party to the dispute:

	Message	Time					
	Hey hope racing is going well. Just letting u no mindy is fine	19/08/2010 3:27:54 PM (+10:00)		Deleted	SIM	1	Incoming
	Call "101" you have 1 new Voice message(s).	19/08/2010 5:15:57 PM (+09:30)		Deleted	SIM	2	Incoming
	Call "101" you have 1 new Voice message(s).	5/08/2010 11:09:25 AM (+08:00)		Deleted	SIM	3	Incoming
	Call "101" you have 1 new Voice message(s).	30/07/2010 3:13:27 PM (+08:00)		Deleted	SIM	4	Incoming

Chat messages and voicemail notifications relating to a civil dispute over the deceased's will

Mobile devices store information and system and application files on solid-state drives, which are small, compact, and physically durable. This format is similar to that of tablet devices and small laptops or netbooks such as Windows Surface Pro, Apple's MacBook Air and Asus netbooks. This and the security encryption of these devices is presently making it problematic to image the devices during a bootup process. A research team associated with me is presently working on a solution and has had some success in making logical copies of Apple desktops and Window's Surface Pro laptops using ISeek technology to recover evidence otherwise difficult to locate and recover.

Mobile phones and tablets are heavily restricted in the amount of data they can store, on average holding a mere 32 to 64 gigabytes of data. The deletion processes on these drives use wear leveling to ensure efficient removal of data in order to maximize the life of the drive. That means that although deleted data may not be evident, it may persist longer on the device, potentially offering more chance of recovery using a physical dump of the deleted sectors. Conversely, the wear leveling and delete feature tends to activate when the phone is switched on and therefore this should be avoided post seizure. Physical extractions from Android phones and iPhones have been thwarted by the security of the devices and unwillingness of phone vendors to assist practitioners in their legitimate endeavors to recover evidence.

Law enforcement agencies process large amounts of telephone intercept data as well as compiling databases of suspects and organized crime syndicates. Processing data recovered from a single device can be time-consuming, but processing a larger number of phones to reconstruct crime events and relationships between suspects is even more so. Sophisticated forensic tools such as Cellebrite and XRY Micro Systemation can filter out irrelevant material from these large collections. These and other tools create relationship diagrams and timelines that assist in reconstructing criminal activities and speedily identifying groups of critical evidence.

Modern mobile forensic tools offer a range of labor-saving functions, such as preparing relationship matrices, reports, data collation reports, and timelines. The timeline shown in the following screenshot, produced by the NewSecure ViaExtract forensic tool, assists the practitioner in overviewing the nature of evidence and key events and filtering data to create meaningful timelines:

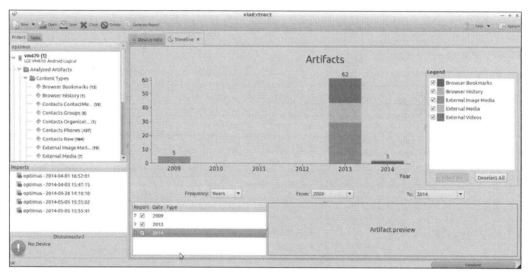

Timeline of key activities recovered from a mobile phone

Some mobile forensics tools, such as MobileEdit, can retrieve mobile backup files from computers used to synchronize iPhones that have passcode-access security enabled. The iTunes application installed on a computer is intended to synchronize music but, by default, the application stores lockdown files of the previously connected iPhone. This is a handy process to use if the phone passcode is unknown but the practitioner has access to the computer or Mac that was used to previously synchronize the specific iPhone. By locating and copying the `lockdown.plist` file, it can be used with the forensic tool to access a locked iPhone.

These iTunes folders are typically stored at the following locations:

* Windows 10: `C:\ProgramData\Apple\Lockdown`
* Mac OS X: `/var/db/lockdown`

Other tools are capable of recovering user access PIN codes by brute force attacks and can also identify the screen swipe access path to allow access to a locked phone.

Managing evidence contamination

Conventional dead imaging of desktop devices is possible but usually impractical for mobile phones. Removing the internal drive is technically challenging and increasingly impractical. External devices and SIM cards, however, may be removed and the contents copied and analyzed with the appropriate tools.

Care should be taken to isolate a mobile phone to prevent it communicating with its telephone provider and local Wi-Fi and Bluetooth services. Removal of the SIM card prevents communication with the telephone provider, but if the device is switched on during recovery, then it is wise to do so in a laboratory insulated from wireless communications—a Faraday bag or container is another favorite protection option. Using the device's flight mode will also isolate the phone from interference, but the practitioner needs to locate this feature speedily to prevent interference.

Mobile phone operating systems can be adversely affected by low battery levels and extremes of temperature, dust, and humidity. It is not uncommon for a device to fail or its connection points to corrode or be affected by static electricity charges causing connection problems.

Mobile phones and certain other handheld devices can be remotely accessed by their owners to locate a lost or stolen device and also to "kill" the phone by deleting private information and resetting it to its factory default state or permanently locking the phone. This may frustrate the thief but it also prevents the practitioner from recovering evidence.

There are some differences, although these are tending to become more blurred, between recovering data from desktop and laptop computers and handheld devices, most notably the following:

- The devices are connected to communications networks such as telecommunication systems and Wi-Fi and Bluetooth connections
- Information stored on the devices can be lost completely as it is susceptible to being overwritten by new data or remote destruction commands it receives over wireless networks

Additionally, to extract information from a mobile device, the device must be switched on to enable live evidence recovery. This may result in the contamination or destruction of some data stored on the device. Forensic tools will often place a small executable file on the device and may also include some alteration to developer options on Android devices, for example. In the following diagram, the developer options of an Android phone are being manually changed before pairing with the forensic software and computer:

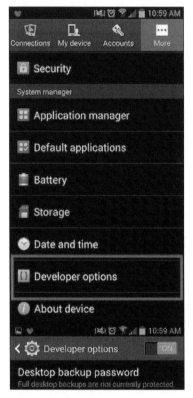

Preparing an Android phone for pairing with the forensic tool

In the following example, the settings of an Android phone have been manually modified to permit forensic recovery of the phone data:

An Android phone being paired with the forensic tool

As seen in the following screenshot, the forensic tool is commencing the pairing process with an iPhone:

An iPhone being paired with the forensic tool

Concealing illegal activities

While law enforcement agencies have successfully prosecuted many criminals using digital evidence recovered from mobile phones, the trend is now reversing. Mobile phones are strongly encrypted and some RIM Blackberry and burner phones are so well protected that it is often not possible to recover any evidence. Some criminals use multiple SIM cards and/or prepaid mobile devices that are used for short periods. This effectively denies practitioners access to any billing or other tracking information associated with normal usage that is provided by telephone network providers:

A RIM BlackBerry 9320 Curve, typically used for secure covert e-mailing

Extracting mobile data from the cloud

The cloud is also becoming a valuable source of digital evidence from mobile phone backup storage as well as social media accounts, such as Facebook, Twitter, and Kik. Cellebrite, for example, provides a forensic process capable of recovering private user data from these types of sites under appropriate legal sanction. This includes logging in to these user accounts with user identification and passwords previously retrieved from other data held by suspects. The process protects the recovered data from contamination during the recovery process and holds it in a forensic state for further examination.

Analyzing GPS devices and other handheld devices

GPS networks are used to navigate and look at various global locations. They form an essential part of mobile phone features, as described previously, and are now commonly installed in the dashboard of motor vehicles, replacing the standalone units attached to windscreens or holders.

Handheld devices, including satellite phones, tablets, and netbooks, also store a limited amount of historical information about the locations visited by the device and timestamps showing that the device was at a specific location. The EXIF data posted to social media sites can also contain information about approximately where the photograph was taken. More advanced mobile forensic tools can verify whether the photograph was taken on the mobile device using what is called **camera ballistics processes**. Digital book readers, such as Kindle, are also subject to forensic examination as they have been found to conceal evidentiary material.

Obtaining data from tablets and other handhelds is relatively straightforward and similar to computers and mobile phones. They provide useful data for evidence reconstruction. GPS devices are becoming more problematic to retrieve data from, particularly those inbuilt in vehicle dashboards. More often than not, the device provides no more data than the home location and locations keyed in as potential destinations. They do not generally record the journey and any meaningful chronology of the journey, but they can add to an investigation by corroborating mobile phone records and Telco logging.

Case study – mobile phone evidence in a bomb hoax

This case study further exemplifies how digital evidence should always be corroborated, verified whenever possible, and certainly never taken at face value.

The defendant in the case was charged with serious offences under telecommunications legislation relating to sending a text message to the defendant's father, claiming that a bomb would detonate at the school attended by one of the defendant's siblings. The threat was reported to the local police, who in turn evacuated the school as a safety measure. A search of the school confirmed that the threat was probably a hoax, but it still was a very serious matter. Unfortunately, these hoaxes are all too common, and, in light of attacks on schools by extortionists, extremists, and persons with serious mental health issues, are always taken seriously by law enforcement and affected parties. However, they are so frequent that one can hardly blame first responders from occasionally adopting a blasé approach in apprehending the perpetrators of these hoaxes.

Prior to the incident, the defendant had been receiving a number of vexatious and sinister text messages on their mobile phone. The messages were partly written in English and partly in another Asian language. They seemed to refer to a former lover who then resided in another country. They also made derogatory comments about the defendant's fiancée, who also started receiving similar text messages.

The defendant, looking more like a victim at this point in time, received a number of sinister text messages on the mobile phone, and a sample of these is shown in the following table:

Number	Name	Message	Time
+614xxxxxxxx		Wheres xxx	8/06/2012 7:44:12 PM
+614xxxxxxxx		Ur not xxx i dont want anything from you	8/06/2012 7:46:32 PM
+614xxxxxxxx		Coz i know xxx,and i know ur not her, dont dupe me	8/06/2012 7:49:36 PM
+614xxxxxxxx		Just tell me wheres xxx	8/06/2012 7:53:26 PM
+614xxxxxxxx		hi	8/06/2012 8:08:04 PM
+614xxxxxxxx		Hello	8/06/2012 8:10:45 PM
+614xxxxxxxx		Hi	8/06/2012 8:12:26 PM
+614xxxxxxxx		I told u iam zzz,tell me wheres xxx and ill stop	8/06/2012 8:42:11 PM
+614xxxxxxxx		Dnt try to hide xxx from xxx iam gonna kill her.	8/06/2012 8:44:14 PM
+614xxxxxxxx		Im in the front of ur housewatching over you	12/06/2012 7:07:22 AM
+614xxxxxxxx		Trying to find me?	12/06/2012 7:14:13 AM
+614xxxxxxxx		Open the light and u'll c me	12/06/2012 7:16:19 AM
+614xxxxxxxx		Getting scared?	12/06/2012 7:30:39 AM
+614xxxxxxxx		Knock knock whos there?its me ur destiny	12/06/2012 7:35:21 AM
+614xxxxxxxx		Open the door	12/06/2012 7:38:45 AM
+614xxxxxxxx		Let me in plz	12/06/2012 7:41:35 AM
+614xxxxxxxx		No battery no carhahahah	12/06/2012 10:42:28 AM
+614xxxxxxxx		Cant even go to the cops	12/06/2012 10:43:14 AM
+614xxxxxxxx		Cant do anything just to stay in the house	12/06/2012 12:09:03 PM
+614xxxxxxxx		U got ur friend huh!!!!!	12/06/2012 10:44:02 AM
+614xxxxxxxx		I put something in your car.....so use it carefully,bomb	12/06/2012 11:55:41 AM
+614xxxxxxxx		One and half our to go tictoc tictoc tictoc	12/06/2012 3:11:49 PM
+614xxxxxxxx		30 minutes and i saw zzz walkingwearing voda jacket	12/06/2012 3:57:39 PM
+614xxxxxxxx		R u trying to run away from me?ur dead	12/06/2012 5:28:10 PM
+614xxxxxxxx		When r u gonna go back to your house,you can run but	12/06/2012 7:09:02 PM
+614xxxxxxxx		I know where you are now ur in ur bf's house 6 brockmil	12/06/2012 9:06:31 PM
+614xxxxxxxx		U cant run but u can hide from me	13/06/2012 9:11:58 AM
+614xxxxxxxx		Ur dead to me when i see ypu	13/06/2012 9:12:13 AM
+614xxxxxxxx		Im not joking i can do it	13/06/2012 9:12:28 AM
+614xxxxxxxx		Ur really dead	13/06/2012 9:12:35 AM
+614xxxxxxxx		Im just in front	13/06/2012 9:12:48 AM
+614xxxxxxxx		And i can see ur dad	13/06/2012 9:12:53 AM
+614xxxxxxxx		I can see ur family	13/06/2012 9:21:29 AM
+614xxxxxxxx		U left xxx alone in the house	13/06/2012 9:35:59 AM
+614xxxxxxxx		Wrong move	13/06/2012 9:36:03 AM
+614xxxxxxxx		Im not gonna leave here	13/06/2012 11:44:32 AM
+614xxxxxxxx		Ur inay inay	13/06/2012 11:44:43 AM
+614xxxxxxxx		Chicken treat xyz	13/06/2012 5:36:38 PM

The defendant's and their fiancée's responses to the messages seemed to goad the caller to make or send more threatening messages, including the following messages extracted from the fiancée's phone:

From	To	Message	Time
+614xxxxxxxx		xxx is hiding to your house u better be	12/06/2012 1:15:54 PM UTC (Network)
+614xxxxxxxx		Why did u try to hide xxx? Im just	12/06/2012 1:25:36 PM UTC (Network)
+614xxxxxxxx		They left xxx alone in the house	13/06/2012 1:37:26 AM UTC (Network)
+614xxxxxxxx		Y did u set me up to the police ur dead	14/06/2012 1:13:33 PM UTC (Network)
+614xxxxxxxx		Wheres xxx now	14/06/2012 8:07:55 PM UTC (Network)
+614xxxxxxxx		Wheres xxx now	14/06/2012 8:07:55 PM UTC (Network)
+614xxxxxxxx		You wont be able to catch me im just	15/06/2012 10:25:05 AM UTC (Network)
+614xxxxxxxx		Ohhhhh cctv camera im scared	15/06/2012 12:39:08 PM UTC (Network)
+614xxxxxxxx		Go run and hide but i can still catch	15/06/2012 12:46:36 PM UTC (Network)
+614xxxxxxxx		Im riding on the bus	15/06/2012 12:46:44 PM UTC (Network)
+614xxxxxxxx		Hahah didnt catch me mga idiots!!!!	15/06/2012 1:27:40 PM UTC (Network)
+614xxxxxxxx		Y theres a police outside	15/06/2012 1:40:02 PM UTC (Network)
+614xxxxxxxx		U r all dead to me !!! I will see u in the	15/06/2012 9:24:42 PM UTC (Network)
+614xxxxxxxx		Ohhh xxx is the only one at home	16/06/2012 2:41:04 AM UTC (Network)
+614xxxxxxxx		Check ur house	16/06/2012 5:17:15 AM UTC (Network)
+614xxxxxxxx		Nice car zzz	16/06/2012 9:23:00 AM UTC (Network)
+614xxxxxxxx		Y r u calling me?	16/06/2012 12:27:58 PM UTC (Network)
+614xxxxxxxx		I will see u in church tomorrow	16/06/2012 3:33:00 PM UTC (Network)
+614xxxxxxxx		Ur gonna pay for evwrything	17/06/2012 12:13:12 AM UTC (Network)
+614xxxxxxxx		I put something under xxx's bed	17/06/2012 12:31:39 AM UTC (Network)
+614xxxxxxxx		Ur dad is keep on watching me on ur	17/06/2012 1:14:29 AM UTC (Network)
+614xxxxxxxx		U gave xxx back to me	17/06/2012 12:46:08 PM UTC (Network)
+614xxxxxxxx		Oh xxx went back home already i saw	17/06/2012 1:15:38 PM UTC (Network)
+614xxxxxxxx		xxx is gonna be alone again :-)	17/06/2012 3:38:38 PM UTC (Network)
+614xxxxxxxx		xxx is so beautiful whn shes sleeping	18/06/2012 12:01:08 AM UTC (Network)
+614xxxxxxxx		Im gonna kidnap her	18/06/2012 12:28:33 AM UTC (Network)
+614xxxxxxxx		Where is ur brother going?	18/06/2012 12:36:55 AM UTC (Network)
+614xxxxxxxx		Theres a bomb on ur brothers school	18/06/2012 2:22:12 AM UTC (Network)

Later messages to the fiancée implied a bomb threat and other sinister actions:

From	To	Message	Time
+614xxxxxxx (2nd phone)		Cant catch me?!	29/06/2012 3:18:40 AM UTC (Network)
+614xxxxxxx (2nd phone)		Poor xxx :-(	29/06/2012 3:19:16 AM UTC (Network)
+614xxxxxxx (2nd phone)		Set	29/06/2012 3:19:57 AM UTC (Network)
+614xxxxxxx (2nd phone)		One press and boom	29/06/2012 3:20:13 AM UTC (Network)
+614xxxxxxx (2nd phone)		Pretty	29/06/2012 3:20:28 AM UTC (Network)
+614xxxxxxx (2nd phone)		Tiktok tiktok on (location)	29/06/2012 3:20:44 AM UTC (Network)
+614xxxxxxx (2nd phone)		Dont run! Dont hide i will still catch	29/06/2012 3:21:03 AM UTC (Network)
+614xxxxxxx (2nd phone)		Im back again	5/07/2012 8:05:31 AM UTC (Network)
+614xxxxxxx (2nd phone)		Idiots	5/07/2012 8:35:11 AM UTC (Network)
+614xxxxxxx (2nd phone)		U cant catch me	5/07/2012 8:35:28 AM UTC (Network)
+614xxxxxxx (2nd phone)		Y da heck u put camera r u trying to	5/07/2012 9:49:05 AM UTC (Network)

The tone of these messages became even more bizarre and intimidating:

From	To	Message	Time
=A44+614xxxxxxxx (2nd phone)		I got xxx's phone and i put it back in	6/07/2012 3:39:04 AM UTC (Network)
	+614xxxxxxxx (2nd phon	Prove it	6/07/2012 3:42:55 AM UTC (Device)
	+614xxxxxxxx (2nd phon	Far out man your terrible	6/07/2012 5:12:06 AM UTC (Device)
+614xxxxxxxx (2nd phone)		U cant catch me right? BecUse the	9/07/2012 4:19:58 AM UTC (Network)
	+614xxxxxxxx (2nd phon	Prove it	9/07/2012 4:20:46 AM UTC (Device)
	+614xxxxxxxx (2nd phon	No proff	9/07/2012 4:49:46 AM UTC (Device)
+614xxxxxxxx (2nd phone)		I have prof	9/07/2012 4:50:09 AM UTC (Network)
	+614xxxxxxxx (2nd phon	Where is it?	9/07/2012 4:50:53 AM UTC (Device)
+614xxxxxxxx (2nd phone)		Its im my hands	9/07/2012 4:51:53 AM UTC (Network)
+614xxxxxxxx (2nd phone)		And i can set up one of u again like	9/07/2012 4:52:29 AM UTC (Network)
	+614xxxxxxxx (2nd phon	U cant do anything all u do is talk	9/07/2012 4:54:04 AM UTC (Device)
+614xxxxxxxx (2nd phone)		I will show u	9/07/2012 4:55:16 AM UTC (Network)
+614xxxxxxxx (2nd phone)		Even you cant do anything right	9/07/2012 4:56:21 AM UTC (Network)
+614xxxxxxxx (2nd phone)		I know you have so many secrets	9/07/2012 4:57:26 AM UTC (Network)
	+614xxxxxxxx (2nd phon	I have nothing to hide, all u do is show	9/07/2012 4:58:40 AM UTC (Device)
+614xxxxxxxx (2nd phone)		How come that i set up xxx into this	9/07/2012 5:00:09 AM UTC (Network)
+614xxxxxxxx (2nd phone)		Poor you!!!!!!	9/07/2012 7:47:16 AM UTC (Network)
+614xxxxxxxx (2nd phone)		R u scared at me?	9/07/2012 7:48:32 AM UTC (Network)
+614xxxxxxxx (2nd phone)		Im gonna kidnap her	9/07/2012 8:02:27 AM UTC (Network)
+614xxxxxxxx (2nd phone)		Ur such a dick	9/07/2012 8:20:58 AM UTC (Network)
+614xxxxxxxx (2nd phone)		Everybody is suffering because of	9/07/2012 8:33:24 AM UTC (Network)

And they continued in a similar vein:

From	To	Message	Time
+614xxxxxxx (2nd phone)		I got evedence that the police is our	10/07/2012 4:06:03 AM UTC (Network)
+614xxxxxxx (2nd phone)		I will show all i asked them to do a	10/07/2012 4:06:41 AM UTC (Network)
+614xxxxxxx (2nd phone)		So lawyer will be distructed	10/07/2012 4:06:59 AM UTC (Network)
+614xxxxxxx (2nd phone)		Do u know hu i am?	10/07/2012 4:09:37 AM UTC (Network)
+614xxxxxxx (2nd phone)		abcde clue number 1	10/07/2012 4:10:36 AM UTC (Network)
+614xxxxxxx (2nd phone)		Kawawa	10/07/2012 4:16:08 AM UTC (Network)
	+614xxxxxxxx (2nd phon	U dont phase me	10/07/2012 4:16:27 AM UTC (Device)
+614xxxxxxx (2nd phone)		Huh	10/07/2012 4:17:26 AM UTC (Network)
+614xxxxxxx (2nd phone)		July 20 is xxxs court trial i will be	10/07/2012 4:18:18 AM UTC (Network)
	+614xxxxxxxx (2nd phon	Look it up in the dictionary... Simple	10/07/2012 4:18:33 AM UTC (Device)
+614xxxxxxx (2nd phone)		No im good at it its ok i dont need to	10/07/2012 4:19:17 AM UTC (Network)
+614xxxxxxx (2nd phone)		Ur the reason of everybodys suffering	10/07/2012 4:20:58 AM UTC (Network)
+614xxxxxxx (2nd phone)		<Share Audio via GO	10/07/2012 4:22:53 AM UTC (Network)
	+614xxxxxxxx (2nd phon	Like i said simple things u cant	10/07/2012 4:23:01 AM UTC (Device)
+614xxxxxxx (2nd phone)		Like u said? Ur not human ur just some	10/07/2012 4:24:18 AM UTC (Network)
	+614xxxxxxxx (2nd phon	Big words for sum1 who understands	10/07/2012 4:25:12 AM UTC (Device)
+614xxxxxxx (2nd phone)		And big word who doesn understand	10/07/2012 4:25:57 AM UTC (Network)
	+614xxxxxxxx (2nd phon	Noone is suffering, although id pray	10/07/2012 4:27:42 AM UTC (Device)
+614xxxxxxx (2nd phone)		Really? Not if u keep them suffering	10/07/2012 4:28:56 AM UTC (Network)
+61424631297		No1 loves u anymore	10/07/2012 4:29:26 AM UTC (Network)
	+614xxxxxxxx (2nd phon	The only one suffering will b u	10/07/2012 4:29:38 AM UTC (Device)
+614xxxxxxx (2nd phone)		Im not because the police are on my	10/07/2012 4:30:19 AM UTC (Network)
	+614xxxxxxxx (2nd phon	The Lord on ours	10/07/2012 4:30:55 AM UTC (Device)
+614xxxxxxx (2nd phone)		So am i	10/07/2012 4:31:32 AM UTC (Network)
+614xxxxxxx (2nd phone)		U not good at all	10/07/2012 4:31:47 AM UTC (Network)
+614xxxxxxx (2nd phone)		Bitch	10/07/2012 4:32:11 AM UTC (Network)
+614xxxxxxx (2nd phone)		They are suffering because of you	10/07/2012 4:33:06 AM UTC (Network)
+614xxxxxxx (2nd phone)		Clue no.2 (phone number)	10/07/2012 4:33:52 AM UTC (Network)

At this point, the defendant made a complaint to the local police about these messages and an apparent burglary at their parents' family home that the defendant shared with a younger sibling. The complaint was recorded and the police visited the home, but they noted that while the defendant's bedroom had been ransacked, nothing had evidently been stolen.

The following day, a bomb threat message was received by the defendant's father, and police took possession of the defendant's father's mobile phone and were later able to identify the subscriber number of the caller. The telephone provider provided a log of calls made between the phone and other contacts, which was restricted to the phones belonging to the defendant, the fiancée, and the father. The phone's IMEI and SIM card IMSI numbers were identified, and further inquiry confirmed that the handset belonged to the defendant, although the SIM card was purchased without identification being provided (not an uncommon occurrence).

A search of the defendant's bedroom (previously burgled) located the handset underneath the defendant's bed. As it transpired, the handset was an old phone that the defendant had purchased and later replaced with a newer model. Consequently, the defendant was questioned and then arrested, and prosecution action commenced. However, the motivation of the defendant, a respectable office worker, was not established — unusual, considering the background circumstances. Moreover, none of the preceding events leading up to the data of the bomb threat were heeded by the police, and I was engaged to seek the truth of the matter.

A reconstruction of the crime commenced with a comparison of the available prosecution evidence with the findings of defense investigation. There was no doubt as to the text message being sent from the seized handset that belonged to the defendant, but no SIM card was ever recovered. The defendant was linked to the crime by the handset, the text messages recorded on it, and the corroborating information provided by the telecommunications provider — strong evidence, but not necessarily conclusive, for motivation for the crime seemed lacking.

The following concerns were raised to the prosecutor by me through the defense legal team:

- The discovery facts provided by the prosecution were lacking essential information for the defense team to make a reasonable examination of the evidence
- There was no forensic report made of the defendant's new phone or the fiancée's phone, which contained exculpatory evidence
- Details of the forensic tools and processes used to extract data from the seized mobile phones were not provided
- Copies of the actual forensic files of the seized phones obtained through these processes were not shared in full
- Details of any Wi-Fi connectivity recovered from any of the phones were not checked and provided to the defense team

- No details were provided of any GPS location data that may have been recovered from the perpetrator's phone, particularly relevant to the time the threatening texts were sent at

- No details were provided of the recorded location of the seized mobile phone to determine its location through connections to telephone towers during the period from the commencement of the sinister and threatening calls received by the defendant and other parties

The last point raised was important to answer so as to determine the location of the person who sent the bomb threat message and compare that with the location of the defendant's phone, which was active at the same time the bomb threat message was sent. The defendant claimed to be in a distant suburb at the time of the threat and had a sound and independent alibi to support the claim. If it could be shown that the threat had been sent from another location, which seemed plausible, then it could be inferred that the defendant did not have possession of the phone at the critical time.

Within a day of the prosecution being made aware of these concerns, the charges against the defendant were unexpectedly withdrawn without reason being provided. Not wishing to be overly critical of the agency involved in this case, there seemed to have been some systemic problems not uncommon with the handling of digital evidence. Certainly, the prosecution investigation was defective, incomplete, and too narrowly focused on obtaining a quick conviction at a lower court to settle what the officers may have decided was a routine nuisance call. Sloppy police work contributed to the low standard of the investigation, resulting in an overreliance on the devices seized and a failure to note or consider other digital and witness evidence.

It is unclear who the actual culprit was, but the following observations seemed to suggest it was the defendant's younger sibling, in that:

- He had access to the defendant's bedroom and could have removed and later replaced the incriminating phone under the bed after sending the threat

- He spoke the foreign language fluently and had an intimate knowledge of the insides of the family home and the movements of family members, as reflected in the text messages

- He suffered some form of mental illness and had a low intellect that seemed to be reflected in some of the text messages

- He disliked the fiancée and was obsessively possessive about his parents and the defendant

In effect, he had the means, motive, and opportunity to implicate the defendant. Curiously, the defendant appeared reluctant to provide all but the phone evidence and appeared to be protecting the sibling. That is speculation, but highly plausible, with some grounds for believing the defendant was hoping the digital evidence could successfully overturn the case without implicating the sibling.

This was an unusual case, which you may find intriguing, and while it does provide a sample of a real case, it leads on to the next chapter, which will focus on the ever-important forensic rule: seek the truth, be led by all the evidence, and do not let investigator bias hide the truth.

Summary

This chapter provided some of the key processes for locating and recovering digital evidence relating to records of personal communications, including e-mails and browsing records stored on computer devices and telephonic communications stored on mobile phones. It outlined the recovery and searching of Internet browsing records and other messaging systems, including Skype. It described in more detail the processes of e-mail analysis and recovery.

Mobile phone forensics was introduced and its importance in forensic examinations along with the growing challenge of evidence acquisition from personal computing devices and GPS devices was explained. The case study provided an insight into some of the key issues with mobile phone evidence. It described the pitfalls of investigators with a poor understanding of the complexity of mobile phone forensics and an overreliance on assumptions about the circumstances surrounding the case.

Chapter 9, *Validating the Evidence*, will reflect on the fundamentals of digital evidence analysis: a thorough examination of the evidence to test its authenticity, relevance, and reliability. You will further recognize and appreciate the importance of the scientific examination of digital devices and evidence to ensure that the best forensic practice is maintained.

In particular, the next chapter will describe some common pitfalls that diminish the value of digital forensics through cursory and biased examinations. A case study will showcase the importance of sound evidence selection and analysis as well as emphasizing the importance of impartiality in selecting evidence to ensure that the courts' expectations are met. Validating the evidence to determine its relevance and authenticity in anticipation of it being tendered in legal proceedings relies on testing and checking the evidence to ensure it is what it purports to be. This includes a more structured analysis of the evidence collected, including the development and testing of hypotheses and counter-arguments in line with forensic standards.

9

Validating the Evidence

The absence of a clear model of digital evidence validation is one of a number of fundamental weaknesses confronting practitioners in the emerging discipline of digital forensics. "Every case is unique!" is a common cry. Well, yes indeed, but there are so many characteristics common to most cases, and that common knowledge can be used better than it is and on a wider scale.

This chapter reflects on the fundamental idea of digital evidence analysis, which is to ensure that irrespective of the circumstances of a case and any prohibitions imposed on a practitioner, as thorough as possible an examination of the evidence is undertaken to test its authenticity, relevance, and reliability.

This chapter describes some common pitfalls that diminish the admissibility of digital evidence as well as affecting the evidentiary weight or value of evidence that has been tendered. Validating evidence relies on testing and checking it to ensure it is what it purports to be. This requires a structured analysis of the evidence collected, including the development and testing of hypotheses and counterarguments in line with forensic standards. Practitioners need to justify their selection of the evidence based on some rational reasoning process that is explainable and free from bias or unsupported comment.

Presenting complex technical evidence to laypersons during hearings in terms they understand is the culmination of many forensic examinations and the endeavor and expertise of the practitioner. Testifying in court requires composure and clarity of careful preparation, and certainty of the evidence is crucial. This book is not intended to be a definitive guide for providing expert witnesses with a mass of advice; that is far too complicated an issue; you are referred to the following repository to find out more:

```
http://legal.thomsonreuters.com.au/expert-evidence-individual-
technical-chapters/productdetail/118878.
```

The case study at the end of the chapter will showcase the importance of sound evidence selection and analysis. It will emphasize the importance of impartiality in selecting evidence to ensure that the courts' expectations are met.

The chapter outlines the difficulty in validating digital evidence and offers some solutions to address the problem. It will describe and discuss the following:

- The nature and problem of unsound digital evidence
- The importance of impartiality and objectivity in selecting digital evidence to meet legal expectations
- The structured analysis of the evidence collected, including the development and testing of hypotheses and counter-arguments in line with forensic standards
- Formalizing the validation process and solutions for best practice
- The presentation of digital evidence
- Ethical issues confronting digital forensics practitioners
- A case study describing the problem and offering tips for the forensic practitioner

The nature and problem of unsound digital evidence

Evidence tendered in legal hearings must meet the expectations of the court. The validity of digital evidence must be tested to determine its admissibility in legal cases in the same way as other established forms of evidence are verified.

As outlined in *Chapter 3, The Nature and Special Properties of Digital Evidence,* for evidence to be admissible in a hearing, it must meet three conditions: that it was obtained lawfully, is relevant to the case, and has not been contaminated.

It must generally be demonstrated that it has not been altered or damaged in any way prior to, during, or after its acquisition and that adequate or sufficient evidence was collected to support a case. If it passes these conditions, it may be argued that the evidence has been validated or at least tested and the likelihood of its validity has been determined. If it is valid, then it may be tendered and judged on its evidentiary merit.

There really is no universally well-established or standard process to guide digital forensic practitioners in the validation of digital evidence artifacts to ensure their admissibility in legal proceedings. However, there is a pressing need for a more scientific measurement of digital evidence validity, as distinct from practitioners' or lawyers' intuition, which may be insightful in simple "yes" and "no" instances of evidence analysis.

It is evident from more intricate or convoluted instances that digital evidence can be misleading because of its special properties. Most importantly, file locations, timestamps, and other metadata containing file antecedents and file data require close scrutiny to ensure that its properties may be fully identified and explained. This becomes more challenging to analyze when correlating file events introduces a degree of uncertainty that must be measured in some way to determine the validity of the exhibit.

To illustrate the problem with what appears at first inspection to be a simple matter, consider the location of an incriminating e-mail found in the **Sent Mail** box of a computer. The computer owner becomes the primary suspect in a suspect-led examination (all too common), since there is a typically implied presumption of guilt because the computer owner is the one most likely responsible for its creation and dispatch. In an evidence-led examination, the evidence is examined objectively without bias and faulty intuition, and an attempt is made to determine its antecedents and links to possible transgressors. Knowing the full processes involved in this alternative type of examination, the courts would prefer such an objective process to mere intuition.

In this example, the simple statement that the e-mail file was in the outbox suggests that it was sent by some user of the computer—well, it was or it wasn't. But in reality, checking its antecedents raises a range of questions, including determining whether there was a "hack", whether it was sent from another computer and synchronized to the suspect's computer, whether the timestamps were anomalous, or whether the message has been manipulated. If the response to each of these questions is a yes or no or even uncertain, it is possible, with careful attention to detail, to make some sense of what happened, but that still requires a measure of likelihood because of the result. If the answers to some or all questions are uncertain, that increases doubt as to the reasonableness of the evidence; consequently, some testing, checking, and, if possible, corroboration of the evidence, is necessary to determine the truth.

Explaining such complexity in terms understandable to the layperson requires clear understanding of the technicalities as well as sound communication skills. This is described in more detail later in the chapter. The literature shows that the difficulties hampering practitioners in effectively validating evidentiary admissibility may be attributed to:

- Challenges explaining the technical complexity of digital evidence to courts
- The immaturity of the forensic subdiscipline
- The ineffective security integrity of computers and networks
- Evidence contamination

Challenges explaining the complexity of digital evidence

It is widely accepted, and certainly borne out by my own research and liaisons with various legal teams, that the legal fraternity and clients really do not always have a clear understanding of computer systems and are often in the dark as to the validity and significance of the digital evidence presented to them. Although it has much in common with other forms of indirect evidence, such as paper documents, the inherent technical complexity of its properties challenges forensic practitioners attempting to present and explain digital evidence in many legal settings. The increasing reliance on digital evidence is likely to increase legal challenges to its admissibility and, ultimately, its evidentiary weight.

The use of diagrams, Toulmin charts (described in the *Presentation of digital evidence* section of this chapter), and other visual aids goes further than a detailed report, which many find confusing; visuals can break through communication barriers.

The immaturity of the forensic subdiscipline

Observers have suggested an imprudent wish by many practitioners to adopt scientific processes and tools too rapidly in digital forensic examinations, together with an undesirable perception that the proper review and validation of methods and processes is not necessary. Such review and testing is often fully and even partially bypassed. Concern about this poor practice is shared by me. It seems that this misperception creates situations where evidence produced by new processes is challenged because the process or new forensic tool used in its recovery and analysis has not been validated to determine its fitness for use in forensic examinations. That does not mean the evidence recovered is invalid but that the processes and tools make it less reliable if they have not been tested and independently and scientifically evaluated.

This is a worldwide problem, with cases relying on information and testimony based on faulty forensic science analyses, which is believed to have contributed to wrongful convictions of innocent persons. The absence of standard protocols governing forensic practice in a given discipline and uncertainty about the validity of many forensic processes and practices is surprisingly not uncommon.

Evidence that is denied admission in court proceedings because of unsound evidence-collection, processing, and preservation processes is evidence of wasted effort. For some time, there has been a perception among informed observers and practitioners that while the discipline has grown, it has not matured. The lack of substantial and significant research into the discipline has failed to identify broad scientific standards. Moreover, there is no clearly established science to underpin and support the use of digital evidence. Fingerprint analysis used for suspect identification has long been an established discipline; however, it has recently come under scrutiny for lacking any robust scientific groundwork.

The immaturity of digital forensics has brought into question its justification as a scientific discipline because of a lack of standardization and consistency within legal jurisdictions and criminal and civil investigation environments.

The ineffective security integrity of computers and networks

Courts have trouble evaluating evidence because it is sometimes difficult for practitioners to provide them with assurances about the integrity and reliability of the computing and network systems where the evidence is stored. It is common when tendering digital evidence that the custodian of the records, or other qualified witness, proves that the records were trustworthy.

Evidence corroboration of the soundness of the computer device and those managing computer networks is assumed by the courts, which also expect assurances attesting the security and integrity of computer and network systems that are known to be vulnerable to a range of threats.

Evidence contamination

Not only must the evidence be lawfully acquired, the courts now recognize the increased risk of evidence tampering and authentication problems with digital evidence. The relative ease with which DNA evidence can be falsified and created, thus creating great uncertainty about its soundness, has been well demonstrated in recent years. It has recently been clearly demonstrated that digital evidence may be modified without leaving any obvious trace of the commission of a transgression, and although the previous existence of evidence may be speculated, if it did exist, it is irretrievable.

The use of valid forensic tools minimizes the risk of evidence contamination during the recovery of data from digital devices, which assists the courts in determining the reliability of the recovered data. However, when applying standard tests, such as those in the United States, to cases involving digital forensic tools and processes, the status of digital forensics as a scientific discipline causes some disputes over the lack of broadly accepted standards and processes. The preservation of digital evidence has been described in some detail in earlier chapters, and its importance cannot be overemphasized.

Impartiality in selecting evidence

The recovery and forensic analysis of digital evidence and its ultimate presentation in court is no different than that of other forensic exhibits. It requires the best forensic standards and expects practitioners to possess special skills, notably:

- The ability to undertake impartial, unbiased, and through examinations of the evidence
- Possessing and adhering to a strong ethical code
- A modicum of sound forensic examination experience
- Having access to other practitioners to cross-pollinate
- Being widely read on digital forensic practices and case studies
- Having access to the best forensic tools and possessing a high level of competence in their use and deployment
- Possessing sufficient understanding of relevant legislation
- Recognizing the limitations of their competence and signaling the need for specialist support

- The ability to understand client needs and define the nature of the examination at an early stage and, if necessary, on an ongoing basis
- Being a sound communicator, with the ability to explain findings to the legal team and, ultimately, the courts
- Being able to satisfy the court that evidence has been checked and tested to determine its validity

All of these attributes are expected of forensic practitioners and, most importantly, they must show that there was no bias in their case examinations. Those practitioners who are basically dirty witnesses throw away their impartiality and get a reputation for serving their clients or organizations, and are certainly in no way servants of the court. Others tend to select evidence that fits a subjective view, often termed **examiner bias**.

Indolence and banality can dominate practitioners' behaviors, especially if they feel their opinion will not be challenged, as well as them developing a sense of superiority. It happens and is a pitfall the conscientious must avoid. These ethical issues are discussed later in more detail in the *Ethical issues confronting digital forensics practitioners* section.

From my forensic experience working on criminal and civil cases, it is abundantly clear that looking for evidence sitting in even smaller-sized datasets requires patience, concentration, and a dedication to doing a good job for the client. The discipline may sound glamorous, and the odd cameo court appearance where the evidence is presented and argued can be a rewarding experience, but sometimes it is harrowing and intimidating. That being said, the presentation of the evidence, irrespective of its value, must be based on a sound professional examination and analysis.

In an ideal world, where time and resources are not restricted, the practitioner can devote time and thought to completing a thorough, unhurried analysis. However, if the client is on a low budget, there may be limited time available to complete a thorough examination. Impending trial dates and other tight schedules often limit the amount of time available to the practitioner. Added to this crippling lack of time to ensure thoroughness of examinations, other factors, such as unreasonably heavy workloads or the unpleasantness of the case topic, such as sexual indecency and violence, sometimes results in practitioners being stressed and disillusioned—not really a situation conducive to maintaining effective forensic output.

Meaning is only clear in context

Patterns of information combine to provide substance, and just like a puzzle, pieces are put together to get a picture. However, such evidential artifacts may be easily misinterpreted, and are sometimes misleading or patently false.

Missed evidence or information not recognized as relevant to the investigation can have catastrophic consequences, and there are common problems caused by a failure to:

- Identify evidence as present
- Collect evidence while it is fresh
- Identify relevant materials for a warrant
- Properly label and record exhibits

Conversely, the practitioner might:

- Identify things as evidence that are not actually evidence
- Collect things that are not allowed by the warrant
- Mislabel exhibits
- Create forgeries

Faulty case management and evidence validation

Since 2008, I have provided expert analysis of digital evidence to defense criminal lawyers in Australia. This involved the reexamination and validation of digital evidence presented in state and federal law enforcement cases. A number of defendants were able to sway the jury and were consequently acquitted. While the deliberations of the jury are strictly confidential, it was thought that the reexamination and testing of the digital evidence, which provided additional explanation and a contrary view of the evidence, and providing all the evidence with greater clarity may have helped the jurors reach fairer or better-informed decisions.

What is evident to me, and my fellow workers in the field, are two related problems:

- Faulty case management through inadequate analysis and presentation of digital evidence
- Incomplete and incorrect validation of digital evidence

In practice, inadequate analysis is often due to a range of factors, such as caseload or practitioner inexperience. However, sometimes it is due to evidence relevant to the case being ignored or not identified. This evidence may be of an exculpatory form, in that it may exonerate the suspect or implicate another suspect. The preponderance of some practitioners to cherry-pick the lowest-hanging fruit when selecting evidence and a lack of analysis of the evidence to ensure it is what it purports to be continues to be a problem. It shows a need for more accountability by practitioners, who are in fact servants of the court.

The real danger when examining evidence, irrespective of its form, is that it can be seductive and can offer what the finder wishes to perceive. What might at first glance appear obvious may be deceptive. The practitioner must stick to the evidence and not become preoccupied with whether it will prove guilt or innocence based on personal feelings. Unsuccessful prosecutions based on what has been exposed as biased and faulty interpretation of digital evidence are not that uncommon. This is unhelpful, as it can aggravate cases where the evidence, if successfully challenged, does not result in the conviction of a guilty person. Conversely, biased evidence can result in the conviction of innocents.

Practitioners must expect their presentations and expert opinions to be challenged and repudiated, because the pillar of law in many jurisdictions is that the defendant is innocent until proved guilty of the offence or transgression. There are some exceptions, such as in drug trafficking and possession cases, where there is a reversal of this fundamental protection. In those cases, the onus is on the accused to explain away the evidence and prove their innocence.

"The defendant is presumed innocent" seems to be a hackneyed expression and a misunderstood term. That the police would not have charged the defendant if there were not a modicum of proof of guilt is another dangerous fallacy. A prima facie case does not presume guilt nor is it the inevitable outcome. It is for the prosecution to establish as compelling a case as possible for the judge or jury to deliberate upon. The defendant does not have to prove innocence; the prosecutor has to establish whether there is a nexus between the events in question and the defendant. In effect, they have to prove that the accused is not innocent.

In terms of cases relying on digital evidence, it is often the case that the evidence, which may well be true, can be easily repudiated. Some validation process is required to determine, among other factors, whether the evidence is accurate, factual, relevant (and consistently relevant), applies to the time of the transgression, and is the complete truth. Other synonyms could be added here, but the gist is that some formal process is needed to assist practitioners to define the validity of the evidence that they present. This is discussed in the following section.

The structured and balanced analysis of digital evidence

Clearly, it is hoped that you, having read through previous chapters, would realize that intuition is not enough and does not impress the court—solid facts are needed and should be supported with logical analysis. Attempts must be made to locate all evidence and intuition alone may not be sufficient for an inexperienced practitioner to locate hidden and hard-to-find evidence. The incomplete identification of all evidence that should be located can thwart an examination of crucial facts. This may be due to the incompetence or inexperience of a practitioner or because of the lack of time and available resources.

Not validating the evidence can destroy a case if it is later challenged successfully. I am especially critical of practitioners who miss *exculpatory* evidence in their pursuit of placing their prime suspect in the "frame". Linking the suspect to incriminating events, assuming the events are really incriminating, is the first hurdle in any examination, and this requires hypothesis testing. Even if the events are incriminating, the relationship between them and the suspect must be also tested.

Developing hypotheses

An internal investigation by a company's systems administrator, for example, will result in a less formal report to management and often leads to evidence contamination. This common phenomenon, which plagues forensic examinations, is highlighted in the case study at the end of the chapter. The task of developing a hypothesis or a line of argument about what may have occurred on the device or network is usually presented to persons other than the practitioners, investigators, and legal team.

The results of forensic examination may be presented in a criminal or civil court, before some legal hearing, or, in the case of an internal disciplinary matter, before a management team. The team leading the action will put forward an ultimate hypothesis supported by hypotheses of various evidence artifacts and arguments. Prior to the hearing, the practitioner may well need to test each hypothesis of the digital evidence that may reject the hypothesis or require corroboration to support it. A true professional will look for an alternative hypothesis or counter-hypothesis to test which is more likely.

More exacting means of measuring and standardizing the evidence may help practitioners, investigators, and jurors decide on the validity of the evidence. For the practitioner, it is essential to always remain objective. Once digital evidence is admitted as evidence, common sense seems to fly out the window.

Developing standard operating procedures for certain types of cases will limit the potential for human error and is often most useful as a general process. There is, of course, a need to develop a set of required actions for various types of cases. It is important that the evidence stand out on its own and point to the truth. Practitioners should avoid selecting which action to undertake as the examination progresses, as it may be considered contentious, not *evidence-led*, far too subjective, and guilt-seeking. It can also miss leads and misinterpret other facts rather than being built on a solid framework.

Modeling arguments

An important question for the practitioner to try to answer is what properties are necessary and/or sufficient for evidence to be viable in a specific investigative content. This will depend to some extent on the following factors:

- The integrity of the data or assuring that the evidence is not modified, intentionally or accidentally, is a primary concern

- The ability to authenticate information must be present

- Being able to reproduce the processes used to gather and examine evidence is yet another consideration

- It is essential to know that the seizure of the evidence does not substantively change the state of either the evidence or system from which it was taken.

- It may also be important to demonstrate that only the information relevant to the investigation was accessed

The Toulmin model of argumentation

I am an advocate of the Toulmin model of argumentation and have found it useful in explaining in diagrammatic form the arguments about digital evidence at different levels of a case to legal teams.

Toulmin's theory defines six aspects of argument common to any type of argument, as described and illustrated in the following figure, which shows a line of argument that the suspect knowingly had offensive images on his computer (the backing for the argument), which is refuted by the unreliability of the data and file timestamps (reservation about the validity of the argument):

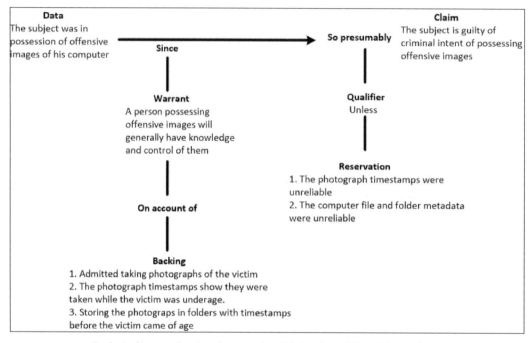

Toulmin diagram showing the ease of explaining the validity of the evidence

An interesting site that provides background and examples of the argument model is located at http://changingminds.org/disciplines/argument/making_argument/toulmin.htm.

The diagram is a simple representation of the evidence and has been used by me to show the ultimate hypothesis, and then each group of evidence can be deconstructed in separate diagrams to show the likelihood of the claim and reservation (or counterargument). It requires the practitioner to show, in visual form, the key issues and counter-issues the layman can comprehend.

Formalizing the validation of digital evidence

The term "validation" in terms of digital evidence is poorly defined. I proffer the following definition of validation:

> *"The validation of digital evidence is a process of ensuring that the digital evidence presented in court cases is legally admissible in that it can be shown to have been lawfully obtained; is untainted, relevant, and, because of its circumstantial nature, corroborated; and that its probative value outweighs its prejudicial effect."*

There are no current processes to guide digital forensic practitioners in the validation of digital evidence artifacts to ensure their admissibility in legal proceedings. My ongoing research and development of an enhanced validation model for digital forensic examinations is intended to enable forensic practitioners to input data in the form of questions about evidence artifacts and, through the calculations embedded in the model, yield a diagnosis of the validity of evidentiary admissibility. Embodied in the model is a software application incorporating a **Bayesian network** reasoning process and a data repository based on a range of case studies and circumstances encountered in digital forensic examinations.

The perceived benefits of a formalized validation process

Implicit in the prototype model is its capability to quantify the process of digital validation and provide practitioners with measurements to diagnose evidentiary validation in a simple and understandable format. Specifically, the model design must:

- Ensure that the conditions of validation applicable to each forensic examination have been satisfied in terms of the thoroughness of checking and testing of the validity of each evidence artifact
- Provide dependable measurements of the validity of exhibits to determine whether each meets the conditions of evidence admissibility

The prototype model presented here is intended to assist forensic practitioners by providing them with a greater understanding and clarity of their own forensic tools, processes, and practices as they relate to the validation of digital evidence. Specifically, the objectives are:

- Developing a formal process for the validation of digital evidence

- Implementing this process in a practical model that is usable by practitioners
- Providing meaningful and understandable prognoses of the evidence helpful to practitioners and, ultimately, the law courts
- Minimizing errors and the misinterpretation of evidence during the validation process
- Providing a thorough validation-checking regime
- Reducing the frequency of lengthy and costly legal challenges by producing more reliable analysis of the evidence and the wherewithal to verify analyses through scientific processes

The **design-based model** is seen to be of benefit to courts and legal practitioners by providing more reliable, scientific evidence analysis.

Rationale for selection

The Bayesian network model was selected for experimentation from a range of reasoning models. Bayesian reasoning has been used as a formal reasoning process to assist forensic experts in understanding and explaining the nature of complex evidence during legal cases. It is helpful when interpreting evidence where uncertainty exists about the reliability of the evidence. The Bayesian model is normative for the ideal court evaluating a new item of evidence and was adopted to separate information and opinion more clearly than has been done previously.

Legal advocates and judges prefer to rely on **abductive reasoning** to develop and evaluate plausible hypotheses based on supporting facts. Nevertheless, the benefits of using **Bayesian probability theory** by forensic practitioners as part of an evidence validation process, as distinct from the courts, has some merit.

Researchers have stressed the appropriateness and importance of distinguishing scientific knowledge from judicial judgment, as the former can be made using Bayesian probability theory. Litigators and judges have tended to avoid statistics based on probability reasoning to interpret the plausibility of evidence, yet is there is not a need for legal practitioners to understand the fundamentals of probabilistic reasoning? Using such processes to enhance the decision makers' understanding of what the evidence most likely suggests may be beneficial in the digital environment.

My research has shown that such a model offers practitioners a useful validation process that would:

- Navigate in a structured way through groups of evidence to identify exhibits requiring validation
- Test and check those exhibits to measure their validity as evidence
- Provide an understandable explanation on how measurements are calculated
- Provide meaningful measurements of validity
- Serve as a training tool for novice practitioners

The likelihood of the soundness of evidence helps the forensic expert provide an assessment of the objective probative value of their evidence. From this, the jury or adjudicator can decide on the probability of guilt or innocence of the accused. Bayes' theorem is based on probability or the likelihood of something happening or being true. It can be expressed in terms of odds, such as predicting the likelihood of India beating Pakistan in a Test match. These odds are not a random guess or inspired guesswork based on threads of evidence, such as abductive reasoning, but based on known and likely outcomes that can often result in a far more reliable prediction than human guesswork.

The evidentiary weight of an exhibit expressed as a likelihood ratio in a legal case seeking to prove guilt can be expressed as:

$$\frac{\textit{The probability of finding the evidence given that the defendant is guilty}}{\textit{The probability of finding that same evidence given that the defendant is innocent}}$$

When that likelihood ratio is combined with the strength of the other evidence known to the decision maker (the prior odds), then the decision maker is armed with **posterior odds**. Bayesian logic can be used to measure likelihood ratios of admissibility in a similar way, as follows:

$$\frac{\textit{The probability of finding that the evidence is admissible}}{\textit{The probability of finding that evidence is inadmissible}}$$

In Bayesian reasoning, every hypothesis under consideration must have some probability of being true. If that hypothesis based on the attached evidence is true, then there is a particular probability that the item of evidence will be observed; by contrast, if that hypothesis is false, then there is another, different, probability that this item of evidence will be observed.

The conceptual framework of the model

My research posits that the validity of each evidence object must be checked before it can be considered admissible. In other words, validation of the evidence in support of a claim about a certain state of affairs is essential. These conditions of the admissibility of digital evidence (and circumstantial evidence in general) may be defined as its legal admissibility, plus its state of being untainted, its relevance to the issues at hand, and, ideally, whether it is corroborated. The conceptual framework describing these four conditions of evidence and the relationship between evidence and claim are set out in the following diagram:

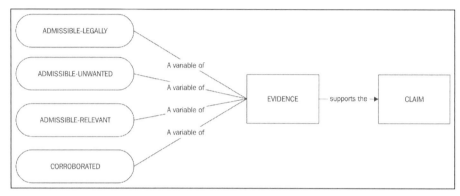

The conceptual framework of the model

Therefore, for the purpose of the model, *all* conditions of admissibility must be fulfilled, namely, if the evidence is legally admissible, untainted, and relevant, then the evidence may be admitted and, if appropriate, the evidence should be independently corroborated. In the following diagram, the highlighted conditions of admissibility and their interdependence are shown:

Conditions of admissibility schema

The prototype model is based on a substructure of the conditions of evidentiary admissibility requiring validation. Proposed subsets of each condition have been included to outline the model structure, as shown here:

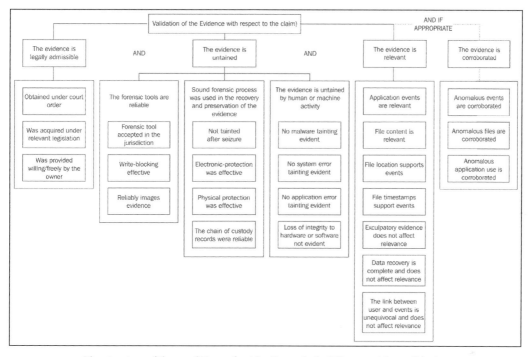

The structure of the conditions of evidentiary admissibility requiring validation

The validation process

The input of evidence exhibits requiring validation is processed by the model based on a response to a set of relevant, predetermined questions, represented as **e1**, **e2**, and so on, stored in the statistical database, as shown in the following diagram. Evidence input is a formal way of selecting evidence and preparing it for interrogation built on preset tests and checks. The interrogation input requires comparison with the statistical database of predetermined events and thresholds to measure evidentiary admissibility:

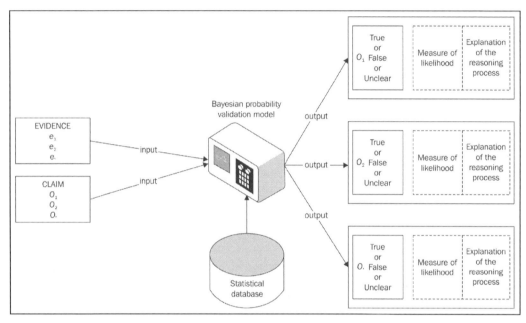

The Enhanced Validation Model for Digital Forensic Examinations

Through calculation completed by the embedded Bayesian network reasoning software application that harnesses the statistical database, the model produces an output statement stating the validity of the evidence artifact. The statistical database consists of a broad collection of information questions relating to the relevance of the evidence objects being examined. The questions require empirical proof to show that they and the range of associated answers were appropriate for inclusion in the statistical database. A wide range of digital evidence artifacts may be validated on the basis of whether they meet specific conditions of admissibility requiring a simple Yes, No, Unsure, Discounted or Cannot Be Determined output statement or response.

The output includes an explanation of the reasoning process in terms understandable by practitioners as well as comments on suggested further investigation processes required if the provided measurement results in a negative prognosis.

Applying Bayesian reasoning to the analysis of validation

The real value of the model presented is to assist the validating of evidence where there exists a degree of uncertainty. The first condition of the model—the legal admissibility of the evidence—is a reasonably straightforward component, unlike the other conditions that often appear complex with no hard-and-fast outcome statement. This relatively uncomplicated condition is described in the following subsection.

The comparative simplicity of the analysis of legal admissibility

In many instances, the validity of evidence is clearly substantiated and unchallenged. The lawful admissibility of evidence requires that some legal process be followed to permit the seizure and examination of exhibits or that the lawful owner grant permission for its acquisition. Except in exceptional conditions, it must normally be confirmed that evidence was acquired lawfully for it to be tendered during a trial. The legitimacy of the circumstances of the seizure of an exhibit, such as a mobile phone under a search warrant, may seem straightforward, provided there are no special conditions that require closer compliance with the order.

In e-discovery, the search order may specify that only certain data may be collected in order to protect the privacy of the custodians and user(s) of the data. Any evidence collected outside the terms of the order may be expected to attract a legal challenge.

These circumstances of lawful authority can be examined through a simple decision tree process and flowcharts and often result in providing practitioners and legal representatives with a positive or negative outcome. The process of checking the legitimacy of evidence collected pursuant to a search warrant is set out in the flowchart shown in the following diagram. The process requires that all checks are met; otherwise, the information gathered may not be admissible. The practitioner must look to other forms of seizure under the legislation and owner's permissions and apply similar checks:

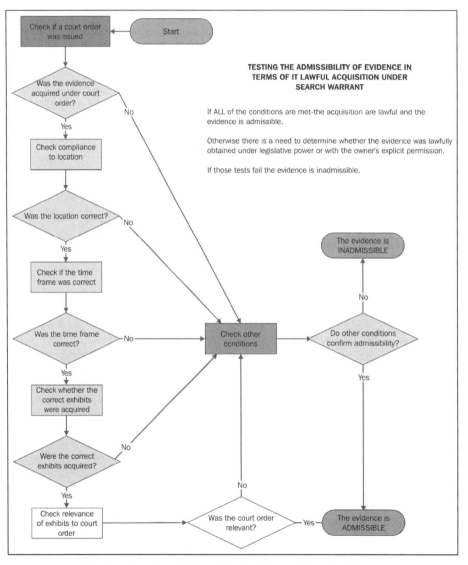

Flowchart to test conditions of the lawful acquisition of evidence

A sophisticated software process is not required in these instances, but examining other conditions of admissibility may require some structured guidance. This is especially so when determining the relevance of file-based events located on a computing device, as explained in the example in the next subsection.

More complex components requiring scientific measurement

The relationship between files and operating and application systems involves complex dynamics and requires close scrutiny. The need for a more scientific measurement of digital evidence validity, as distinct from practitioners' or lawyers' intuition, is evident in more intricate or convoluted instances, when the nature of digital evidence can be misleading because of its properties.

Such properties include the examination of the file location; timestamps; creation, transfer, and storage antecedents; and other software and user-generated events that help reconstruct device or system usage. This becomes even more challenging to analyze when correlating file events (or their absence) and introduces a degree of uncertainty that must be measured in some way to determine the validity of the exhibit.

The assessments of evidential value that may be applied to untangling these complexities, if based on intuition and experience alone, may not be right. There may be a tendency for subjective and expedient treatment of the basic facts. Interpretations about relevance will also vary among practitioners with little or no thought to testing their hypotheses. There is certainly no central repository for practitioners to consult outside of their own organizations or teams, so a tendency for defensive egocentricity amongst some practitioners exists—hardly an ideal scientific setting, but there may be security reasons for not sharing such case details.

It has been demonstrated, for example, that web-based e-mail messages can be relatively easily falsified and supplanted, and with some basic knowledge, evidence of such intervention is easily obfuscated.

If, to highlight the model, we break down one of the conditions of admissibility, such as the relevance of the evidence, shown in the following diagram, there are seven identified subconditions that must be checked for relevance. If we take, for example, the subcondition **r7**, the link between user and events is unequivocal and does not affect relevance.

There are a number of possible remote-access instances that should prompt the practitioner to verify whether the statement holds good. Checking for the likelihood of linkage between a suspected user and key events may require checking to determine whether other users had access to the computer through physical access, remote access through hacking, and other remote access through the presence of software applications such as TightVNC:

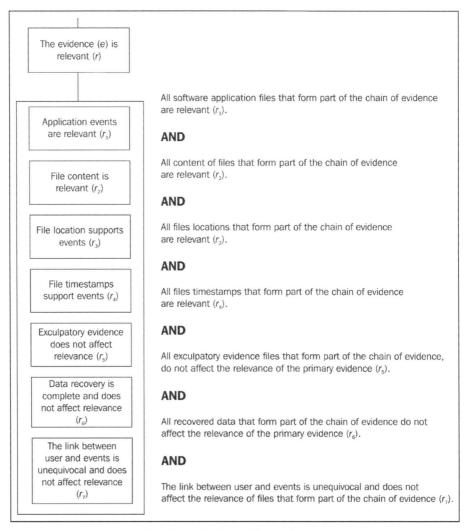

The evidence (e) is relevant (r)

Application events are relevant (r_1)

File content is relevant (r_2)

File location supports events (r_3)

File timestamps support events (r_4)

Exculpatory evidence does not affect relevance (r_5)

Data recovery is complete and does not affect relevance (r_6)

The link between user and events is unequivocal and does not affect relevance (r_7)

All software application files that form part of the chain of evidence are relevant (r_1).

AND

All content of files that form part of the chain of evidence are relevant (r_2).

AND

All files locations that form part of the chain of evidence are relevant (r_3).

AND

All files timestamps that form part of the chain of evidence are relevant (r_4).

AND

All exculpatory evidence files that form part of the chain of evidence, do not affect the relevance of the primary evidence (r_5).

AND

All recovered data that form part of the chain of evidence do not affect the relevance of the primary evidence (r_6).

AND

The link between user and events is unequivocal and does not affect the relevance of files that form part of the chain of evidence (r_7).

Conditions of admissibility – relevance

These instances of possible remote access have the potential to show that a sole user did not have exclusive access to the computer, requiring more certainty to establish a link between a specific user and evidence of the transgression. In practice, the practitioner, as part of the case examination, should check all of these potential links. To illustrate the process, the following demonstration is set out using the hypothetical instance of measuring the likelihood of a remote-access exploit through the presence of software applications.

The flowchart is shown in the following diagram, which shows the process required to check applications and files to determine whether other user access occurred at times relevant to the transgression. The various outcomes of the checking process assist the practitioner in determining whether the evidence is admissible, because it is more likely than not that remote access did not occur. The results of the checking can also show that the evidence is less likely to implicate the computer owner as other user access is implied through remote access. The process may also show that the likelihood of other user access is uncertain or may not be possible to determine.

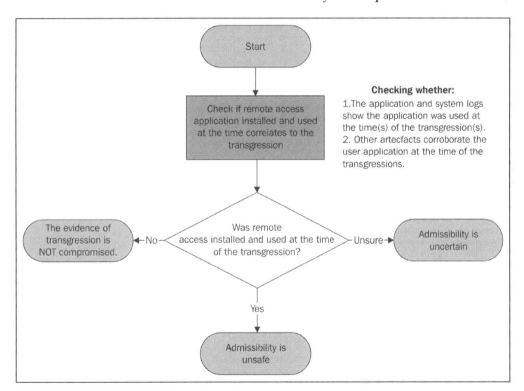

The process of checking remote access through applications installed on a device

The overarching question is whether the remote application has been installed and used during a period the transgression took place. The practitioner may or may not confirm the existence of the application on the computer, because it may have been uninstalled or deleted without a trace and the logging files may not be present. If that proves inconclusive, checking other system records, such as the Event Viewer and Registry, may reveal the previous use of the application. Some indication that remote access was enabled by the application at or close to the time of the transgression of course raises the possibility of unauthorized use of the computer. This example is used to demonstrate the model's ability to process reasoned input and provide a useful output prognosis.

In this selected sample scenario, it is important to determine whether remote access applications were ever present on the computer. If this is confirmed, the implications this may have on the nature of transgression events should, as a matter of course, be considered. A diligent practitioner would check whether the application file metadata shows that the application was installed prior to the installation. If its previous installation were confirmed, then the focus would be on whether the application and system logs show that the application was used at the time of the transgression.

A positive response to evidence of the application running should trigger some alarm, and if other artifacts corroborate the use of the application at the time of the transgression, then the practitioner should consider the activities of another user of the computer.

If it can be established that the application was not used at the time of the transgression, this would allow the practitioner to conclude that this matter does not degrade the value of the evidence. Moreover, if the application has been present on the computer and not used, then there is no degradation of validity.

If, however, the application was installed, this would raise some concern as to its use at the time of the transgression and require further checking. The likelihood of the application degrading the evidence has increased and may be measured, the more so if it can be shown that it was installed and used at the time of the transgression. If its use was uncertain, this affects the likelihood ratio and has the implication of an uncertain prognosis.

If other evidence corroborates the application's use at the time of the transgression, a different likelihood ratio is presented. It is the cumulative result of these questions and the output measurements provided that allows the practitioner to gain an insight into the implications raised, but sometimes, the human brain needs extra help.

Determining prior probability

Each hypothesis has a prior probability of being true, that is, the probability of that hypothesis being true before anything at all is known about the evidence that might be associated with it, and this may be modified at any time. Setting the prior probability in the hypothetical example of the vulnerability of a remote user exploit by the installation and operation of remote-access software on a target computer is the first priority.

Each subcategory in the model will have different thresholds to show the expert the different outputs.

In trying to determine whether there was a remote application to exploit the device, it may be decided that the probability of such an occurrence is infrequent or highly improbable, and other scales may be selected, but within the realm of reasonable expectation. The question is whether a remote application allowed an external exploit of the user's computer. The practitioner must decide whether the probability of such an event having taken place was infrequent, highly improbable, probable, most likely, and so forth. These predictions must be reasonable and within the bounds of what may be expected to occur on a computer.

If the occurrences are infrequent, a low threshold of prior probability of 0.01, which represents odds of exactly 1 in 100, may be selected. If the likely occurrence is greater, a higher threshold of prior probability of, say 0.1, which represents odds of exactly 1 in 10, may be selected. A lower threshold tells us that such an occurrence is infrequent, whereas a higher threshold suggests greater frequency.

There is flexibility embedded in the model to enable adjustments to meet criminal and civil standards of certainty, such as "beyond reasonable doubt" in criminal cases or "on a balance of probability" in civil cases. In criminal cases, if the evidence is not beyond reasonable doubt, then the defendant should get the benefit of the doubt.

Setting post probabilities

The next process is to determine the posterior or post probabilities based on alternative hypotheses. There are two items of evidence related to this proposition:

- Was the remote application running at the time of the transgression?
- Do system logs confirm a remote application running at the time of the transgression?

If either were running, this would suggest a measure of certainty that a remote user had accessed the computer at the time of the transgression (which may or may not be an unauthorized hack). We could set that probability at 0.8 or 8 in 10 for either. We could set the threshold at 1.0, which would mean that when either of these events occurred during the period of transgression, there was a certainty that a remote exploit had occurred. However, such certainty cannot be predicted without compelling corroboration.

At the other end of the scale, we can set it at 0.01, which means that odds of 1 in 100 that the application was running at the time of the transgression will be observed even if a remote application compromise does not occur. In the test sample, the prior probabilities were set at 0.1 and 0.01 to see whether there were any significant differences in calculating the output to these two questions. The post probabilities for each question were set at 0.8 and 0.1, as the significance of both questions was considered identical to determining the likelihood of a remote exploit.

These post probability ratios were calculated on the perception that if the answer to either question was in the positive, then the likelihood of a remote exploit was high, and if it was positive in both instances, highly probable. A higher threshold of 0.8 supported this measurement, while the 0.01 threshold was considered representative of the fact that the concept should not be dismissed to lightly.

The model presents these thresholds based on this question: Was the remote application running at the time of the transgression? In this case:

- A probability of 0.8 of observing the application running at the time of transgressions will be observed if it does

- A probability of 0.01 of observing that the application was running at the time of transgressions will be observed even if a remote application compromise does not occur

It will also consider this: Do system logs confirm remote application running at the time of the transgression? In this case:

- A probability of 0.8 of observing the system logs showing the application running at the time of transgressions will be observed if it does

- A probability of 0.01 of observing system logs showing the application was running at the time of transgressions will be observed even if a remote application compromise does not occur

The output from the model based on the complete range of responses to the prompts **Yes**, **No**, and **Uncertain** is shown in the following table. Some differences were observed between the use of the prior probability ratios of 0.1 and 0.01, as shown in the table. Using the lower likelihood ratio of 0.01 showed a lower range or odds to support the hypotheses than with using the high threshold or 0.1.

The following nine output reports consist of:

- **The hypothesis is possible**: one result from instance **D**

- **The hypothesis is uncertain**: six results from instances **B, C, F, G, H,** and **I**

- **The hypothesis is discounted**: two results from instances **A** and **E**

Application status and odds instance	The remote application was running during the period of the transgression	Other system data shows that the remote application was running during the period of the transgression	Prior odds (posterior odds 0.8 and 0.01)	Odds observed by the model calculations	Prognosis of remote application compromise
A	No	No	0.1	2 in 443	This hypothesis is discounted
			0.01	1 in 2,427	
B	Yes	No	0.1	9 in 14	This hypothesis is uncertain
			0.01	8 in 57	
C	No	Yes	0.1	9 in 14	This hypothesis is uncertain
			0.01	8 in 57	
D	Yes	Yes	0.1	712 in 713	This hypothesis is possible
			0.01	66 in 67	
E	Uncertain	Uncertain	0.1	1 in 100	This hypothesis is discounted
			0.01		
F	Yes	Uncertain	0.1	53 in 59	This Hypothesis is uncertain
			0.01	17 in 38	

Application status and odds instance	The remote application was running during the period of the transgression	Other system data shows that the remote application was running during the period of the transgression	Prior odds (posterior odds 0.8 and 0.01)	Odds observed by the model calculations	Prognosis of remote application compromise
G	Uncertain	Yes	0.1	53 in 59	This hypothesis is uncertain
			0.01	17 in 38	
H	No	Uncertain	0.1	7 in 319	This hypothesis is uncertain
			0.01	1 in 491	
I	Uncertain	No	0.1	7 in 319	This hypothesis is uncertain
			0.01	1 in 491	

Checking whether the remote access application was running at the time of the transgression

The analysis of the results as to whether the remote-access application was running at the time of the transgression analysis of the results from the checking process provided a range of outcomes, described as follows:

- The hypothesis is possible: From these results, the practitioner would recognize that in one instance (D), which reflects that both questions were positive inputs, there was a high likelihood of a remote exploit.

- The hypothesis is uncertain: Instances B, C, F, G, H, and I should suggest to the evaluator that there is now some uncertainty as to whether a remote exploit had occurred. In instances B, C, F, and G, the 0.1 result shows a greater possibility of support for the hypotheses than against it, whereas the 0.01 result shows the inverse. The remaining instances show a minimal support for the hypotheses using either likelihood ratio. The level of uncertainty of the results in the catchment are measurable a with some favoring to discount the hypotheses, notably instances H and I, whereas B, C, F, and G are more borderline results, suggesting that a remote-access exploit was possible but not proven.

- The hypothesis is discounted: Instances A and F show that the hypothesis is highly unlikely.

Notes for the practitioner regarding the significance of the input question and some background information to assist in checking and testing the evidence on which the response to the question was based are also made available in the output report.

Here is a sample note regarding the application having been running at the time of the transgressions:

> Evidence: Application was running at the time of transgressions
>
> Question: Was the application running at the time of the transgressions?
>
> Response: Yes
>
> NOTE: The operating logs for the application may provide confirmation that the application was active during the period of the transgression. The examination of available volume shadows in Windows may also provide some confirmation that the application was active at key times.

Here is a sample note regarding the application having been running at the time of the transgressions, based on system logging:

> Evidence: Other system logs confirm remote application running
>
> Question: Do other system logs confirm remote application running?
>
> Response: Yes
>
> NOTE: This information may be derived from Windows Event Viewer files. Windows Registry may also provide additional information.

Present limitations and scoping

The model addresses admissibility and not the evidentiary weight of an exhibit per se. The weight of the evidence, including its plausibility, is beyond the scope of the model and a matter for the investigation team and legal practitioner to debate and discuss, and ultimately for the jury to decide upon.

The results from the prototype and other models must enhance understanding of the complexity of the evidence and likelihood ratio about the validity of the digital evidence artifacts. This is seen as enhancing the communication of the practitioner's findings to others as part of the evidence presentation.

The presentation of digital evidence

There are two main types of testimony given by professionals at a trial, deposition, or hearing:

- Technical or scientific witness testimony
- Expert witness testimony

Digital forensic practitioners may be called upon to act in either or both roles. The technical or scientific witness provides evidence of facts that were uncovered during the investigation and describes what was found and how it was obtained. The expert witness provides opinion about what was observed based on experience, using deductive reasoning with observed or examined facts.

It is important to reiterate that in presenting a report or testifying in person, the practitioner must ensure that exculpatory as well as inculpatory evidence is presented to the other party. The practitioner must make the following things certain when presenting the evidence:

- Conclusions are technically sound
- The evidence solidly supports them and is properly preserved
- Any exculpatory evidence that may have been found has been considered

Preparing digital forensics reports

In preparing forensic examination reports, it is important to aim for clarity and simplicity and be certain that the evidence is easy to access and properly cross-referenced. The report should make recommendations, including those for preventing a recurrence of the incident, and describe the root causes, if any, that permitted it to occur.

It is prudent to present the evidence in the best possible light and to demonstrate the examination processes progressively. It is also appropriate to describe the strengths and weaknesses of the case along the following lines:

- The most-favored position first and last
- Alternatives in the middle
- Summarizing the evidence in the context of the process
- Addressing anomalies before the other party does
- Drawing conclusions, if any
- Providing the basis for drawing those conclusions

- Addressing other possible interpretations and their basis
- Clear conclusions including understandable and justifiable reasoning
- Whether the results and conclusions change if any of the information given is incorrect or changes

A sample report outline is shown here:

TABLE OF FIGURES

TABLE OF TABLES

A specimen forensic report layout

It contains an **EXECUTIVE SUMMARY** that concisely and clearly outlines the purpose of the report, the processes involved, and the analysis of evidence recovered and any other key facts. The body of the report provides a more detailed background to the case and the objectives for the forensic examination.

The report should also include the evidence-recovery process, including chain-of-custody information if a separate register has not been maintained. The results of the examination are then described in specific detail, with some discussion at the end of this section and embedded in the report at the relevant parts. Recommendations, if any, and conclusions complete the report, along with a table of figures, tables, and attachments of files, as appropriate.

Court appearances

Juries place enormous weight on practitioners' evidence, thanks to CSI. We *all* have a duty to help them understand *and* not to overrate it. Just because practitioners know their field of endeavor does not mean the juries and legal teams will understand.

Cardinal rules for experts are:

- Know your stuff
- Never underestimate lawyers
- Think first before answering questions
- Be honest
- The outcome doesn't matter

Remember, practitioners are impartial and are expected to justify:

- What scientific principles underpin the processes used
- The process or validation data for the technique
- Reference databases used and the reason for using them
- Their ability to calculate the statistics and likelihood ratios (justifying a need for such processes, as previously described in the validation model!)

A practitioner should also practice the following:

- Use plain language and avoid jargon.
- Stay within the bounds of their expertise.
- Ensure their research on a specific matter of relevance is up to date, especially if it is an area that keeps changing.

- If there is an error in the report or the practitioner has a change of mind about something before the trial, notify the lawyer urgently.

- If the practitioner has a change of mind in court, so be it: be brave. Be prepared to change your stance if that is what the truth requires.

- Admit a lack of knowledge or uncertainty and accept other reasonable propositions.

- If the question asked is unclear or complex questions are posed, ask for it to be repeated and broken down—refuse to answer if its meaning still remains unclear.

- Look out for assumptions in questions and misquoting, and make sure the information being relied on is easy to locate, such as when sharing information on a computer as a visual aid.

- Try not to get defensive.

- Answer questions such as "Isn't it possible?" with "I've seen no evidence to support that assertion." or "It is highly unlikely."

- Look out for ambiguous or multi-part questions.

- Be prepared for the judge to ask questions and then for further cross-examination.

- Keep initial notes and review them before the trial.

- Tag the notes, bring them to court, and ask to refer to them during testimony.

- Listen, pause, think, and only answer what is asked.

- Tell the whole truth and don't talk down to the lawyer.

- Do not just answer "Yes" or "No" if it is misleading—seek the judge's help.

- Practice on a friend before the trial.

- Don't act too smart.

- Don't argue or lose the plot.

- Don't try to second-guess.

- Be consistent within and between cases.

- Treat each question as the most important one in the case.

Jurors dislike it when practitioners:

- Talk down to the lawyer
- Display obvious bias
- Are cocky, lose their tempers, and become defensive
- Are unprepared
- Present confusing, unreadable, and cluttered visual aids

The court and legal teams will want to see the practitioner's qualifications, which should include:

- Your title and years employed
- Years employed in that area
- Number of analyses of this nature done
- Qualifications, including academic and training courses
- Skills and certifications in competency in digital forensics processes and tools
- Professional experience
- Publications
- Lectures and presentations to professional societies
- Prior expert testimony, including the types of courts such testimony was given in
- Memberships of professional organizations
- Seminars/symposia attended

Ethical issues confronting digital forensics practitioners

Ethics is concerned with right and wrong behavior and makes us reflect on how a person should act in various situations where an ethical dilemma arises. Often, there are persuasive arguments both for and against every course of action open to a person in each circumstance.

Among other conduct, ethical behavior requires:

- Honesty
- Fairness
- Good reputation
- Consistency
- Goodwill
- Diligence
- Proficiency
- A sense of community

Ethics is the branch of philosophy that deals with the interrelationships of humans to each other, animals, the environment, and all that exists in the universe. It asks whether an action is:

- Good or bad
- Right or wrong
- Acceptable or unacceptable
- Virtuous or evil

Ethics is actually very hard to define, and different interpretations and environments complicate attempts to define a universal meaning. Each of us may derive our own personal ethics from many sources, including family and culture, religion or faith, the legal system, and where we live. Slothfulness and banality in undertaking forensic examinations are inexcusable considering the need for the very highest standards.

Practitioners will experience situations that test their ethical standards as shown in the following case study. Impartiality and service to the court may sound quaint, but it is a solid barricade to defend when pushed to drop standards. The expert's overriding duty is to the court, not to those who instruct.

Case study – presumed unauthorized use of intellectual property

This recent case study exemplifies some of the problems that occur during examinations and provides some tips on avoiding certain pitfalls that occur.

The background to the case

This was an industrial espionage case involving a member of staff who was suspected of stealing the intellectual property of the employer. Suspicion arose when the CCTV footage of the office detected the employee's presence at his workstation during out-of-office hours for a 2-hour period—unusual activity for staff members. Scrutiny of the CCTV footage showed a partial view of what appeared to be the employee's laptop, on which could be observed the opening of files on the desktop.

Examination of the company's server confirmed the download of a number of files, including images, spreadsheets, and some text documents, at the same time as the CCTV footage. The server logs also showed synchronization between the server and the e-mail account on the laptop. The employee's service was terminated 3 months later after the employer became aware that the employee was joining a rival company and of other innuendo as to his disloyalty.

Prior to the employee's departure, the company covertly installed an application on the laptop, its property, to monitor browsing activities of interest. The legality of this action is questionable. After the departure of the employee, the IT administrative staff carried out an examination of the laptop to seek information that might incriminate the employee. They installed various applications in an attempt to recover deleted files, but with no success. At this late juncture, the services of a forensic practitioner were sought to look for evidence to decide whether there were sufficient grounds to lodge a complaint to police.

The forensic recovery

The laptop was subsequently examined, but it proved impossible to obtain a physical image of the hard drive by bootup or by removal of the drive, which appeared a tedious process with some risk of damage to the device. Ideally, a physical image will recover deleted data, but on this occasion, there was no guarantee that the operating system peculiar to the device installed on a solid-state drive would offer up much extra evidence.

Not all devices are amenable to recovery through the bootup process, and device removal, if possible, is a last resort. ISeekDiscovery installed on a specially configured external drive was proposed to capture a logical image of the device, but as the insertion of the drive may have overwritten the attached drive logs, this was of concern.

The company's legal team was advised that there may be some small contamination of the evidence, but that as the device had already been accessed by other personnel, the damage was done and the forensic process was unlikely to further contaminate the data to any greater extent. Permission was provided to proceed with the extraction, which was duly completed.

The forensic examination

The examination recovered some data, and the following observations were made:

- There was confirmation that the laptop was switched on during the period of the after-hours server download. The times matched other evidence relating to the employee's physical presence in the office workplace.

- The location of a number of picture files that bore some resemblance to the information downloaded from the server was found. Some of the picture file names recovered from the laptop appeared be identical to those recorded in the server log.

- Other picture files that appeared to be the intellectual property of the organization were located on the laptop.

- A number of similar filenames recorded in the server log were located on the laptop, but the timestamps did not match.

- A number of the filenames recorded in the server log were not located on the laptop.

- A number of e-mail and calendar files were located on the laptop and appeared to relate to the business of the organization.

- There was some evidence of cloning software on the device that indicated copying of the organization's property.

Linking the suspect to the device and the device to the server

The IT administrator could not confirm that the files recorded in the server log were opened and accessed by the employee's laptop based on the IP address shown in the server log. According to the IT administrator, this was an IP address issued to various employees when they logged on to the server. However, despite an intensive search, no trace of this IP address was located on the laptop, which was most likely removed during the process of decommissioning the device after the employee's departure. The IT administrator also confirmed that apart from the IT administration team, no members of staff had remote access to the server. Confirmation that the IT administration had not accessed the server was made.

It was also recommended that a backup copy of the access log be retained as potential evidence. The CCTV footage of the office, but not the building in which it was housed, showed the employee in the workplace, whereas other staff were recorded as having earlier departed. The laptop was nondescript and had no identifying features to confirm that it was the one shown in the CCTV footage, even though the suspected employee could be seen using its keyboard. There was no record on the laptop showing any connections to the server other than what could be presumed from e-mail synchronization and data owned by the company, later identified through search terms.

Other data recovered for the date in question showed that the employee's e-mail account had been used to send and receive work messages. A plausible nexus between the employee, the laptop, and the server was established, which would be hard to contradict. However, confirmation that files were downloaded to the laptop and later used without authorization was not so straightforward.

Analyzing the downloaded files

Only some of the files downloaded were recovered on the laptop, and the timestamps did not match the download time, with some pre-dating and others post-dating the server records. Similarly, none of the synchronized server e-mails shown in the log were located on the laptop.

Connected storage devices

No information regarding the connectivity of an external device, such as a thumb drive or external storage device, was detected on the device prior to the period when the IT administration personnel installed data-recovery devices on the laptop. This information would have been helpful to determine whether an external device was used to copy the company's data.

This lack of connectivity logging may be attributable to these factors:

- The operating system not maintaining a fuller list of previously attached devices, such as on Windows systems.

- The IT administration team attaching external devices in an attempt to recover deleted files and examine the laptop prior to the forensic examination. This would have the effect of overwriting and removing any previous logging events.

- In the 3-month period between the date of the alleged transgression and the employee's departure, the system may have also recorded attached devices, but such events may have overwritten any earlier connectivity of relevance and shortly afterwards.

- The log may have been manually deleted, but that would require some knowledge of its existence and some technical skill.

- USB ports were present on the left and right-hand sides of the keyboard close to the screen. Evidently, there was no reported sighting of any such connected devices based on the CCTV footage.

No micro-SD card port was fitted to the laptop, and so, that process of data transfer was not available. Alternatively, if the pictures and other documents such as spreadsheets and PDF files were present on the desktop and deleted afterwards, it is unlikely they would be recovered if they had been deleted and then removed from the recycler—simply put, the evidence was not present.

The illicit copying of data

The installation files for a cloning application were located on the laptop after the alleged transgression, and earlier browsing records linked to the software website. The application makes a clone of the laptop, which means if it was used, it would allow the user to keep a full record of the data for possible future use. Data saved by such a process allows the user to reinstall the data on another machine and make the data available. It was not possible to determine whether the application was used to clone the device; however, the possibility exists that this may have occurred. Who loaded and installed the application could not be determined, and it may not have been the employee, as the integrity of the laptop data had been compromised, to some extent, by the handling of it by personnel prior to the forensic examination.

The outcome

There was some evidence that was recovered of the employee's most likely having possession of the company's property and using it to exploit business opportunities kept private from the company. Whether this information was sufficient to substantiate a case of theft or misuse of intellectual property is uncertain, but actually, it was not the concern of the practitioner. Why this unremarkable, but not uncommon, type of case is presented here is because it showed the company in a poor light and highlights some of the challenges confronting practitioners:

- The client was suspect-driven and had already decided that the employee was guilty based on gossip and innuendo in the first instance, whereas the practitioner was evidence-led and neutral.

- The client expected confirmation of these suspicions and was disappointed when the evidence was not clear-cut and decisive in part.

- The evidence proves the suspicions to a point, but only to a point, and the case looked weak, with the client expecting that the forensics would provide more collateral—sometimes it does; sometimes it has the opposite effect.

- The client asked that comments about evidence contamination be excised from the practitioner's report. This was refused on ethical and procedural grounds, with the client being sharply told that the practitioner was the servant of the court, not of the client, and was not an investigator subject to client manipulation. This denial by the practitioner was supported by the client's lawyer.

- There is some question about the lawfulness of installing a web-browsing tracking application on the laptop in this particular jurisdiction, which required a magistrate's warrant.

Consider if you will, dear reader, that had the practitioner not made a full and honest account, the legal team would have charged ahead, ready to prosecute or litigate with a reasonable chance of cowing the employee into admitting some responsibility and guilt.

Had the practitioner succumbed and deleted the contamination information, it was suspected that the client would have filibustered the employee with what appeared to be a sound case, hoping to cower the employee into admitting the suspected transgression. But once the practitioner becomes aligned with the wishes of the client, it is a slippery slope into perdition. Often, the opposing legal team will discover that full and open disclosure of all the evidence was not made. This can result in the case being thrown out of court and the reputation of practitioner being damaged, perhaps permanently.

Summary

This chapter described some problems of unsound digital evidence, the need for impartiality in undertaking forensic examinations, and some common pitfalls that diminish the value of digital forensics through cursory and biased examinations.

The pressing need for structured and balanced analysis was outlined, as was the need to validate evidence to determine its relevance and authenticity in anticipation of it being tendered in legal proceedings. The process stressed the importance of testing and checking the evidence to ensure it is what it purports to be. This included the discussion of a more structured analysis of the evidence collected, including the development and testing of hypotheses and counterarguments in line with forensic standards.

A prototype model of validation was presented, intended to benefit practitioners in handling complex evidence, in which the process of testing and checking digital evidence was presented through a sample scenario. The presentation of evidence reports and court attendance were briefly discussed.

Ethical issues were outlined and then emphasized in the case study that showcased the importance of sound evidence selection and analysis as well as emphasizing the importance of impartiality in selecting evidence to ensure that the courts' expectations are met.

Chapter 10, Empowering Practitioners and Other Stakeholders, will summarize the topics covered in the book and discuss trends affecting practitioners and stakeholders, and reinforce the need for a more pragmatic approach to manage digital information that may be relied on in legal hearings. It will describe ways of empowering digital forensic practitioners and other stakeholders through better processes. I will highlight trends in digital forensic practice and the need to adopt better strategies for managing increasingly large and complex datasets. Also introduced will be processes, tools, and forensic contingency strategies that increase stakeholder awareness of and competency in managing digital information held in their trust.

10
Empowering Practitioners and Other Stakeholders

This chapter will review the key aspects of the book and emphasize current issues that challenge practitioners. We will cover the following topics:

- The evolving nature of digital evidence vis-à-vis the role of the practitioner
- Solutions to the challenges posed by new hardware and software
- More efficacious evidence recovery and preservation
- Enhanced evidence selection and analysis tools
- Challenges posed by communication media and the cloud
- The need for effective evidence processing and validation
- Contingency planning

The chapter will also discuss processes, tools, and forensic contingency strategies that increase the awareness of stakeholders and engender competency in managing digital information held in their trust.

The evolving nature of digital evidence vis-à-vis the role of the practitioner

This is a truly exciting and rewarding vocation—the skill of an investigator, the wisdom of a lawyer, and the knowledge of a computer analyst, all rolled into one. Being able to advise legal counsel or the investigation team on the outcome of an examination puts the practitioner in a unique and privileged position.

Irrespective of the outcome, the practitioner's advice cannot be ignored. It is not uncommon for the examination to reveal very little information of value; nothing had been present to recover in many instances. However, it is common for the client and lawyer to say that the venture was productive in that it could be set aside and the search for evidence could focus elsewhere. It is also pleasing to secure evidence that helps secure a conviction or acquittal too, depending on the party who engaged the practitioner.

Practitioners do not work in a vacuum. They do follow standard processes and develop their own through case experience and court outcomes. The question is whether the standards are adequate and easy to interpret and apply in practice. Practitioners are constantly updating their knowledge of new and evolving applications and devices. Accumulating expertise is a journey of discovery for them.

Chapter 3, The Nature and Special Properties of Digital Evidence, presented processes for recovering data from devices using sophisticated tools such as ILookIX and described the nature of digital evidence: where it could be found, how it could be recovered, and how it could be used in an investigation. Much information was condensed into that chapter, all of which could fill a book in itself. It would suffice to say that an understanding of the characteristics of digital evidence is a prerequisite for an entrée to the discipline. Furthermore, digital evidence is not static: new types of files, applications, operating systems, storage repositories, communications networks, and processes emerge with surprising frequency.

The practitioner must keep up with these trends, yet little is published or shared, leaving it to the individual to explore new formats and processes and determine the best way to recover and process evidence. Exchanging discoveries is slow and tedious and usually restricted to publications and reviews, and they normally take an eternity to publish after peer review, are made into a quick blog post but not properly reviewed, or are kept "within house" because of confidentiality and privacy issues. This book does not provide encyclopedic coverage of digital evidence, but it has covered a considerable cross-section of the discipline.

The practitioner needs to be able to explain the properties of digital evidence and the role it plays in adding to the weight of a case but must ensure that it passes the admissibility rules. Explaining the soundness and authenticity of the evidence, as well as being able to provide some corroboration to assist the court in assessing its worth, goes beyond merely selecting and presenting the evidence, for it is the role of the practitioner to interpret and explain the full and likely meaning of the evidence and metadata to the layperson.

As the discipline evolves and hopefully matures, it is practitioners who will lead the charge, but if they do not research and share any knowledge, it is going to be a ponderous exercise for them. Not all practitioners have the time even if they have the inclination to share their discoveries and experiences, and as mentioned before, there are confidentiality impositions too. In *Chapter 9, Validating the Evidence*, an evidence-validation process was introduced, and there may be merit in adopting such a process as a training tool for novice practitioners as well as a navigation tool for the more experienced. The process could be updated as new issues arise and used beyond its admissibility-checking design.

Solutions to the challenges posed by new hardware and software

Chapter 2, Hardware and Software Environments, described different operating systems and filesystems and introduced processes for locating evidence of potential value. Filesystems have become ponderously complex, perhaps unnecessarily so, but in doing so, they do retain information about past transgressions that may have otherwise been erased. The challenge is knowing where to look—assuming the practitioner knows how to navigate new operating systems and applications.

The traditional processes of imaging-indexing-searching or imaging and manually searching are becoming untenable; the sheer size and complexity is time-consuming and not necessarily guaranteed to locate the evidence, except by chance in many instances. There will always be a place for "deep rinse" analysis, but there are more effective ways. My research and fieldwork has shown that while it is difficult to part with familiar processes such as these, there exists a better way of recovering potential evidence.

The ISeekDiscovery automaton is presently being modified to be used in criminal investigations in addition to its role in e-discovery. The automaton is capable of recovering deleted files and registry files as well as collecting all specific file types. Several criminal defense cases have been tested using ILookIX and ISeekDiscovery, and the recovery rates were high, but ISeekDiscovery was able to capture just what was needed and was far more effective in cataloging and processing the recovered data.

While traditional tools can catalog and zero-eliminate duplicate files to reduce the dataset, they fall short of the automaton's ability to seek and return results in shorter periods and undertake follow-up searches based on preliminary analysis. Putting this in an e-discovery and network setting, the automaton can be launched remotely and the results viewed securely and remotely for extraction to legal process teams. Savings in time, travel, expensive practitioners, and inherent system challenges are eliminated. This enables the practitioner to access and analyze evidence more quickly and devote more time to evidence analysis.

More efficacious evidence recovery and preservation

What seems certain is the challenge of new technologies and the ability to recover evidence from an unabated increase in large and complex datasets. This requires a pragmatic approach to evidence recovery, and existing forensic tools for criminal and e-discovery do not achieve this. In my opinion, they are obsolete processes and really do not provide the support needed for speedy evidence analysis. This book has introduced new technologies and processes of preserving digital evidence and making recovery quicker and more reliable.

The imaging of drives has been the traditional means of collecting digital information from desktop, laptop, and networked computers for most criminal investigations. Mobile phones and other handheld devices require different data extraction processes. For e-discovery, where it is common to seek evidence from networked systems, imaging is impractical, and indexing and copying massive datasets using complicated software installed on the networks has been normal practice.

Imaging using existing technology does not provide the best protection for collected evidence. Mobile phone extraction tends to capture only logical data and now rarely recovers the physical data needed for deeper analysis. E-discovery is proving to be too costly for many organizations in terms of time, experts, and disruption to networks using existing data recovery tools.

Extracting data from tablets and even certain desktop devices is becoming problematic because of system encryption and difficulty in booting a device for imaging. They are becoming frequent stumbling blocks, making it difficult and sometimes impossible to recover data from these devices. My research colleagues are constantly finding ways to overcome these obstacles, but it is a sad fact that the discipline usually lags some way behind the introduction of new types of devices and systems.

The tools presented by me, including the IXImager and ISeekDiscovery suites, preserve evidence securely and conveniently. The `.ASB` forensic container format is the only forensic image type secured inside a container that is self-authenticating as well as tamper-proof. The peace of mind this gives a practitioner, who always faces the trauma of having the record of custody challenged, is that the logging process has provenance: its authenticity can be verified.

Similarly, the ISeekDiscovery `.ISK` format is a secure vault that is transportable, leaves no footprint of data on the system, and is relatively small compared with tradition e-discovery datasets. Not only are these tool processes soundly secure, but they are smaller in size, being compressed, and, in the case of the `.ISK` vaults, require significantly less storage space.

Challenges posed by communication media and the cloud

It is evident that mobile phones and other handheld devices are rivals of desktop and laptop computers, because they are portable, relatively affordable, and easy to use. Storage size is no longer a barrier to using these smaller devices because of the compactness of external storage media and the trend to store more personal and organizational data on remote servers such as the cloud.

This raises a number of scenarios. Those countries whose jurisdictions provide no safeguard for the privacy of data stored or transferred to and from these devices have unbridled access to private data, the main problem being the difficulty of recovering encrypted data. Other jurisdictions are more mindful of their citizens' right to privacy but still face the problem of recovering evidence from encrypted devices. The discipline is now probably at a watershed, with the storage of data being transformed into remote network hubs, less convenient to access than in the past and certainly infeasible to image!

Mobile telephony has posed its own obstacles to forensic recovery, adding to the general frustration of practitioners, who are denied access to the evidence that hides within a device.

Mobile phone evidence recovery

Recovery of data from Apple iPhones, in particular, is nearly impossible to accomplish. Android and other operating systems are heading the same way. New models and versions now make it virtually impossible to recover a logical extraction of these phones unless the passphrase or PIN has been decoded or provided by the device owner — often not an option. The days of recovering a full physical dump containing erased data have long since passed for iPhones and Android devices.

I have been evaluating a number of mobile phone forensic recovery tools, and none seem close to dealing with the problem. Disappointingly, the vendors are unusually quiet as to what progress is being made to gain access to these devices. My research colleagues are working hard towards a solution to decrypt some of these devices and recover a physical dump capable of being processed by ILookIX and ISeek. ILookIX has been able to recover, for example, some 60 percent additional data from an iPhone 4 that other mobile forensics tools could not. It is hoped that this recovery success is extended to new versions of the iPhone. So, dear reader, keep an eye out for updates, particularly in light of the FBI versus Apple debacle regarding access to iPhones.

The cloud - convenient for users but problematic for practitioners

Access to cloud resources to recover digital evidence is often through the normal access protocol used by consumers to connect to the host server, even if it is not owned by the consumer. However, it is not a simple matter to identify the path that the data takes from the source storage device to the target storage device, and this path may not remain fixed. Moreover, the owner of the data usually does not have physical control of the server where it is held, thus complicating the desired imaging of stored data, which may be stored in another jurisdiction and may require travel and extra resources. This also means that the data is accessed and recovered by a non-practitioner with limited understanding of what should be recovered and who may be unreliable in protecting the admissibility of the evidence.

A more viable alternative is to recover data remotely using the ISeekDiscovery automaton, which is non-intrusive, can be launched remotely, is secure, and can segregate data to ensure compliance with court orders and warrants, compared to conventional recovery processes. These processes often require the server to be shut down for extended periods and can be intrusive and may contaminate the evidence and other data.

The need for effective evidence processing and validation

This book has presented a range of digital forensics tools and introduced some lower-level processes used in the recovery, preservation, and analysis of potential evidence. *Chapter 9, Validating the Evidence*, presented a candidate model for validating digital evidence that could be considered a foundation for developing a model to assist practitioners in mapping their analysis processes and navigating digital evidence datasets and images. The need to test and check evidence is so important but sometimes paid mere lip service to.

Research by *Adams* (2012) produced a formal and timely generic model for the forensic acquisition of digital data in criminal and civil environments, particularly in incident response, a field that is constantly evolving. The lack of any standard model across all areas of the discipline is vexing and Adams' **Advanced Data Acquisition Model (ADAM)** has much to commend it to practitioners.

ADAM incorporates the following strictures relating to evidence acquisition:

- The activities of the practitioner should not alter the original data
- A complete record of all activities associated with the recovery and handling of the original data and any copies of the original data must be maintained, including compliance with the appropriate rules of evidence, maintaining a chain of custody record, and verification processes such as hashing
- The practitioner must not undertake any activities that are beyond their ability or knowledge
- The practitioner must take into consideration all aspects of personal safety while undertaking their work

ADAM consists of three stages of acquisition of digital data: the initial planning stage, the onsite survey, and the acquisition of digital data. It is intended to provide clarity of the acquisition processes for presentation in legal hearings. More information about this innovative model may be located here:

`http://researchrepository.murdoch.edu.au/14422/2/02Whole.pdf`.

Contingency planning

Strategic business management identifies assets at risk and anticipates the threats to them. Prudent organizations predict the risk and set up processes to mitigate the threat in advance or better manage the consequences after a security breach. An organization's IT team is often engaged in profiling the threat to electronic information and implementing threat minimization and management processes. Their primary role is to restore the functionality of electronic resources and networks after security breaches, including physical and personnel security.

Management and IT personnel are increasingly involved in investigating breaches of security, crime incidents, and personnel misconduct, as presented in the case study in *Chapter 9, Validating the Evidence*, yet they seldom possess the experience and wherewithal to preserve and recover evidence.

Difficulties confront business managers and non-forensic practitioners, who are often the unwitting custodians of digital evidence later relied upon in court. Organizations are not always familiar with the complexity of digital evidence and how to locate and recover it without altering its integrity. Without some preparation for the eventuality of an incident requiring the preservation of digital evidence, it becomes problematic for organizations to handle evidence in the organization's best interest.

Having seen organizations' lack of readiness to deal with incidents involving digital evidence recovery firsthand and with depressing regularity, I note here that those organizations that have a forensic contingency plan recover more quickly from an incident, with a greater probability of bringing offenders to account. It is really a prudent strategy for organizations big and small to have some form of forensic response in addition to a security incident contingency plan. While existing risk-assessment standards may be useful, they generally do not encompass a digital forensics response.

In civil e-discovery cases, the lack of preparation to meet discovery demands can be a costly experience and disruptive to an organization's information-management routine. Software programs are available that anticipate the likelihood of discovery, and this helps sanitize the discovery search process and reduce cost somewhat.

Such programs are not always affordable or thought necessary by smaller-sized businesses. Searching for e-mails is expensive during discovery for both parties, and in the Monica Lewinsky case, the cost of searching for relevant e-mail files was more than US $17 million. There is no doubt it would have been a fraction of that cost if the investigators had had access to the ISeekDiscovery automaton!

Some form of pragmatic forensic contingency plan is highly recommended, and may include the following:

- A contingency plan and the appointment of a team responsible for researching, maintaining, and testing it
- Using a **Computer Incident Response Team** (**CIRT**) to provide a professional investigation and response to investigate security incidents and recover and preserve digital evidence
- Raising standards and awareness of the problem
- Maintaining tightly configured network security to protect information assets and potential digital evidence
- Validating the security configuration of systems and the digital evidence by digital forensic practitioners

References

Adams, R. 2012. "The Advanced Data Acquisition Model (ADAM): A process model for digital forensic practice." School of Engineering and Information Technology, Murdoch University. PhD thesis.

Summary

This chapter summarized the key topics presented in the book and reviewed trends affecting practitioners and stakeholders.

Practical Digital Forensics has introduced the discipline of digital forensics in such a way that the technical mystery has to some extent been moved aside to provide you with greater clarity about the fundamentals of the discipline. Case studies have been liberally peppered throughout the book, together with examples of analyses to highlight key recovery and analysis processes.

The book strongly endorses the need for a more pragmatic approach to manage digital information used in legal proceedings. It has described various ways of empowering digital forensic practitioners and other stakeholders through better processes and forensics tools.

New forensic tools that are emerging to enhance forensic examination have been shared with you, and these tools, especially ILookIX and the ISeekDiscovery automaton, are making the task of the practitioner more manageable and productive.

This has been a "warts and all" introduction to the discipline, as it would be unfair not to mention some of the heavy challenges facing practitioners. It is not a profession; it is a vocation, and one that can be very rewarding despite these challenges. I hope that some of you will find the book insightful and be encouraged to look towards digital forensics as your true vocation. For the seasoned practitioner, I hope that something within these pages strikes the right chord as well as providing you with a view of new tools and processes.

I and my colleagues are disappointed with the lack of professionalism of some practitioners. Whether this is attributable to arrogance, ignorance, complacency, or some other cause, they are clearly not acting as servants of the court. As intimated in *Chapter 9, Validating the Evidence*, he who pays the piper does not call the tune— practitioners answer to a higher authority than their clients and employers. The objective of the book was to make a positive contribution to the field of literature relating to the discipline by presenting processes and tools to enhance the professionalism of practitioners.

However, it is a sad fact that the immaturity of the discipline includes a complacency about standards and accountability — all too frequent within government and private organizations. This book would be glorifying the discipline far in excess of its present stature by not mentioning these deficiencies, notwithstanding the really positive work of most practitioners and the benefits offered by emerging processes and tools.

To stress the point, in a recent case, a colleague of mine engaged by a defense legal team was tasked to authenticate audio files of conversations covertly recorded by a government agency. The colleague, an experienced forensic practitioner, formerly trained and working in several government forensic teams, found that the audio files were not the original data but copies produced by data-archiving software. Having the original data was essential to examine the audio for any possible alteration post recovery.

After several months of procrastination from the government agents and their consistent insistence that the data provided was original, they conceded that it was not, despite earlier assurances that the hashing logs related to the original data, when in fact they did not. Moreover, it was not possible for the agents to provide any form of provenance as to the authenticity of the hashing logs, unlike the forensic image container protection afforded by the `.ASB` forensic container file described in *Chapter 4, Recovering and Preserving Digital Evidence*. The agent had apparently hashed the copied data and not the original, bringing into question the integrity of the data. It appeared the agents did not know, did not care, or possibly lied about the preservation and recovery processes for some obscure reason.

A validation test, such as that described in *Chapter 9, Validating the Evidence*, to test the integrity of the imaging or preservation process, was evidently not applied. What really amazed the practitioner was a statement from one of the agents, evidently irritated that the evidence was being challenged to such an extent, to the effect of, "We're not employed to be forensic analysts — we just collect intelligence."

This book has highlighted trends in digital forensic practice and called for better strategies for managing increasingly large and complex datasets — obviously needed, considering the agent's outburst above!

Those in the profession and those contemplating joining should not be overly disconcerted by these recurring examples of poor practice, for this is a very rewarding discipline, especially when receiving recognition for a job well done. The sense of achievement in locating and analyzing information that was hard won adds to the experience, which in turns builds a secure foundation for practitioners. The discipline needs fresh blood that questions everything and is not satisfied with the "enough is good enough" outlook that exists. Most importantly, it should never be overlooked that a practitioner's learning, like in other professions, is never complete.

Index

enhanced digital evidence
preservation 143-146
enhanced digital evidence recovery 143-146
for assisting practitioners 140

R

RAM slack 115
random-access memory (RAM) 27
Redundant Array of Independent Disks
(RAID) 153
Registry Explorer
about 212, 213
devices, mapping through 216
hibernation and sleep files 226
hidden data, recovering from VSS 221-224
jump list activity, reviewing 219
most recently used list, reviewing 219
pagefiles 226
prefetch files, examining 224, 225
steganography, detecting 227
USB removable storage, detecting 218
useful leads, seeking 213-216
user activity 219
Windows Event Viewer logs, observing 220
wireless connectivity, detecting 219
remote access 233, 234
research repository
reference link 124

S

Sally Clark case
reference 6
Scientific Working Group on Digital
Evidence (SWGDE) 11
search category
archive files 44
audio 44
databases 45
e-mails 45
internet browser files 45
link files 45
Microsoft Office suite 45
recycler 45
registry files 45
system files 45
video 45

security protection
reference link 88
Service Set Identifiers (SSID) 219
software application
connecting, to operating systems 31
connecting, to operating systems and
device 31
solid-state drive (SSD) storage devices 28
steganalysis 227
steganography 227
structured and balanced analysis, digital
evidence
about 300
arguments, modeling 301
hypotheses, developing 300, 301
Toulmin model of argumentation 301, 302
structured processes
for locating digital evidence 165-167
for selecting digital evidence 165-167

T

tapes 26
technical complexities, digital evidence
about 71
date and time problems 79, 80
files, recovering from unallocated
space 76-78
malleability 72
metadata, avoiding as face value 72-75
Technical Working Group on Digital
Evidence (TWGDE) 11
testimonial evidence 64
Transmission Control Protocol (TCP) 118

U

unallocated data analysis 47
unsound digital evidence
about 292
challenges 294
evidence contamination 296
immaturity, of forensic
subdiscipline 294, 295
ineffective security integrity, of computers
and networks 295
issues 292, 293

Made in the USA
Columbia, SC
28 November 2020